Jane Martin
Collected Plays

1980-1995

Jane Martin
Collected Plays

1980-1995

Contemporary Playwrights Series

SK
A Smith and Kraus Book

A Smith and Kraus Book
Published by Smith and Kraus, Inc.

Manufactured in the United States of America
Cover and Text Design by Julia Hill
Cover art *Portrait of a Woman,* detail, by Pablo Picasso. Charles H. Bayley Picture and Painting Fund, and Partial Gift of Mrs. Gilbert W. Chapman. Courtesy, Museum of Fine Arts, Boston.

First Edition: October 1995
10 9 8 7 6 5 4 3 2

Library of Congress Cataloging-in-Publication Data
Martin, Jane.
[Plays. Selections.]
Jane Martin: collected plays, 1980-1994. --1st ed.
p. cm. --(Contemporary playwrights series)

ISBN 1-57525-002-5 (cloth). -- ISBN 1-880399-20-2 (alk.paper)
I. Title. II. Series.

PS3563.A72433A6   1995
812'.54--dc20   95-30492
CIP

Contents

LIVES IN HIDING
The Work of Jane Martin

*Oh, I've flown high and known tragedy both. My daddy says it's put
spirit in my soul and steel in my heart. My left hand was crushed in a
riding accident by a horse named Big Blood Red, and though I came
back to twirl I couldn't do it at the highest level. That was denied me by
Big Blood Red who clipped my wings. You mustn't pity me, though. Oh,
by no means! Being denied showed me the way, showed me the glory that
sits inside life where you can't see it.*
        "Twirler," 1981

Jane Martin's *Twirler* was the first of 12 monologues produced
under the group title *Talking With* by Actors Theatre of Louisville in
its 1982 Humana Festival of New American Plays. Each monologue
is self-contained and, but for the fact the voices are all female, unre-
lated to the next. The combined impact of the piece was tremendous.
"Martin's is a unique sensibility," reported *The Washington Post.* "It
mixes a kind of primitive religious ecstasy with a cutting anger and a
disturbing surrealism." "Each monologue is invested with a generosity of spirit and originality of imagination that is unique," wrote
David Nowlan of *The Irish Times.* Said William B. Colins of *The
Philadelphia Inquirer*, "With Jane Martin, the monologue has taken
on the aspect of a new poetic form, intensive in its method and reve-
latory in its effect."

Martin has amplified the convention of the monologue, a theatrical device akin to the aside or the stage whisper. Characters confront the audience directly with revelations not simply truthful but deeply spiritual, hauntingly private, embarrassingly funny, frighteningly exotic and bizarre. These are nit the elevated denizens of tragedy, not even the absurd abstractions of tragicomedy. Martin's characters are the unredeemable freak side of the American Dream. The very meanness of their lives is set in vivid relief by the extremity of their metaphorical obsessions. A young girl carries on her father's ministry, handling water moccasins and rattlesnakes to prove the spirit within her. A middle-aged woman, tattooed on every visible part of her body, describes her emergence from an unmarked life:

> *And these people, life-engraved, are drawn to each other and pass the time interpreting their signs. And those moments of sharing are the best of life. And this unraveling of hieroglyphics, personally I call it love, lasts only so long as there are marks to read. Then it is gone.*
> "Marks," *Talking With*, 1982

Over the next five years, Martin wrote *Coup/Clucks*, two related one-acts, and five shorter works: *Summer, Shasta Rue, Boy Who Ate the Moon, Travelin' Show*, and *Cul de Sac*, originally published under the collective title *What Mama Don't Know*. From the later work, *Summer*, produced by Actors Theatre of Louisville as part of the 1984 Shorts Festival, interweaves monologues with more complex multi-character scenes pitting male and female characters in shatteringly lonely and violent interaction. The play takes place over a four month period from May to late August during the year 1949 and moves between a garden in Philadelphia, a ranch outside Billings, Montana, a Cunard Liner, and various locations in France. It foretells many of Martin's future preoccupations: the salacious potency of innocence, the brilliancy of repressed female consciousness, and the isolating cruelty of machismo.

> *You know your father's been disappearing all his life, if you remember. Bit by bit. Despite our best efforts.*
> *Summer*, 1984

Vital Signs, produced by Actors Theatre of Louisville in the 1990 Humana Festival of New American Plays, marked Jane Martin's prolific return to and redefinition of her monologue form. Six actresses perform thirty-four monologues each approximately two minutes long. With the flash and thunder of fireworks on the Fourth of July, *Vital Signs* peoples the stage with a bizarre display of the American spirit. An aging woman invites encyclopedia salesmen to her parlor, believing them to embody the manners and intellectualism of a bygone age. A lesbian trick artist finds herself "travelin' alone" because her jealousy and her talent are too dangerous a combination. A cautious swinger incorporates written sexual histories into her foreplay and laughs indulgently at the memory of the lover who used a condom on his tongue for oral sex. Martin achieves her effects through the wild creativity of her characterizations coupled with her tremendously visceral, idiomatic language. The German critic Peter Iden attempted to define the linguistic impact of *Vital Signs* for a non-American audience, "Martin's particular idiosyncrasies in her use of the American language create a tension in which jargon, developed through schematized speech patterns, belies a deeper reality, which is only partially alluded to in the words themselves."

> *They tested me twice on account of their dumbfoundedness the first time. And those results they came out the same both times. Within a fraction of a point, so they told me. 'How'd I do?' I'd say and they'd get this startled look and they'd say, 'Well, Miss Latonia, we're pleased to say it's conclusive and definite, you don't have a personality.'*
> Vital Signs, 1990

With the production of *Cementville* one year later, Jane Martin found the perfect area in which to combine a panoply of her peculiar characters in one full-length dramatic situation. Stranded in a grimy locker room below a run-down sports arena in the nowhere town of Cementville, Tennessee, a group of second-string females wrestlers suit themselves in the iconographic costumes of their "professional" personas as their manager struggles to find a replacement for their headliner attraction who reportedly has had his penis bitten off in a sexual mishap the previous night. Enter Mother Crocker with her daughters, The Knockout Sisters, two blonde ex-porn stars whose ambition to be Hollywood "Sex Goddesses" is so bloodthirsty as to make painfully explicit the link between glamour and self destruction. When the sexuality and violence spills out of the ring, into the audience and down to the locker room below, Martin whips her comic sideshow into a more dangerous satirical frenzy. America's unappeasable appetite for violence, preferably laced with sexuality, in its popular entertainments is called into question as the line between fantasy and reality is crossed.

Well, that poor man didn't have a thing in the world but that dick and now its bit off.
Cementville, 1991

Misfit female solidarity is again the norm in *Criminal Hearts*, produced in 1992 by The Theatre Company, Detroit, Michigan. Sex and violence are also at issue but directed mainly at property rather than person. The felonious comedy pairs Bo, a ballsy, streetwise grifter, with Ata, a condo-bound agoraphobic. Ata could be the later day of Miss Latonia of *No Personality*, validated by a closetful of designer labels and violated by a philandering husband who's as plastic as his cash flow. She's certainly a precursor of Mona in *Middle-Aged White Guys*, jarred out of her normal orbit by an inspired lust for revenge. The play posits the last resort of the disinherited and disrespected.

You smile, you agree, you ask questions, you praise him, you debase yourself, you go down on him, and then they marry you.
Criminal Hearts, 1992

The critical success of *Cementville* and *Criminal Hearts* put to rest questions of whether Jane Martin was capable of work with a traditional dramatic structure. But speculation resurfaced and amplified as to the playwright's identity. Jane Martin was known to be a pseudonym for an author described by her producer as intensely private and uninterested in discussing her work. Was Jane Martin a man, a woman, or a group? The one surety, that Jane Martin was a wildly funny writer, was exploded with the production of *Keely and Du*.

Tackling one of the most hotly debated and violently fought issues on the political and religious battleground of America, Keely and Du, first produced in the Actors Theatre of Louisville's 1993 Humana Festival, turned post-theatre chats into tearful remonstrations and caused audience members to boo and hiss as antagonistic characters acted their beliefs. The issue is abortion. But this is no schematized political view. Martin insistently works from the gut. Consistently, her characters are deeply passionate; though they exist on the extreme edge of everyday reality, the empathy they evoke is powerful and universal. Keely, pregnant from s rape by her estranged husband, is kidnapped from an abortion clinic. She is drugged, blindfolded, transported to an unknown place and handcuffed to a bed. When she awakens to confront her masked captors she is told that she has been taken into "protective custody" by Operation Retrieval, "a group of Like-minded Christians motivated by a belief in the sanctity of life and the rights of unborn children. She will be held until she is past the point of abortion. Du is an elderly nurse left to care for Keely. Over months, their unlikely symbiosis warms, deepens, and prompts them to search desperately for mutual understanding. The play ends with Keely aborting herself with a hanger and Du paralyzed by a stroke and imprisoned. Their violently forged bond endures the moral and intellectual incomprehension of both women.

LIGHTS up immediately. Du is in the chair by the bed. SHE takes a pair of baby shoes out of her purse. SHE puts one in the palm of her hand and holds it out to Keely. KEELY looks. SHE takes it. SHE smells it. LIGHTS out.
    Keely and Du, 1993

Keely and Du won the 1993 American Theatre Critics award for the year's best play. It has been produced in Lithuania, Germany, Poland, Ireland, and in 1994 was the most produced new work in America. After a two year hiatus, Martin reverted to her bawdiest comic form with *Middle-Aged White Guys*, produced by Actors Theatre of Louisville in its nineteenth Humana Festival of New American Plays. The play, a surreal comic allegory, is darkly serious in its intent and hatefully funny in its effect.

In *Middle-Aged White Guys,* back are the warped icons of Americana: a corrupt mayor dressed up like Abraham Lincoln for his local Independence Day celebration, a Vietnam Vet turned mercenary soldier back to his midwestern hometown after twenty years "out there killin' people for the free enterprise system," a local business tycoon made rich from Gun World, "the biggest handgun retail outfit in a three-state area." The three are brothers drawn together on a local garbage dump, beneath which is buried the baseball field where they played out the American Dream. The occasion is the twentieth anniversary of the suicide of RV, wife to the mayor, lover to the mercenary, goddess to the businessman. To their surprise, RV comes back and with her she brings a host of heavenly messengers to deliver God's ultimatum to the White Man. This vengeful God is female and she's pissed and eventually gets her way. The play's final image: three, middle-aged men standing naked holding a sign which simply says, "I'm sorry." The moment is richly cathartic.

> *Everybody's wife leaves him, Roy. It's a shit job.*
> *Middle-Aged White Guys,* 1995

The Jane Martin of the ten-minute *Pomp and Circumstance* seems another creature entirely from the more familiar, raucous, Southern voice. The play is unique in her repertoire as it involves not a single female character. But the plight of the composer Bachweist in his struggle to adapt his identity to the pleasure of his King seems a poignant explanation of Martin's celebrated anonymity. What part of an artist's life does s/he owe to the marketplace, to the critics or to the public? How is a voice compromised by celebrity and expectation? If Jane Martin is a woman, her anonymity has bought her the freedom to be politically incorrect, to castrate, to violate, to satirize a society in all its heinous specificity. If Jane Martin is a man, his anonymity has bought him the freedom to be not in charge, to be out of control, to be intuitive, to give voice to the mysterious femina within all of our species. Perhaps the Jane Martin has bought the freedom to see "the glory that sits inside life where you can't see it."

MARCIA DIXCY has been an Assistant Literary Manager and a Literary Associate for Actors Theatre of Louisville. Among plays by Jane Martin, she served as dramaturg for the original productions of *Vital Signs, Keely and DU,* and the upcoming *Tumblin' After.* She designed costumes for *Shasta Rue, Summer, Vital Signs, Cementville, Keely and Du,* and *Middle-Aged White Guys.* She is a graduate of Wellesley College and New York University School of the Arts.

Jane Martin
Collected Plays

1980-1995

Talking With…

ORIGINAL PRODUCTION

Talking With..., by Jane Martin; directed by Jon Jory; set, Tony Straiges; costumes, Jess Goldstein; lighting, Pat Collins; production stage manager, Elizabeth Ives. An Actors Theatre of Louisville production presented by the Manhattan Theatre Club, Lynne Meadow, artistic director, and Barry Grove, managing director. At 321 East 73rd Street, New York, N.Y. Opening night: October 1, 1982.

FIFTEEN MINUTES............................ with Laura Hicks
SCRAPS.................................. with Penelope Allen
CLEAR GLASS MARBLES................... with Sally Faye Reit
AUDITION................................ with Ellen Tobie
RODEO ....with Margo Martindale
TWIRLER........................... with Lisa Goodman
LAMPS ....with Anne Pitoniak
HANDLER............................... with Susan Cash
DRAGONS........................... with Lee Anne Fahey
FRENCH FRIES........................... with Theresa Merritt
MARKS .... with Lynn Milgrim

TALKING WITH...

FIFTEEN MINUTES

A theatrical dressing room. A table and chair. Makeup for the evening's production is laid out on the table. Over the loudspeaker we hear the Stage Manager call, "15 minutes, please. The call is 15 minutes." The actress enters hurriedly and goes to the table. She wears a kimono over a slip. During the course of the piece she completes her makeup and dresses for the play she is doing. Though not actually present she looks into a mirror and thus directly toward the audience. She speaks to an unseen dressing room partner.

ACTRESS: Anyway, this guy, the director, actually used a buzzer. ZZZZZZZZZZ. Really. He would sit there wearing a Yankee's baseball cap and push this buzzer after each laugh line for as long as he thought the laugh would last. Laugh line, ZZZZZZZZZ. This was to train us not to step on the laugh. Can you believe it? Really. Oh, he trained us, believe me. The show opens, there are no laughs but we are waiting for the buzzer. A two-hour play lasted three hours while we paused for laughs that didn't exist. I aged seven years in a night. Directors! Last year I did Katrin in Mother Courage for this really *dour*, silent, unapproachable, East German woman. She sat on a camp stool, immovable, for hours during rehearsal. With her eyes closed yet. No reactions. Really. I felt like a radio show. Anyway, after a week she asks me out for a beer and suggests that we should sleep together to get in tune with the play. I tell her she wants to get in tune with the play she should sleep with the author. She says, 'My dear, Bertholt has been dead for thirty years!' I said, 'In that case you're perfect for each other.'

(S)HE called fifteen right? My! Sooooooo, we're really going to do this? Of course we are. It's really mysterious, you know? I mean they're already out there right? Sitting out there. Eating little candies. Peering in pocket mirrors. Who are they? Who knows. What are they expecting? Who knows. We do it. They watch it. We finish. They applaud. They go home. We go home. What was it? Who knows.

What I want to know, is how the hell do they live in a town like this without a decent Chinese restaurant?

O.K., O.K., O.K., O.K.,…so, it's fifteen and I am in here getting ready for an evening of 'lacerating self exposure' and there are people out there reading the program, reading my bio, you know getting a little personal insight, getting to know me. And what I want to know…you think this is enough eyes for this house? Great. And what I want to know is who are *they*? Fair's fair, right? What I would like…other than some decent light in this dressing room…what I would like is a program delivered to me every night with bio's of the audience, you know, so we'd start out even…I am really a mutt, you know it?…where they live, last play they saw, favorite color, sexual preference, last relationship they screwed up, you know just basic stuff. Because then we'd be in this together, right? I do a little lacerating self exposure, they do a little lacerating self exposure and afterwards who knows maybe we get together for a drink, because then…O.K., what you see is what you get…because then there would be an exchange, an exchange and not this unilateral crap, this "I'm in the light, you're in the dark" stuff, which truth to tell is beginning to wear on me. Me. Moira, the semi-Taurus from Julliard, with two Broadway credits, this baby, and an unreleased horror film where I am eaten by stone griffins on the towers of Notre Dame. (*Stage manager's voice: "5 minutes. The call is 5 minutes, please."*) Right; five minutes, right. (*She begins to put on her clothes.*) I mean I have nothing against these people, these humans who have paid their money, some would say too much money, for an evening of…for an evening of…(*She pauses a moment transfixed by a memory.*) Entertainment. Wow. Y'ever think of it like that…what you are, you, are an entertainment? I strike me as a number of things, but I do not strike me as…look, what I would like…once…just after my entrance, is to walk downstage…(*She does, right to the footlights.*) and say, "Excuse me. Excuse me, could we have the house lights for a second please?" (*They come up.*) Hey, O.K., thanks. And I would like to look at them, the people who seriously believe that I am an entertainment…Hi…How are you? I would just *look* at them, you know, take them in…(*She does. A fairly long pause.*) And then I would say…see this would be better already…I mean it's better to have seen their faces. I would say that I'm…a little fragile…freaked out, you know…sort of at the end of a personal relationship…I mean not the character, well I mean the character is too but…you've all been through that, right? The end of a crucial relationship? You know, the self-doubt and everything…the feeling that you're not lovable…that you're a mutt, too much of a mutt to be loved…and that you have…I don't know…a crisis of confidence…is that a good description? That it's hard to *act*…hard to be the entertainment for people you don't know…haven't looked at. So I just needed to see you tonight, O.K.? Just see you for a minute. That's all…O.K.? (*The stage manager calls places: "Places, please. The call is places. Places, please." She stands a moment longer and then moves back up to the dressing table. The house lights fade.*) Soooooooooo. Hey, O.K.! Ready to Rock-and-Roll, right? Ready to do it in the dark. For whoever and whatever, whoever makes of it. Hey, that's the way it's 'sposed to be. They got a law on this thing. Besides, hey listen, I ain't a mutt. I am *supremely* self-confident. I lacerate with my self exposure. Listen, don't screw with me, they said it in the *newspaper*! I am the entertainment and when I ope' my lips, let no dog bark! Plus, fuck 'em if they can't take a joke right? (*She checks the mirror one more time.*) And me, hey, I'm the joke! (*She loses herself again for a moment, staring in front of her, just for a moment.*) On the other hand, I'm in the light. (*She crosses out right. Lights fade out, sound of vacuum, which continues during scene change.*)

END OF FIFTEEN MINUTES

SCRAPS

The lights come up on a woman in a multi-colored patchwork costume. Red, blue, green, yellow. Even the head. Button eyes, yarn hair, pearls for teeth. It is the Patchwork Girl of Oz. She is using a stand-up vacuum cleaner. She turns it off and looks at the audience.

THE PATCHWORK GIRL OF OZ: I spend more and more time in Oz. Since I've turned thirty-five. Since Suzanne is in high school. This is Scraps. I had a dressmaker do it. It's not the only one I have. I have Ozma, I have Dorothy, I have Glinda the Good Witch. I'm even beginning to go out in this stuff. The midnight Rocky Horror Show, St. Patrick's Day parades. I went down one night to a gay bar and they waved the cover charge. Always as Scraps. My face doesn't show. Jack doesn't even know I have the books. He sure as hell doesn't know I do this. You know about the Patchwork Girl? It's the seventh Oz book. She was made from a patchwork quilt by Dr. Pipt, the crooked magician, to be his servant. He sprinkled the "powder of life" on her. But what nobody realized is that Ojo had dumped a bunch of *cleverness* into the Patchwork Girl's head. Too much for her to be satisfied as a servant. So she set off for the Emerald City with Ojo and the Transparent Glass Cat with the ruby heart and pink brains and the Living Phonograph. They called her Scraps and sometimes Patches.

I wish I was clever. Oh, I know how to hide nail holes with toothpaste, and how to spray cut flowers with hair-fix to make them last longer, but I've never had a job because I don't know how to do anything. I mean anything they pay you for. I'm not too good at learning new things either. I just freeze up or something.

God, I loved the Oz books when I was a kid. Do you know the countries? Well you know the Munchkins. Everybody knows the Munchkins. The Winkies where everything's yellow. Jack Pumpkinhead, the Tin Woodman, The Scarecrow, they all have their castles there. Gilliken Country, Quadling Country. I can get around better in any one of those places than I can in downtown Cleveland. When Jack goes I just sit looking out the window for a long time and then I close the drapes and spend the day in Oz. I can clean and stuff and still be there. Jack doesn't understand why I put yellow linoleum in the kitchen.

Nobody dies in Oz. No matter what's happening to you Ozma watches on her magic picture and you always get saved. Listen, there are great bad guys! Old Mombi, The Gnome King, The Skeezers. You think I'm ill don't you? You want to send me to group therapy or self-improvement seminars or off to take night classes towards a law degree. God I hated school! How could anybody like it? Hell, you can live a whole life and never have to subtract. Have you noticed that nobody ever talks about anything? I bet I haven't heard anybody talk about anything in two years. God knows Jack doesn't. In the morning he reads me the cereal boxes out loud. He thinks *I'm* boring. He wouldn't think I was so boring if he came home and found me in this. What would he do I wonder? Call his mother for advice. She'd tell him to buy me a Cuisinart and an exercycle.

I live in Oz. I see it all. I've even gotten so I can smell it. "Two or three hours walk along this trail brought Ojo and Scraps to a clear level country where there were a few farms and some scattered octagonal houses, all bright Quadling red and smelling of peppermint." I can live in that sentence for a full 3 hours. You know what? I like that a lot better than life.

Someday I'll be at the front door when Jack comes home. The Chevette will pull up and he'll have the week's charts, the Southeastern sales figures, the demographics under his arm. And there I'll be to give him a nice kiss, holding the spatula, me, Scraps. "You certainly are a wonder, my dear, and I fancy you'd make a splendid pin cushion. If you belonged to me, I'd wear smoked glasses when I looked at you." (*She takes the "Scraps" head off.*) But I do belong to you Jack. I'm your helpmeet, your homemaker.

The thing that frightens me is I'm getting flashbacks, just like combat or acid.

We had some people over. Jack had bought an Atari. You know, those television computer space games? Asteroids, Space Invaders, Cosmic Cadet. God, I hate the sound of it. They were talking about municipal bonds or something. We were all around the T.V. with the pretzel mix. Jenny, Allen, Marty, Turk, Jack, me. And I went to Oz. I was in trouble and I was being rescued from a whirlpool by this Ork…a bird with four wings, four legs and a propeller tail, and I guess Jack was talking to me and I didn't answer. He had to shake me. I really didn't know where I was. I ruined his best score in the Atari. I suppose he'll leave me when he finds out. Take the Irish setter. He's the provider. Jesus, I'll have to make a living, won't I? Maybe Ozma will see me in her Magic Picture. Then they'll send the Scarecrow to come get me and we'll ride the Sawhorse all the way back to the Emerald City. We'll lunch with the Hungry Tiger and the Cowardly Lion. And the Scarecrow will say, "Why here's a right curious creation, midway between a ragbag and a rainbow. Why my dear, (*She puts the "Scraps" head back on and sings.*) you are quite bedazzling!" The Scarecrow has the very best brains the Wizard ever made. Perhaps we'll be married.

> Kizzle-Kazzle Kore
> The Wolf is at the door
> There's nothing to eat
> But a bone without meat
> And a bill from the grocery store.

(*She freezes for a beat and then begins vacuuming.*)
(*Lights Out.*)

END OF SCRAPS

CLEAR GLASS MARBLES

A young woman is standing next to an end table with a lamp on it,
holding a crystal bowl filled with ninety clear glass marbles.

LAURIE: The day my mother found out she was dying she asked me
to go out and buy her these clear glass marbles. Dad and I hadn't
even known she was ill which was nothing new. Whenever you
asked my mother if she was ill she would throw things at you,
sesame buns, the editorial page, a handful of hair ribbons. 'Do
not,' she would say, 'suggest things to suggestible people.'
Anyway, I brought her the marbles and she counted ninety of
them out and put them in this old cut-glass bowl which had
been the sum total of great Helena's estate. Apparently, the
doctor had given her three months and she set great store by
doctors. She said she always believed them because they were the
nearest thing to the Old Testament we had. 'I wouldn't give you
two bits for these young smiley guys,' she'd say, 'I go for a good,
stern-furrowed physician.' She wouldn't even have her teeth
cleaned by a dentist under fifty. So she counted out ninety clear
glass marbles and set them in the bowl on her bedside table.
Then she went out and spent twelve hundred dollars on
nightgowns. She said, 'In my family you are only dying when
you take to your bed, and that, my darlings, is where I am
going.' And she did. Oh we hashed it around. Dad said she
couldn't possibly be dying but the doctors convinced him. I told
her it seemed a little medieval to lie in state up there but she said
she didn't want to be distracted from what she loved, us, and
what she wanted to mull...And she said there was nothing
outside except drugstores and supermarkets and drycleaners and
that given her situation they were beneath her dignity. I asked
her what she intended to do up there and she said study French,
visit with us, generally mull and maybe call a few pals. Study
French. She said she had made a pledge to herself years ago that
she would die bilingual. Dad and I cried a lot, but she didn't. He
was fun to cry with. From then on the doctors had to come see
her because, as she put it, she *came in* with a house call and she
was *going out* with a house call. And all day, every day, she would

hold one of these marbles in her hand. Why? She said it made the day longer. Mother had her own bedroom. That was the way it always was, for as long as I can remember. She called my father 'The Thrasher.' Dad could really get into a nightmare. Apparently early on in the marriage he had flipped over and broken her nose and that was it. Separate beds. Her room was very spare really. Wooden floors, an old steel-and-brass bed, oak dresser, bedside table, and don't ask me why, a hat rack. No pictures on the walls. She never understood how people could look at the same darn thing day after day. She said it was bound to 'deflate the imagination.' We'd sit with her after dinner and talk about 'issues.' She told us she was too far gone for gossip or what we ate for lunch. Then we'd all turn in and in a little while, just before I'd drift off I'd hear this...* (*She rolls one of the marbles across the stage floor.*) Happened every night. After the third or fourth day I saw one on the floor and started to pick it up but she said 'leave it.' She said it very sharply. I asked, 'How come?' She said she was 'learning to let go of them.' (*From now on the actress frequently rolls marbles across the stage, indicated hereafter by an asterisk, ending up at last with only one.*) Oh, she passed the time. There were things she wanted. She made out a list of children's books from her own childhood and we got as many of them as we could find from the library. She said they were still the only good books she'd ever read.*

She wrote notes to, I don't know, maybe sixty or seventy people, and they told us later on that they were sort of little formal goodbyes, each of them recalling some incident or shared something, not very significant, but the odd thing was that in each one she included a recipe. A recipe in every one of them.

We got out the big cookie tin full of snapshots that somehow never became a scrapbook. She liked that. She showed my father how to do the medical insurance and how she handled the accounts. We went through her jewelry.* She wrote down the names of the roofers and plumbers and air-conditioning people. She called it 'wrapping it up.' 'Well, this is good,' she'd say, 'I'm wrapping it up.'*

She had the television moved up in her room and she called me aside to say that it was entirely possible that she might reach a stage where she really wouldn't know what she was watching but that I must promise her that I'd keep it on P.B.S.

Later on, when it started getting hard,* she told Dad and me that she would like to spend more time alone. 'I'm afraid,' she said, 'that I'm going to have to do this more or less by myself.' She said that she was glad, and she hoped we would be, that this was arranged so that you got less attached to the people you loved at the end. The next period isn't worth going into, it was just...hard. (*She picks up the bowl of marbles.*) Do you know that from the very beginning down to the very last she never admitted to any pain. Never. She called it 'the chills.' The last thing she asked for was a picture we had in the front entrance hall of a labrador retriever she and Dad had owned when they were first married. He was, she said, a perfectly dreadful dog. 'When you are young,' she said, 'you believe in the perfectibility of dogs.'

I was in bed two weeks ago Wednesday toward dawn, then this...(*She pours the rest of the marbles on the floor. When they have stopped rolling, she speaks.*) Dad and I ran in there. The bedside table was turned over and she was gone. Dead. When the emergency medical people got there they found this...(*She opens her hand to disclose one more marble.*) The rest spilled when the table fell, but this one was still in her hand.

I keep it.

I keep it in my hand all day.

It makes the day longer.

(*Blackout.*)

END OF CLEAR GLASS MARBLES

AUDITION

An actress in her late twenties runs up on the stage. She is nervous. She shields her eyes against the light. She is dressed in a slightly bizarre and trendy style. She carries in her arms a cat on a leash.

ACTRESS: Hi. Hey Hi. Wow. All Right. Nice Place. Nice, uh, nice theatre. Good Vibes. Yowsa me yesirree. Toy boat, toy boat, toy boat, toy boat. Now…Let's see here. For my…can you hear me? Can you? No? Yes? You are out there, right? (*She puts the cat on the floor, her foot on the leash.*) O.K., so we're all here. Well, I mean, you're *there* and I'm *here* but we're all…forget it. Let's see…Audition, RAH! Get that part! O.K., my *name* is…shit, I forgot my name. Right. This…this would be construed as craziness. My name is…I did, I forgot my name…my stage name…see I decided to use my new stage name for this audition…for uh, for luck, it was…it was very…look what d'you care, right? My human, world name is Mary Titfer. Titfer. You got it? Goodo! O.K., can you hear me? All the way back? Loud and clear Captain Marvel? A-O.K.!…Now, one more introduction and we're under way. The uh, the small person on my leash is my cat 'Tat.' My cat, 'Tat.' Get it? (*Points to herself.*) Titfer (*Points to cat.*) Tat. Right, you got it. Hey, we're waking up here. We're demonstrating consciousness. O.K., O.K., now you…the imperial you…have a part. I, Titfer need a part. We are thus in tune. Synchronicity. Sooooooo, it's audition city! Now I've got two pieces for you today, and here's the surprise, I've got one classical piece…late greats, and I've got one contemporary piece…dispatches from the front. Good. For my classical piece I will take off all my clothes. 'Crude Rube Protrudes Dubious Boobies.' Beep-Beep. O.K., O.K., but all kidding and joshing aside I will take them off. Now, why is this classical? Surely, you jest. The body, the body is classical…it goes all the way back…and all the way front. Har, har. It starts the art, the body does. But there's no argument there, eh? Naturally not. O.K., O.K., now in the great tradition of auditions you may stop me at anytime. You can stop me one second after I start. But, *BUT*…and here is the stinger…(*She takes a hammer out of her purse, and a nail.*) Bear with me, O.K.? Little hyped-up. A simple task and I'll be back with you. (*She nails the cat's leash to the floor.*) There. Tat the cat, that's that. Nice kitty. Where were we? Toy boat, toy boat, toy boat, toy boat. O.K., stop me at any time. Right, O.K. Just yell 'Thank you Miss Titfer.' Firm but courteous and zaparoonie...I stop. I nip the strip. *But* when I stop my classical piece, I shift immediately into my contemporary piece which is...full attention now...beating the cat's head in with the hammer! Yipes! Holy Mackerel! 'Is this broad kidding?' Wellllll, I wouldn't want to spoil it for you but I don't think she's kidding. So, dear listeners, that's the full menu...that's all she wrote. But the tickle in the tushy are the options...Option A...we will let this poor, desperate, deluded girl debase herself...and I would, will, be debased...mortified...I mean...*no clothes*...here? In front of strangers? Crummy, yucky, hateful! Or...Option B...we can yell out 'Thank you Miss Titfer' and watch her clonk the kitty...and remember, Miss Titfer is fast. It will happen in a flash...kittyplasm...and haven't we, you, 'fess up now' actually killed little puss? Responsibility! Or Option C, the second-to-last option, we could give Mary Titfer the crummy, undemanding, twelve-line, two-scene part, which, let me assure you, any mildly competent average workday actress could do while standing on her head humming 'You can take this job and shove it'...backwards. O.K., last option...now this is just too tawdry but we are nothing if not thorough. We could give her the part *now*, and then when she splits, she and the furry hostage, we could take it away from her on the basis that she needs...shhh, psychiatric attention. But if you did that...if you did *that*, Mary Titfer would find you and Jacobean revenge, kill the feline, and, perhaps – disturbing thought – herself in a particularly garish and oriental manner RIGHT IN FRONT OF YOU. Now she might not have the nerve but on the other hand we don't know. We just don't know. O.K., O.K. We're ready to go in the wooden O. We're out of the exposition and into the meat of the matter. Denouement. Everybody has their work cut out for them. The dialectic. You have a part. I want a part. We have serious business here. Right? Right.

Now, I will begin my classical piece by unbuttoning my Jordache blouse. Watch me closely, both my hands are connected to my arms. (*She begins to unbutton her blouse as the lights fade out.*)

END OF AUDITION

RODEO

A young woman in her late twenties sits working on a piece of tack. Beside her is a Lone Star beer in the can. As the lights come up we hear the last verse of a Tanya Tucker song or some other female country-western vocalist. She is wearing old worn jeans and boots plus a long-sleeved workshirt with the sleeves rolled up. She works until the song is over and then speaks.

BIG EIGHT: Shoot – Rodeo's just goin' to hell in a handbasket. Rodeo used to be somethin'. I loved it. I did. Once Daddy an' a bunch of 'em was foolin' around with some old bronc over to our place and this ol' red nose named Cinch got bucked off and my Daddy hooted and said he had him a nine-year-old girl, namely me, wouldn't have no damn trouble cowboyin' that horse. Well, he put me on up there, stuck that ridin' rein in my hand, gimme a kiss and said, "Now there's only one thing t' remember Honey Love, if ya fall off you jest don't come home." Well I stayed up. You gotta stay on a bronc eight seconds. Otherwise the ride don't count. So from that day on my daddy called me Big Eight. Heck! That's all the name I got anymore…Big Eight.

Used to be fer cowboys, the rodeo did. Do it in some open field, folks would pull their cars and pick-ups round it, sit on the hoods, some ranch hand'd bulldog him some rank steer and everybody'd wave their hats and call him by name. Ride us some buckin' stock, rope a few calves, git throwed off a bull and then we'd jest git us to a bar and tell each other lies about how good we were.

Used to be a family thing. Wooly Billy Tilson and Tammy Lee had them five kids on the circuit. Three boys, two girls and Wooly and Tammy. Wasn't no two-beer rodeo in Oklahoma didn't have a Tilson entered. Used to call the oldest girl Tits. Tits Tilson. Never seen a girl that top-heavy could ride so well. Said she only fell off when the gravity got her. Cowboys used to say if she landed face down you could plant two young trees in the holes she'd leave. Ha! Tits Tilson.

Used to be people came to a rodeo had a horse of their own back home. Farm people, ranch people – lord, they *knew* what they were lookin' at. Knew a good ride from a bad ride, knew hard from easy. You broke some bones er spent the day eatin' dirt, at least ya got appreciated.

Now they bought the rodeo. Them. Coca-Cola, Pepsi Cola, Marlboro damn cigarettes. You know the ones I mean. Them. Hire some New York faggot t' sit on some ol' stuffed horse in front of a sagebrush photo n' smoke that junk. Hell, tobacco wasn't made to smoke, honey, it was made to chew. Lord wanted ya filled up with smoke he would've set ya on fire. Damn it gets me!

There's some guy in a banker's suit runs the rodeo now. Got him a pinky ring and a digital watch, honey. Told us we oughta have a watchamacallit, choriographus or somethin', some ol' ballbuster used to be with the Ice damn Capades. Wants us to ride around dressed up like Mickey Mouse, Pluto, crap like that. Told me I had to haul my butt through the barrel race done up like Minnie damn Mouse in a tu-tu. Huh uh, honey! Them people is so screwed-up they probably eat what they run over in the road.

Listen, they got the clowns wearin' Astronaut suits! I ain't lying'. You know what a rodeo clown does! You go down, fall off whatever – the clown runs in front of the bull so's ya don't git stomped. Pin-stripes, he got 'em in space suits tellin' jokes on a microphone. First horse see 'em done up like the Star Wars went crazy. Best buckin' horse on the circuit, name of Piss 'N' Vinegar, took one look at them clowns, had him a heart attack and died. Cowboy was ridin' him got hisself squashed. Twelve hundred pounds of coronary arrest jes fell right through 'em. Blam! Vio con dios. Crowd thought that was funnier than the astronauts. I swear it won't be long before they're strappin' ice-skates on the ponies. Big crowds now. Ain't hardly no ranch people, no farm people, nobody I know. Buncha disco babies and dee-vorce lawyers – designer jeans and day-glo Stetsons. Hell, the whole bunch of 'em wears French perfume. Oh it smells like money now! Got it on the cable T and V – hey, you know what, when ya rodeo yer just bound to kick yerself up some dust – well now, seems like that fogs up the ol' TV camera, so they told us a while back that from now on we was gonna ride on some new stuff called Astro-dirt. Dust free. Artificial damn dirt, honey. Lord have mercy.

Banker Suit called me in the other day said "Lurlene ..." "Hold it," I said, "Who's this Lurlene? Round here they call me Big Eight." "Well, Big Eight," he said, "My name's Wallace." Well that's a real surprise t' me," I said, "Cause aroun' here everybody jes calls you Dumb-ass." My, he laughed real big, slapped his big ol' desk an' then he said I wasn't suitable for the rodeo no more. Said they was lookin' fer another type, somethin' a little more in the showgirl line, like the Dallas Cowgirls maybe. Said the ridin' and ropin' wasn't the thing no more. Talked on about floats, costumes, dancin' chor-eog-aphy. If I was a man I woulda pissed on his shoe. Said he'd give me a lifetime pass though. Said I could come to his rodeo any time I wanted.

Rodeo used to be people ridin' horses for the pleasure of people who rode horses – made you feel good about what you could do. Rodeo wasn't worth no money to nobody. Money didn't have nothing to do with it! Used to be seven Tilsons riding in the rodeo. Wouldn't none of 'em dress up like Donald damn Duck so they quit. That there's the law of gravity!

There's a bunch of assholes in this country sneak around until they see ya havin' fun and then they buy the fun and start in sellin' it. See, they figure if ya love it, they can sell it. Well you look out, honey! They want to make them a dollar out of what you love. Dress *you* up like Minnie Mouse. Sell your rodeo. Turn *yer* pleasure into Ice damn Capades. You hear what I'm sayin'? You're jus' merchandise to them, sweetie. You're jus' merchandise to them.
(*Blackout.*)

END OF RODEO

TWIRLER

A young woman stands center stage. She is dressed in a spangled, single-piece swimsuit, the kind that is specially made for baton twirlers. She holds a shining, silver baton in her hand.)

APRIL: I started when I was six. Momma sawed off a broom handle, and Uncle Carbo slapped some sort of silver paint, well, grey really, on it and I went down in the basement and twirled. Later on, Momma hit the daily double on horses named Spin Dry and Silver Revolver and she said that was a sign so she gave me lessons at the Dainty Deb Dance Studio where the lady, Miss Aurelia, taught some twirling on the side.

I won the Ohio Juniors title when I was six and the Midwest Young Adult Division three years later and then in high school I finished fourth in the nationals. Momma and I wore look-alike Statue of Liberty costumes that she had to send clear to Nebraska to get and Daddy was there in a T-shirt with my name, April. My first name is April and my last name is March. There were four thousand people there, and when they yelled my name golden balloons fell out of the ceiling. Nobody, not even Charlene Ann Morrison, ever finished fourth at my age.

Oh, I've flown high and known tragedy both. My daddy says it's put spirit in my soul and steel in my heart. My left hand was crushed in a riding accident by a horse named Big Blood Red, and though I came back to twirl I couldn't do it at the highest level. That was denied me by Big Blood Red who clipped my wings. You mustn't pity me though. Oh, by no means! Being denied showed me the way, showed me the glory that sits inside life where you can't see it.

People think you're a twit if you twirl. It's a prejudice of the unknowing. Twirlers are the niggers of a white University. Yes, they are. One time I was doing fire batons at a night game, and all of a sudden I see this guy walk out of the stands. I was doing triples and he walks right out past the half-time marshalls, comes up to me, he had this blue-bead head band, I can still see it. Walks right up, and when I come front after a back reverse he spits in my face. That's the only, single time I ever dropped a baton, dropped 'em both in front of sixty thousand people and he smiles, see, and he says this thing I won't repeat. He called me a bodily part in front of half of Ohio. It was like being raped. It shows that beauty inspires hate and that hating beauty is Satan. (*Breaks focus, identifies person in audience; focus, pause, line.*)

You haven't twirled, have you? I can see that by your hands. Would you like to hold my silver baton? Here, hold it.

You can't imagine what it feels like to have that baton up in the air. I used to twirl with this girl who called it blue-collar Zen. The 'tons' catch the sun when they're up, and when they go up, you go up too. You can't twirl if you're not *inside* the 'ton.' When you've got 'em up over twenty feet it's like flying or gliding. Your hands are still down, but your insides spin and rise and leave the ground. Only a twirler knows that – so we're not niggers.

The secret for a twirler is the light. You live or die with the light. It's your fate. The best is a February sky clouded right over in the late afternoon. It's all background then, and what happens is that the 'tons' leave tracks, traces, they etch the air, and if you're hot, if your hands have it, you can draw on the sky. Charlene Ann Morrison, God, Charlene Ann! She was inspired by something beyond man. She won the nationals nine years in a row. Unparalleled and unrepeatable. Last two years she had leukemia, and at the end you could see through her hands when she twirled. Charlene Ann died with a 'ton' thirty feet up, her momma swears on that. I did speed with Charlene at a regional in Fargo and she may be fibbin' but she says there was a day when her 'tons' erased while they turned. Like the sky was a sheet of rain and the 'tons' were car wipers and when she had erased this certain part of the sky you could see the face of the Lord God Jesus, and his hair was all rhinestones and he was doing this incredible singing like the sound of a piccolo. The people who said Charlene was crazy probably never twirled a day in their life.

Twirling is the physical parallel of revelation. You can't know that. Twirling is the throwing of yourself up to God. It's a pure gift, hidden from Satan because it is wrapped and disguised in the midst of football. It is God throwing, spirit fire, and very few come to it. You have to grow eyes in your heart to understand its message, and when it opens to you it becomes your path to suffer ridicule, to be crucified by misunderstanding, and to be spit upon. I need my baton now.

There is one twirling no one sees. At the winter solstice we go to a meadow God showed us just outside of Green Bay. The God-throwers come there on December twenty-first. There's snow, sometimes deep snow, and our clothes fall away and we stand unprotected while acolytes bring the 'tons.' They are ebony 'tons' with razors set all along the shaft. They are three feet long. One by one the twirlers throw, two 'tons' each, thirty feet up, and as they fall back they cut your hands. The razors arch into the air and find God and then fly down to take your blood in a crucifixion, and the red drops draw God on the ground and if you are up with the batons you can look down and see him revealed. Red on white. Red on white. You can't imagine. You can't imagine how wonderful that is.

I started twirling when I was six but I never really twirled until my hand was crushed by the horse named Big Blood Red. I have seen God's face from thirty feet up in the air and I know him.

Listen. I will leave my silver baton here for you. Lying here as if I forgot it, and when the people file out, you can wait back and pick it up, it can be yours, it can be your burden. It is the eye of the needle. I leave it for you.
(*Blackout.*)

END OF TWIRLER

ACT TWO
LAMPS

The room is filled with lamps. Some are on tables. Some are floor lamps. There would have to be a minimum of a dozen. A woman of sixty-five, nicely dressed, stands among them. They are all on. There is no other theatrical illumination.

LILA: The older I become, the more I'm drawn to light. To radiance of all kinds. Both the light and the shadows, they fascinate me. Perhaps it's a sort of primitive fire syndrome or, I suppose, simply fear of the dark. I've rented this loft and filled it with lamps. I spend most evenings here. It is both eccentric and childlike, isn't it? I would prefer to think of it as a kind of playing. The hours fly. I draw enormous energy from it. And there's the actual heat of course. (*She begins to move through the room.*) I hope I'm not embarrassing you. May I show you? It's delightful to move at random, extending a hand, weaving in and through these pools of warmth. Each lamp gives its heat differently. Unique. And then in between, and there are many betweens, you can receive, feel, several sources at once. Any movement and the balance is changed. And then when you've exhausted these relationships, why you can change them, don't you see? I'm a little...a little frightened this will bore you...sharing this...it's so difficult to share our enthusiasms don't you think? Does light interest you? Do you respond to it? Night flying? Like costume jewelry on velvet. Wet neon. Trees covered with ice under street lamps. I suppose these are sentimental images of my generation. Might I show you something? It won't take a moment. (*She turns several of the lamps off.*) There. Now, moving through. (*She walks a pattern through the lamps.*) Now this. (*She moves again, holding a handled mirror in each hand.*) Now see. (*She turns two or three off and another on.*) I can *feel* the difference. Acutely. Pleasurably. Is this senility on the hoof? Look. (*She hunkers down on the floor and looks up.*) Seeing the lights above me makes me laugh. Why, do you suppose? (*She stands up.*) You probably suspect that it's a history as well. Of course. Some of these are from the Catsafall Farm. Catsafall, that's Iowa. Several of these are from family and

friends. And my son. (*She touches a lamp.*) My husband. Oh, fiddle, they're all personal. No, I won't bore you. Memories, I believe are patterns of a sort. And these, you see, make patterns and are memories. (*She sits in a rocker off to one side.*) I endlessly wondered what older age, later years, would *be*, feel like. As have you. A diminishment? A narrowing? There are so many things one obviously cannot do. Many of the people once central to one's life are gone or dispersed. One is less often…useful. My grandfather, when he was very rich in years, used to call himself 'deneeded and unpacked.' There are necessarily fewer people. Thinking about it, it seemed sensible then to invest more feeling in objects, enrich my relationship to them so that I…so that I wasn't without intimacy. I have one sister, Amelia, and she resides in a sort of Leisure World, a planned community in Albuquerque…New Mexico. Her husband was a thoracic surgeon and she is very well off. She moved there from Catsafall and tells me that she is ever so busy with…activities. She has many, many friends there she says. Imagine. Amelia has not a single, solitary acquaintance who knew her before she was sixty. There she is, a sort of amnesiac with many friends and no memories, baking herself in the sun like a pop-tart. Quite beyond me. Several years ago she visited me here. She sat there, just where you are, and shared this odd mixture of patterns, heat and memory. I showed her, for instance, how extraordinarily hands take light. Lovely. Well, after a very long silence, a very nice silence really, she rose and said, 'Lila, you are mad as a March hare.' She flew home to a card tournament. (*She stands up behind the one remaining lamp.*) It has been my experience that light is the more pleasurable as you diminish it, and that when a single glow remains there is an agony of pleasure and anticipation while you wait for the moment it will be extinguished. It is ever-so-lovely, ever, ever, so. It bewilders and thrills me, this light, radiance, that has become my friend to succor and sustain me. The warmth! The fascination of the waiting. And then, finally, of course…(*She stands above the lamp, illuminated for several seconds and then turns it off.*)
(*Darkness.*)

END OF LAMPS

Handler

A young woman in a simple, country-print dress. On the floor before her is a handmade wooden box about two feet long and eighteen inches high with a sliding wire screen top.

CARO: My Dada (*Pronounced "Dád-aw."*) was gonna do this tonight but the Lord froze his face so he sent me. I learned this from my Dada and he learned it up from great Gran, who took it on from the Reverend Soloman Bracewood, who had him a mule ministry 'round these parts way back when. Dada taught Miss Ellie, my ma, and my brother Jamie...he was in it too, 'fore he went for Detroit.

See, what I got in here is snakes. Lotta people don't like snakes. Gives it its nature, I guess. This here is water mocs. Jamie, he said they got the dirtiest, nastiest bite of all...well, rattlers is yer biggest. Lotta venom. You milk you a rattler, you can half fill up a juice glass. Dada said Jamie should do rattlers, but he never. Did 'heads, copperheads. Now they're slower and safer but it ain't such a good show. You know those dang snakes smell like cucumbers? Well, they do. Miss Ellie, she favored mocassins. Dada too...well, Dada he did all kinds, all ways. Your mocassin now, he's your good ol' boy snake. Flat out mean an' lots of get up n' go. Heck, they'll chase ya. They will. Ol' Dada he didn't like Miss Ellie doin' 'em. 'You lay off them mocs 'fore they lay you down.' Made Miss Ellie laugh. Lotta handlers think mocassins are slimy. Couldn't get me to touch one. They'll do rattlers...got him a nice dry feel. Little bit sandpapery. Rattler can find ya in the pitch dark though. They git on to yer body heat. Snake handlin'. *All* my blood does it. Only Dada an' me now though. Snake handlin', with the Holiness Church. Down where I come from we take God pretty serious. If you got the spirit, snake don't bite. If he bites you, you know you ain't got the spirit. Makes the difference real clear, don't it?

It's right there in the scripture...Mark, Chapter 16, verses 17 and 18, 'And these signs shall follow them that believe. In my name they shall cast out devils; they shall speak in new tongues; they shall take up serpents; and if they shall drink any deadly thing, it shall not hurt them; they shall lay hands on the sick and they shall recover.' Don't figure it could be much clearer than that. There's some churches don't use snakes, use strychnine, powdered poison, same idea though. They mix it with Cherry kool-ade, sing 'em a hymn, drink it off, and then just stand around waitin' to see if they fall over. Ain't much of a show. Not like snakes. Dada does fire but I can't do it. Pours some kerosene in a coke bottle, sticks a rag in the top and lights it up. Holds that fire under his chin, passes it down the arm, puts his hand in it, you know, that kind of stuff. He says there's people do blow torches down to Tennessee. I don't know. Jamie give it a try 'fore he went to Detroit. Just about burned his ass off. Sorry.

When I handle, I keep 'em in this box. Dada gimme this and some Heidi doll on my ninth birthday. Sometimes I'll just open up the lid and put my foot in or, uh, maybe stick it open side to my chest. There's some lay it to their face. I don't. Scares my eyes. Durin' service we take 'em right out, pass 'em around. It's more dangerous than a single handler. Snake gets to comparin' who got the spirit a whole lot an' who jes got it some. Somebody's jes about bound to come in second. Don't get me wrong now. Y' don't die everytime yer bit. I been bit seven times. Four times by the same serpent. Dada says he got the sweet tooth for me. Dada been bit thirty-two times an' never saw him a doctor. Used to let me kiss him on the marks. Last one got him here. (*Points to eye.*) Froze him right up. Dada says he'll thaw but I don't know.

Day after Jamie took off Miss Ellie did mocassins standin' in the back of the pickup over to Hard Burley. Shouldn't ought to 'cause her mind weren't there. Coal truck backfired and she got bit. Snake bit her three more times 'fore she hit the ground. Dada layed hands on her but she died anyway. There was ten of us handled right there at the funeral. Snake handlin'.

Snake knows what you feel. You can fool a person but you can't fool a snake. You got the spirit, God locks their jaws. Keeps you safe. Tell you what though…I don't believe in a God. Left me. Gone with Miss Ellie. I was handlin' when I knew it sure. Snake was jes comin' on down the line. Marita she yells out, 'The Lord. Lord's in me and with me. In me and with me.' Noah he was ululatin', talkin' in tongues. Couple of folks was rollin'

and singing. Dada was doin' switch grips. Had Miss Ellie's weddin' ring on his little finger. And it came on me, heck, there ain't no God in here. There's just a bunch of shouters gettin' tranced. There ain't no God in here at all. 'Bout that time they layed that serpent to me. Felt fussy. Nasty. Just lookin' for an excuse y'know? An' I was an empty vessel, worse nor a pharasee, grist for the mill. My blood went so cold I coulda crapped ice-cubes. Snake knew. Started to get leverage. So I said, 'Snake. You Satan's hand-maiden. You're right, there ain't no God in me. I'm just a woman, but I'm the only woman in my Dada's house and he needs me home. Outta his faith and his need, you lock yer jaws.' I let that snake feel a child's pure love and it sponged it up offa my hands and then ol' wiggley went limp. I tranced it. It was a real good service. Didn't nobody handlin' get bit. (*Takes snake out of the box.*) Yes, you got to believe. Holiness Church is dead right about that. Make me wonder, you know? I git to lookin' at people and wonderin' if they got anything in 'em could lock a serpent's jaws. Any power or spirit or love or whatever. I look at 'em and I wonder, could they handle? Tell you what though, you can see it in a face. You can read it. You look me full in the face it don't take me 30 seconds. It's like I was the snake, some ol' pit viper, an' I can read yer heart. Maybe you could handle and maybe you can't, but there's but one sure thing in this world...yer empty, yer gonna get bit.
(*Fade Out.*)

END OF HANDLER

DRAGONS

A young woman, nine months pregnant, is lying on a hospital trolley waiting to be moved into the delivery room. We hear the sound of a heartbeat throughout.

MARTI: Dear St. Margaret, patron saint of childbirth, let me live, let my child live, and enough with the labor O.K., St. Margaret? I get the idea, you know what I mean? Ow. Ow. God, I must look like a drowned gerbil. I thought after 23 hours of this they either had to give you a C-section or a hairdresser. Ow. St. Margaret? Don't let Dr. Gussler gasp or faint or throw up or anything when he sees the baby. I mean he hasn't delivered a woman of a dragon lately and he is not ready for this! 'You must abort, my dear lady. One must think of one's husband, one's lifestyle in these cases. An abnormal child will scar your psyche and spoil your dinner parties.' Creep! (*A contraction starts. She begins to pant and blow.*) Ow. Ow. I thought we just did this? Oh boy. Hey St. Margaret, send Wally back from the coffee shop, O.K.? Oh. Ow. Coming down. Coming down. Lawsa mercy. (*Releases a breath.*) Hey baby, you got the classical nine resemblances? Horns of a stag, head of a camel, eyes of a demon, neck of a snake, belly of a clam, scales of a carp, claws of an eagle, soles of a tiger, ears of a cow? Wait'll Dr. Gussler tries to count your toes, huh? Will you cause the owls to cry and the horses to run mad? Sure, you betcha. (*Calls out.*) Wally? (*a moment*) It's my body, Jane Fonda said so. (*A contraction starts. She starts to go with it and then laughs.*) Ow. Ow. False alarm. Why have these doctors gotten so affronted by the extraordinary, huh? Desperate for order Wally says. Why you, Gussler? Where is the *magic?* You won't even rub yourself all over with crocodile doo-doo and dance around me or anything. Oh. Oh. (*Contraction starts.*) Ow. Ow. Wally you bastard, I know you're at Baskin-Robbins. (*Pattern-pant blows.*) Short. Shorter. Back pain. (*A moment.*) The Shively Suburban Hospital of the Immaculate Conception. Gives me a certain ironic pleasure to give birth to a dragon in a Catholic hospital. Look Gussler, I know, you told me I'm going to have a baby that isn't right. You deliver and I'll cope. Just get off my back, O.K.?

Normal baby. Where do you think all the dragons went, huh Gussler? St. George lanced 'em 'cause they weren't normal. (*Heavy contraction.*) Ow! Single combat. Ow. Bright orange, seventy feet tall, wings obscuring the sun, nostrils flaring, radiant with its own fire. Villagers screaming, drawbridges slamming shut, divines shrieking prayers in the market place, nurses telling jokes by the coffee machines, goddamnit this is a long contraction, and here I come, unarmed, vegetarian, hey it's O.K., I can handle this, it's the fruit of my womb, Gussler. (*She lies breathing hard.*) Oh boy. Oh boy. Let me love this child, God, for all beauty is in the eye of the beholder. Let me live with my husband in mutual concern and generosity. Let us be love's fools. I pray that my life, my one life, will not be normal. Amen. Oh, and all forgiving Jesus, I would like Dr. Gussler on a platter, medium-well with a side order of home fries. O.K.? (*A moment.*) Hey, St. Margaret? When I told Wally about the tests, and how I still wanted it, he just touched my arm and said 'Sure.' That's all he said. And then he smiled. The most beautiful, unforced, heartfull, miraculous, beautiful smile. That Wally, he's O.K. in my book. (*Contraction*) Oh my Hannah, burst from my stomach on your night-dark wings, quicken the new spring with your scarlet breath...ow, ow, ow...(*She pattern-pant blows as the lights fade.*)
(*Blackout.*)

END OF DRAGONS

FRENCH FRIES

An old woman in a straight-back chair holding a McDonald's cup.
She is surrounded by several bundles of newspapers. She wears thick
glasses that distort her eyes to the viewer.

ANNA MAE: If I had one wish in my life, why I'd like to live in
   McDonald's. Right there in the restaurant. 'Stead of in this old
   place. I'll come up to the brow of the hill, bowed down with my
   troubles, hurtin' under my load and I'll see that yellow
   horseshoe, sort of like part of a rainbow, and it gives my old
   spirit a lift. Lord, I can sit in a McDonald's all day. I've done it
   too. Walked the seven miles with the sun just on its way, and
   then sat on the curb till five minutes of seven. First one there and
   the last to leave. Just like some ol' french fry they forgot.
      I like the young people workin' there. Like a team of fine
   young horses when I was growin' up. All smilin'. Tell you what I
   really like though is the plastic. God gave us plastic so there
   wouldn't be no stains on his world. See, in the human world of
   the earth it all gets scratched, stained, tore up, faded down. Loses
   its shine. All of it does. In time. Well, God he gave us the idea of
   plastic so we'd know what the everlasting really was. See if there's
   plastic then there's surely eternity. It's God's hint.
      You ever watch folks when they come on in the
   McDonald's? They always speed up, almost run the last few
   steps. You see if they don't. Old Dobbin with the barn in sight.
   They know it's safe in there and it ain't safe outside. Now it ain't
   safe outside and you know it.
      I've seen a man healed by a Big Mac. I have. I was just sittin'
   there. Last summer it was. Oh, they don't never move you on. It's
   a sacred law in McDonald's, you can sit for a hundred years.
   Only place in the world. Anyway, a fella, maybe thirty-five,
   maybe forty, come on in there dressed real nice, real bright tie,
   bran' new baseball cap, nice white socks and he had him that
   disease. You know the one I mean, Cerebral Walrus they call it.
   Anyway, he had him a cock leg. His poor old body had it two
   speeds at the same time. Now he got him some coffee, with a lid
   on, and sat him down and Jimmy the tow-head cook knew him,

see, and he brought over a Big Mac. Well, the sick fella ate maybe half of it and then he was just sittin', you know, suffering those tremors, when a couple of *ants* come right out of the burger. Now there ain't no ants in McDonald's no way. Lord sent those ants, and the sick fella he looked real sharp at the burger and a bunch *more* ants marched on out nice as you please and his head lolled right over and he pitched himself out of that chair and banged his head on the floor, loud. Thwack! Like a bowling ball dropping. Made you half sick to hear it. We jump up and run over but he was cold out. Well those servin' kids, so cute, they watered him, stuck a touch pepper up his nostril, slapped him right smart, and bang, up he got. Standin' an' blinkin'. 'Well, how are you?,' we say. An he looks us over, looks right in our eyes, and he say, 'I'm fine.' And he was. He was fine! Tipped his Cincinnati Reds baseball cap, big 'jus'-swallowed-the-canary' grin, paraded out of there clean, straight like a pole-bean poplar, walked him a plumb line without no trace of the 'walrus.' Got outside, jumped up, whooped, hollered, sang him the National Anthem, flagged down a Circle Line bus, an' rode off up Muhammad Ali Boulevard wavin' an' smilin' like the King of the Pharoahs. Healed by a Big Mac. I saw it.

McDonald's. You ever see anybody die in a McDonald's? No sir. No way. Nobody ever has died in one. Shoot, they die in Burger Kings all the time. Kentucky Fried Chicken's got their own damn ambulances. Nooooooooooo, you can't die in a McDonald's no matter how hard you try. It's the spices. Seals you safe in this life like it seals in the flavor. Yesssssss, yes!

I asked Jarrell could I live there. See they close up around ten, and there ain't a thing goin' on in 'em till seven a.m. I'd just sit in those nice swingy chairs and lean forward. Rest my head on those cool, cool, smooth tables, sing me a hymn and sleep like a baby. Jarrell, he said he'd write him a letter up the chain of command and see would they let me. Oh, I got my bid in. Peaceful and clean.

Sometimes I see it like the last of a movie. You know how they start the picture up real close and then back it off steady and far? Well, that's how I dream it. I'm living in McDonald's and it's real late at night and you see me up close, smiling, and then you see the whole McDonald's from the outside, lit up and friendly.

And I get smaller and smaller, like they do, and then it's just a light in the darkness, like a star, and I'm in it. I'm part of that light, part of the whole sky, and it's all McDonald's, but part of something even bigger, something fixed and shiny...like plastic.

I know. I know. It's just a dream. Just a beacon in the storm. But you got to have a dream. It's our dreams make us what we are.

(*Blackout.*)

END OF FRENCH FRIES

MARKS

A woman sits on a bar stool. She is in her early forties but attractive. She wears a plain, black cocktail dress. On every visible part of her body we see blue and red tattoos. The tattoos include twining snakes, demons, flowers, birds in flight, etc. The left side of her face is without tattoos but bears a single scar about three inches long below the cheek. She holds and sips a glass of red wine.

ALAIN: Until I was thirty-five there was nothing out of the ordinary, nothing remarkable about my life. My days were very like one of those baroque string quartets. Soothing. Placid. Repetitive. School years without protest or excess. Prom years. Not so much as a single evening's anarchy. My uncle, a Connecticut lawyer, was heard on the eve of my nineteenth birthday to raise a toast which described me, in a positive way he thought, as 'unsurprising.' In college, an unexceptional college, I appreciated. Appreciated music. Appreciated art. I was, if memory serves, a major in a subject whose actual point or content now escapes me, cultural geography. Had I died at that time, perhaps of acute boredom let us say, in the school cafeteria, eating peas, it would have been agreed, by all who knew me that my epitaph should read, 'She did as she was told.' Or blander yet, 'She did as she supposed she might be told.'

I met my husband, Arthur, at a festive tea held to honor the retiring faculty advisor of the Christian Youth Center. He proposed a toast, grapeade I think it was, and we were married two years later after weekly dates shared out among three restaurants of vastly ordinary cuisine. We were, I'm sure, the last of our generation to save ourselves for marriage. We had two children. First a girl and then a boy. Two job transfers. Two homes. Two subdivisions. And then on our 15th anniversary Arthur left me, saying I had nothing further to give. I was, he said, unmarked by life.

In the weeks that followed I suffered most because I could not seem to suffer. I became an acolyte to sangria, made brief, nervous forays into singles bars and one evening was walked to my car by a musician who suggested that we make love there in the parking lot, between two yellow lines, as he was, as he so delicately put it, 'between sets.' Well, I resisted, and much annoyed, he cut me here. I stood, horrified and somewhat embarrassed, at sea in the midst of asphalt, staring at drops of blood on my beige shoes. When the scar, this scar, formed I was astounded to find that for the first time people looked at me. Not unkindly, and with interest. And they were not the sort of people that I had known before. Oh no, these were interesting people, people who were not unmarked by life. And my mark, my scar, made me in some way approachable; this blemish gave me confidence. And it occurred to me then, or very shortly thereafter, that perhaps it might be best to wear our lives upon our skin. And so I do. This serpent is Muhammed Kastapha, who coiled his life around mine and taught me that there are pressures, and dangers, even a sort of degradation so delightful that it seems ungrateful to resist. This bird in flight, horror-struck, would be my mother. This scythe, the ritual likeness of my musician of the parking lot. This day lily, which blooms, decays and is remembered, is Marian, who instructed me with her death. Taught me with her going. On the palm of my left hand, a crucified Christ, for Brother Shelton, who reached out a hand to save me, he thought, and was repaid with pain. A rising sun for Alex, Charybdis and Scylla, for Jimmy and Cal. An orchid for...isn't that odd? I know her scent but can't recall her name. They have all marked me. Well, of course, you see that. May I advise you? Please. Let them mark you. Because, you see, the best among us have had so many imprints left upon them that it is like...embroidery. And these people, life-engraved, are drawn to each other and pass the time interpreting their signs. And those moments of sharing are the best of life. And this unraveling of hieroglyphs, personally I call it love, lasts only so long as there are marks to read. Then it is gone.

Sometimes the unmarked are attracted to me. They stare...briefly. Fascinated and a little frightened. And in the parking lots, I cut them. Make a small mark. (*She touches her cheek.*) Like this. And it is then their lives begin. With a little pain. That is, if there is any understanding in them. You understand me? Yes, I think you do. Salud. (*She toasts them.*) (*Fade Out.*)

END OF PLAY

The Boy Who
Ate the Moon

ORIGINAL PRODUCTION

The Boy Who Ate The Moon premiered November 22, 1981 as part of the *SHORTS* Festival at Actors Theatre of Louisville and featured Laura Hicks as Nurse Baines and Allen Evans as James.

CHARACTERS

JAMES
NURSE BAINES

THE BOY WHO ATE THE MOON

A doctor's receptionist greets a new patient.

NURSE BAINES: Good morning.

JAMES: Morning. (*He sits. She works.*) Are you the doctor?

NURSE BAINES: I work for the doctor. (*No reaction from him.*) You have an appointment with Doctor Keane?

JAMES: How do you get one?

NURSE BAINES: An appointment? (*No reaction.*) You would...you would call for an appointment. (*He rises, picks up his stuff and begins to leave.*) Excuse me?

JAMES: Yes, ma'am?

NURSE BAINES: Did you want to see the doctor?

JAMES: I saw a phone downstairs.

NURSE BAINES: You need a phone?

JAMES: To get an appointment with the doctor.

NURSE BAINES: We're getting a little confused, aren't we?

JAMES: You said to call.

NURSE BAINES: Could I have your name, please?

JAMES: My name is James.

NURSE BAINES: James what?

JAMES: Could you tell me how many days...I mean from now... before the moon will be full?

NURSE BAINES: Well...no, I couldn't.

JAMES: But the doctor knows, right?

NURSE BAINES: Mr. James, the doctor isn't in. He makes rounds today. I mean that he will be in but...can I make an appointment for you?

JAMES: What's your name?

NURSE BAINES: Is it an appointment that you want, Mr. James?

JAMES: My first name is James.

NURSE BAINES: I see.

JAMES: The moon is inside me.

NURSE BAINES: I see.

JAMES: I never gave it much thought until I realized it wasn't full.

NURSE BAINES: Would you care to take a chair?

JAMES: No thanks, I have some. (*No reaction from her.*)

NURSE BAINES: My name is Susan.

JAMES: I'm James.

NURSE BAINES: James, if you sat down...you know, sat in a chair...I think I could find a doctor for you.

JAMES: That would be fine. I'm dying.

NURSE BAINES: (*Takes out a form.*) Would you answer a few questions for me?

JAMES: It says Ear, Nose and Throat...the door.

NURSE BAINES: Yes.

JAMES: It went down my throat but it's not there now.

NURSE BAINES: Have you been to see us before, James?

JAMES: No, ma'am.

NURSE BAINES: Have you ever used drugs of any kind?

JAMES: No, ma'am.

NURSE BAINES: What day is it?

JAMES: You mean the date?

NURSE BAINES: That would be fine.

JAMES: The 17th. Have you ever used drugs of any kind?

NURSE BAINES: (*A pause.*) Yes, I have.

JAMES: I'd be afraid.

NURSE BAINES: Why are you dying, James?

JAMES: Distension. I'll explode, I suppose. I have something in me...you know, pressing, pressing out. It grows in there and it presses out…presses the feeling out. The feelings. Plural. Is my hand hot?

NURSE BAINES: (*Hesitates an instant and then takes his hand.*) It's warm, yes.

JAMES: The pressing makes me hot. I've been getting a little hotter each day for several years.

NURSE BAINES: I'll call…get a doctor for you. (*She dials and then talks quietly on the phone during the following.*)

JAMES: It used to be I could control it with ice cream. I would eat ice cream but now it melts without cooling and I don't like the sweet taste. Winter was good. Lying down in the snow was good, but I got so hot that steam…steam came out of me like I was smoking. I can boil water with my right hand. I can't take a bath anymore…showers, sure…I mean I'm not dirty or anything… but a bath, after a few minutes, it could boil me like a lobster. I warm the air. Can you feel it? Melanie can't touch me anymore. Well, I mean for a second, sure…like you touched my hands… But for longer…you know…not anymore. People only want you to give off so much heat…

NURSE BAINES: James…

JAMES: I'll move further back if you want me to.

NURSE BAINES: I found Doctor Keane for you. He's coming.

JAMES: Last night I could see my hands in the dark. It suddenly occurred to me that I was going to ignite. I think it must be very painful to burn…I mean that's different from heat. I would be very afraid to burn…

NURSE BAINES: James…

JAMES: Remember how they taught you that by rubbing two sticks…well that's…my inside rubs against my outside. It was raining last night so I figured it would put me out. I went out… went out in the rain and down by the laundromat…down by Spring Street there was a pool and the moon…I was pretty sure that if the rain on the outside, the outside of me didn't…well then I'd just drink the water…put me out that way…but I wasn't…you know…thinking clearly and I…and I swallowed the moon. Well just the beginning of one…part of a moon. It's going to grow inside me…you know…for however many days… making pressure…making me hotter…I'm uh…I'm uh going to leak flame…I'm pretty sure it will set me on fire…you know, in my condition…see the thing is that once you start getting hot it's really hard to cool down.

NURSE BAINES: James?

JAMES: Yes, ma'am?

NURSE BAINES: Would you let me try something?

JAMES: Yes, ma'am.

NURSE BAINES: (*Moves out around the desk toward him.*) Put out your arms like this.

JAMES: Am I doing it right?

NURSE BAINES: Yes. Yes, that's just right. (*She moves directly to him and embraces him.*)

JAMES: Listen…

NURSE BAINES: Shhhhhh. No talking.

JAMES: (*Still holding his arms out away from her.*) I don't want to hurt you.

NURSE BAINES: You won't. Put your arms down.

JAMES: I'm not burning you?

NURSE BAINES: No, you're getting cooler.

JAMES: Melanie can't even touch me.

NURSE BAINES: SHHHHHHH. (*They stand for a moment, several moments. She moves back.*) There.

JAMES: I didn't burn you.

NURSE BAINES: No.

JAMES: I'm still hot.

NURSE BAINES: It's probably just left over heat. (*She reaches out and touches his cheek.*) You're quite cool to the touch.

JAMES: What should I do now?

NURSE BAINES: You should sit down now. (*He does. She goes back behind the desk.*) The doctor's coming.

JAMES: But I'm cool now.

NURSE BAINES: He'll just make sure the moon's gone.

JAMES: (*They sit in silence for a few moments.*) Thanks.

NURSE BAINES: You're very welcome. (*She goes back to her forms. He watches. The lights go down.*)

END OF PLAY

Cul de Sac

ORIGINAL PRODUCTION

Cul de Sac premiered November 22, 1981 as part of the *Shorts* Festival at Actors Theatre of Louisville and featured Christine Rose.

CHARACTER

MAGGIE

CUL DE SAC

A well-dressed woman in a winter suit with a light topcoat over it, carrying a leather purse enters through the audience. She walks up on the stage without looking back and then suddenly pivots. She holds a thirty-eight special in the two-handed police firing position.

MAGGIE: Freeze! Sorry sucker. You figured you had a real kleenex here didn't you? A real three-minute special? Dressed up pretty and straight. Walking home from her recorder society or her E.S.T. meeting maybe. Carrying, oh, sixty, seventy dollars in cash plus the odd gold chain, coral ring, malachite pin. Three, four credit cards, a checkbook and what, a key, keys…car, house, safe deposit box. Perfection. Big petrified eyes. Funny little terrified smiles. Hit and run. Why you'd be back on the West Side, watching the Jets and snorting coke and it wouldn't even be eleven o'clock. You're white. How nice. Take off your clothes. Your clothes. Take them off. Imagine your delight…some cuckoo broad cutting between buildings instead of staying out where the people are. She doesn't even hear you behind her. Well this is your lucky day. Now your shirt. Ah-ah. In this .38 are exploding bullets that will create something very like the Lincoln Tunnel where your chest used to be. That's better. And the undershirt. Poor thing, you need mending. Tell me, is that how you usually get undressed? When you're about to service your women? You take the pants off over your shoes like that? Men never fail to amaze me. Is this your first time as the victim? I bet it is. Well I'm going to take your cherry. I snack on virgins. Listen hairless, I am extremely powerful and confident. Do you get off on that? The shoes. The socks. I am one of our country's leading research chemists and the spine and provider for a family of five. You apparently mistook me for some other century. Lovehandles. You could lose a little weight. Now, I have observed in lab mice that long-time learned and reinforced behavior can only be modified by shock, pain, fear and disorientation. For you, all four. Lie down. Do it! On the pavement. Flat. On your back. You want bone fragments over a fifty foot area? Good. You follow instructions nicely. A few years of Pavlovian training you could probably become a human. Here. (*She throws another object to him.*) It's my uncle's straight razor, pick it up and cut off your dick. Lie down! It's really sharp; it won't take a second. I'd suggest about an inch from the end. Then you can take this hair ribbon and tourniquet it about three inches below the wound. After that you can go over one block to Eighty Sixth and then two blocks down to St. Michael's Hospital where they will be intrigued enough to take good care of you. You'll like it. You'll meet a lot of nice Pakistani interns. You ventured to smile? Fine. I know it is very hard for you to take a woman seriously because of cultural stereotyping and your internalized male models, but I am one of many women who mean exactly what they say. I'm going to give you fifteen seconds and then you'll be a dead mugger. Believe me Reagan doesn't care. Go on. Cut. Cut! Very good. The ribbon. The ribbon! Tighter. That's my brave boy. The thing to remember here is that you made me. I am your creature. I am what they call backlash. You didn't move fast enough. You didn't change things. You thought you could wait me out. You thought I had a short attention span. I really cannot abide being patronized. That's sweet, you're crying. Here. Cab fare. Thanks for everything. I enjoyed it. (*She walks off. Blackout.*)

END OF PLAY

Shasta Rue

ORIGINAL PRODUCTION

Shasta Rue premiered November 1, 1983 as part of the *Shorts* Festival at Actors Theatre of Louisville and featured Theresa Merritt.

CHARACTER

SHASTA RUE

SHASTA RUE

A fifty-year-old black woman in a flowered summer cotton dress made vague with age. Over the dress she wears a beauty contest sway reading Miss Prettybelle Kentucky. In her hair is a gold bead tiara. In one hand she carries a golden scepter and in the other several slightly wilted long-stem yellow roses. She is a plain woman with a mountainous energy that contains elements of the traditional Southern tent revival.

MAMA: So what you think's wrong with this picture? (*Adjusts her tiara.*) Yeah, that's right, Miss Prettybelle Kentucky. Struck three to four million citizens of this here Commonwealth dumb with admiration. Uh-huh! The considerable number who was dumb already jes' got theyselves struck dumber. Yes, yesssssss! Oh, I got the beauty! My big ol' daughter Shasta Rue, she got it for me. "Don't cry, Mama." "I ain't cryin', Shasta Rue." "Cryin' make you wet an' ugly." "Ugly already, missy, so I'll jes' get wet." "You cryin' at the TV, Mama?" "No, jes' cryin' for the sheer life of it, honey." Sittin' in the trailer, drinkin' flat Falls City beer, watchin' the Dukes, licken' on a taffy apple, switchin' them channels an' jes' cryin' all over my miserable low class life. "Hold on there, Mama." "Say what?" "Miss Kentucky Pageant." "Uh-huh." "Looky them beauties. All them white beauties." "Reason is, ain't enough black people got them a bathin' suit." Yes, yesssssss! Me an' Shasta lookin' on the beauties. Lookin' at all that fine horse flesh. Chilled me to the bone, baby. Made us mean, you know? Gave me an' Shasta the blood lust for straight bourbon whiskey. Oh black Jesus, didn't we knock it back! Didn't we drain the cup? Yes. Oh yes! Ol' Shasta she got down to pantin', started in sighin', started in rockin', rockin' back to front, way she does. "How come you didn't be no beauty, Mama? How come you ain't the Monroe County contestant, huh? How come you ain't up there doin' the sugar-sweet bird calls of the Kentucky cardinal in your apricot one-piece bathin' suit, huh?" "Cause first, God made him the pretty. Then he make him the plain to make the pretty shine, an' then he made us, Shasta Rue, to give them plain folks a laugh on Saturday night."

Then Shasta she bang on the table. She's a big strong girl, Shasta, an' she yell, "An' you made me, didn't you, Mama? You give me my poundage and my six-foot-one an' my hand can close up over a tea pot so y' can't see it, din't you, Mama?" "Yes, I did do that!" An' she yells, "Butcha lef' out m' glory, lef' out my beauty, lef' out my swim suitability." An' I stood up like Moses on the Mount, an' I point at the TV beauties an' I holler. "*They* got it. They got it all!" An' she yells, "Let's git it!" And we do! We haul ass outta that trailer over to Loco Boys' pick-up an' we hotwire that sumbitch, an drive eighty million, lead-footin' bumpity-squealin', lay-rubber miles-an-hour downtown. An' we kill that Kentucky Lucky half-pint dead on the way, singin' "Amazin' Grace" and "Deep Soul Kisses" and yellin' about them beauties, tears running down our faces, and then we see it. See where they got the pageant. Loomin' up. All shiny like a jewel box. Name up in lights. Search lights criss-crossin'. Shasta rockin', doin' little whoops. "Hit them brakes!" she yells. An' I do, I slam 'em. I bang 'em and we go smashin' our heads through that pick-up windshield like a kiss through Kleenex, an' we're bleedin' an' cryin', and we're outta the pick-up, an' this shrimped-up tuxedo doorman says, "Y'all cain't go in there." An' I stomp on's foot and Shasta rips off his li'l blond toupé an' we wipe off the blood wif it an' we're through that lobby eatin' usherettes on the way an' Shasta she hauls open these big ol' oak doors an' there it is! Yes Lord, there it is! We in the theatre with the Miss Kentucky Prettybelles pageant.

An' there's them beauties straight in a line, rainbow dresses and 'lectric bouquets, smile-to-smile like one big long picket fence, an' they waitin' on the envelope for they fate to be delivered by one a' them A.C./D.C./Emcees. An' ever' single one a' them ding-dong beauties is blonde. Look like a police lineup for Palomino ponies. White folks must jes' kill them brunettes at birth. An' Shasta she goes crazy! Sound come through her throat like an ash from a volcano, an' the rivers dry up, an' all the dogs and cats turn to stone, an' all over town the trees start glowin' in the dark an' Shasta an' her mama start down that aisle, pickin' up speed, an' it's downhill, gettin' steep, rollin', roarin', and there's ushers step up and we blow 'em away, poppin' up, goin' down, poppin' up, goin' down, an' we speedin', and we fly over this pit, this fifteen-foot hole an' the audience is screamin' and then there we are, we up there, we up there with the beauties.

An' Shasta stops, an' the audience it stops, an' the man with the envelope he stops, an' the big clock on the balcony it stops, an' it's grave-closin' low moanin', down deep, well-water quiet. An' Shasta spreads her arms, she lets out her wing span, an' her eyes bug out and she say in this deep bass voice, "I come for my beauty." An' they all still smilin' but they got pee-pee seepin' outta the corners of their eyes. An' then Shasta she throw her head back an' crows like a rooster, an' we're amongst 'em like bears in a hamster hutch.

Oh, there's bouquets flyin', an' strips of chiffon like a blizzard, an' falsies floppin' out like burger patties. Store-bought eyelashes gittin' stuck on boobies an' ol' Shasta, she stuff two fuck-me pumps in the emcee's mouth and kick his Miami-tan ass right into the orchestra pit. I got this one blonde beauty by her prissy French-braids and I'm hootin', "Gimme that uptown wig you Baptist bitch!" And then, right from up on this high place, clear like a tornado alert comes this voice sayin' "Y'all hold on there Batman, you and Robin back your blackness off!"

I look up and Shasta looks up, and there she is, lightnin' zappin' off her tiara, radiation round her head, Miss Kentucky, last year's model, got her gown on, got her crown on, got her sash on, oh so white looks like she been bleached once a day since creation, an' she got crimson red hair like the Grand Klan Dragon just set her to fire, and them neon blue eyes flashin' on and off, blinkin' and winkin', and baby sparkles like fireflies midst the hairs on her arms, and she say, "What you niggers want?" An' Shasta she shake her ham-fist up in the air, and she stamp on the floor an' she say, "I come for my mama's beauty!"

An' Miss Vanilla she walk her pretty perfume tallow-candle self down her red carpet paradise stairs 'til she nose-to-nose with Shasta Rue, an' she say, "Shit, honey, you want this raggedy crap, you can sure as hell have it. You can have the crown, the gown, and the chicken à la king. *You* can pull that parachute off them new Toyotas, dress like Scarlett O'Whatsit at the Kosair luncheon, an' chap your lips at the kiss-a-queen booth at the Twitchelltown Fair. You ain't chaos and confusion darlin', you the goddamned marines!" Then she turn to the multitude an' she say, "Y'all redneck trash, hesh up, you hear?" An' she lay that sash on me, gimme her rhinestone scepter and gold bead tiara, an' then she smile on Shasta Rue and give her her ear bobs.

Lordy, it was lessez faire! An' the three of us walk on out, hand-in-hand like ol' Hubert Humphrey's wet dream a' racial equality, an' the Red Sea parts an' we under the marquee with them searchlights goin' and I say, "Thank you, Miss Pale," an' she say, "You entirely welcome, Aunt Jemima," an' she unzip her strapless aquamarine dot-sequin formal an' she say, "They ask you where I gone, Sweet Ebony, you tell 'em I gone to Houston to the Spoon Gravy debutante ball." An' she walks off down Third Street naked as a jaybird in her lime green heals, an' that white pickaninny's whistlin' "Dixie." Lemme tell you one thing, it takes a real lady to walk bare naked through downtown Louisville after 'leven o'clock at night an' git home with two arms and legs. Yes, yesssssss!

Well, that's how Shasta Rue got me the beauty. White missy lay it down like it was spit or ol' gum, but I know better. Beauty beats smart. *Beauty* is the *life*. *Smart's* jes' talkin' about it. Uh-huh. See, now I got the beauty an' *you* ain't got shit. You want it, you go hunt some up for y'self. Ain't that right, Shasta Rue? Yes it is, it's right. (*Blackout.*)

END OF PLAY

Summer

ORIGINAL PRODUCTION

Summer premiered October 31, 1984 as part of the *Shorts* Festival at Actors Theatre of Louisville and featured the following cast:

Jennifer Landis..Gretchen Kehde
Esposito...Michael Kevin
Lilian Landis..Dorothy Holland
Driver...Lanny Flaherty
Dilly McGregor..Gretchen West
Marta McGregor.......................................Kathleen Chalfant
Cairn McGregor...Bob Burrus
Doc...Rob Knepper

CHARACTERS

Jennifer Landis
Esposito
Lilian Landis
Driver
Dilly McGregor
Marta McGregor
Cairn McGregor
Doc

SUMMER

The Scene: The play takes place over a four month period from May to late August during the year 1949. The scenes move between a garden in Philadelphia, the McGregor ranch outside Billings, Montana, a Cunard Liner and various locations in France. There is no scenery, only specific pieces of furniture which always remain on stage but are rearranged to indicate several locales. The furniture includes four bentwood chairs, a small but attractive country side-table, a delicate antique armchair, an iron and brass single bed covered by a country quilt, and two filled feed sacks that together act as a settable.

At Rise: The central acting area is clear except for a pair of gardening shears, a hoe and work gloves. Lilian Landis, an attractive woman of 38, dressed in a light white or pastel gardening frock stands upstage holding cut flowers and a trowel. Downstage is her daughter Jennifer, 16, similarly dressed and holding cut flowers. Jennifer, in a fury and out of control, throws the flowers at her mother as she speaks.

    Others on stage (and it is worth mentioning that no character ever leaves the stage, except for costume changes, but adjust themselves while remaining in character and watch scenes in which they take no direct part) include: Esposito, a well-to-do Guatemalan, dealing in copper claims. He is in his early forties, seemingly gentle, somewhat evasive, gracious and keenly focused. He dresses mainly in summer white. Cairn McGregor, 45, a Montana rancher, worn, watchful, hunted in an odd way. Marta McGregor, his wife and Lilian's sister, 36 years of age. She is warm, fearful of the future, delicate with children and radiates a kind of unfulfilled promise. Dilly, Marta's daughter of eighteen, is a pistol. Bright and cosseted, newly aware of her sexual powers, and demanding but easily embarrassed or angered. She is home from her first year at the university and made edgy by constraint. Doc, twenty-two years old, he is deaf and signs to communicate. Marta, Dilly and Cairn can sign as well. He is a barometer of atmospheres, part Indian, and works for Cairn, raising, training and handling his game fowls, a consuming interest to them both. The "Driver," a man in his forties with the high color that often marks an alcoholic. He was a non-commissioned officer in the recent great war. He has a cynical manner and a flat delivery.

During the course of the play of fifteen scenes, there are no blackouts but only shifts of light while Lilian "corresponds" with Jennifer, all her dialogue being in actuality letters. She can stay in or near the antique chair or move through those who effect the brief scene changes. None of the other characters interact with her, though Jennifer reacts. She alone does not watch the action in progress but writes in her journal when she is not speaking. The lights come up on the two women, standing on an empty stage.

Scene 1

JENNIFER: Because it's you. Not him. God, mother, don't you know that? Don't you see what you do? What he does? Because you don't love him, that's why. You love lupines and delphiniums and sweet williams and marguerites and times when we aren't around and your own privacy. Don't you know what people do when they're not loved? It's you. Don't tell me it's him. Don't you dare. You – bitch. Don't you dare.

END OF SCENE 1

Scene 2

The light leaves them and immediately Esposito strikes a match to light his cigar and is picked up by the stage lights. He is dressed in a white linen summer suit and highly decorated cowboy boots. He is seated on a feed sack. Before him is Doc, seated on the floor and watching Esposito's face intently. He also smokes a cigar. Esposito speaks slowly. He indicates his mouth.

ESPOSITO: You understand me? Si? Fuedes leer mis labios? (*The boy nods. Esposito points to a note the boy has given him.*) I also understand. Perhaps she cannot love, hah? She is the mimic of love. You pretend to be in love, you may even fool yourself, hah? Not everyone hears, not everyone loves, you see? Some can only be loved. This is their food. (*Doc holds up a warning hand so Esposito will speak slowly.*) Ah. Yes. El iman? The magnet. You understand? They give nothing, only attract. Only. A very bad thing perhaps, but their fate. They give the lesson, these ones. Hah? But no one likes. No one learns. (*He laughs.*) You see? But part of life this fate. We accept this, hah? Whatever comes. Whatever. Those who cannot love they also serve God. Tambien servimos a Dios. (*Doc looks down. Esposito puts a finger under his chin and raises his head until their eyes meet. Esposito smiles.*) Sometimes those who cannot love seek love from those who cannot love. Hah? This makes the big comedy, yes? What a dance this is! (*He laughs and ruffles the boy's hair.*) You need boots my friend. (*He reaches in his pocket and fishes out a fat roll of bills.*) Black boots, hah? With decorations. The Field-of-Lillies. Or the Climbing Rose. A man accepts his fate if he has boots. Toma'lo. (*He holds out several bills. The boy reaches toward them as the light fades. Lilian now appears in a single spot in a more elaborate and sophisticated traveling dress.*)

END OF SCENE 2

LILIAN: My Dearest Darling Jen',
   As soon as you had disappeared in a curl of steam down the platform, I began to cry buckets, and continued like a great

yawping baby all the way home. Your father, as usual, called me "La Tragedious," which rhymes I think with tedious, and said he would send for a bilge pump unless I desisted, but we packed without further incident or argument and, wonder of wonders, he held my hand in the dining car enroute to New York and was more than solicitous while we boarded the Queen Mary at dock. Don't be too angry with me, Jen. I couldn't bear it. Really. I need your warm heart, my darling. Particularly now. Such journeys we both have, Jen. And so much to learn.

Scene 3

Four bentwood chairs create a taxicab.

DRIVER: ...bout sixteen, seventeen miles. That wall a rock got prehistoric fossils in it. That over there's the outside edge of the Bitteroot Forest. All pretty bare nekked, huh? Hard damn place is what. 'Scuse my French. You want a Life Saver? (*She hesitates.*) I ain't spit on 'em. Any one but a red one. Only ones I eat.

JENNIFER: Thank you.

DRIVER: Please this, thank you that. Hell on manners, ain't ya? Tell you what, I don't like that stuff. Never know what the hell somebody's thinkin'. Guy said thank you one time an en hit me with a claw hammer. Last words outta his mouth, "Thank you." Wham!! 'Bout three weeks later I run the S.O.B. over, 'scuse my French, got out, said pardon me. That's what I said. Pardon-E-MWAW! (*Laughs.*) You ain't from here, that right?

JENNIFER: My family is from Philadelphia, but I've come to visit for the summer with my Aunt.

DRIVER: McGregor Ranch. (*He lights a cigarette.*)

JENNIFER: Do you know them?

DRIVER: I know Cairn. That old Scot, he takes him some money off me time to time.

JENNIFER: (*Coughs.*) Excuse me.

DRIVER: I take a gentleman out there sometimes. South American gentleman… (*Laughs.*) Now there's a fella takes some money offa Cairn. Them damn roundheads of his.

JENNIFER: (*Coughs.*) Could you open the window?

DRIVER: Ain't Montana summer yet, young lady. Time I get you there they'd have to chip you out with an icepick.

JENNIFER: Please. I'm allergic.

DRIVER: Allergic, huh? All in people's heads, you ask me. One a them made up diseases rich people get to pass the time. (*Jennifer has a coughing fit.*) Tell you what, you're in for a summer, way your uncle smokes.

JENNIFER: Do you know my cousin Dilly?

DRIVER: (*Noncommittal.*) I know her. Your people comin' out later?

JENNIFER: My father and mother are touring Europe.

DRIVER: Yeah? (*Chuckles.*) I toured Europe. Got but one eye to show for it. Stood up and yawned at the wrong time outsidea Cherbourg, France. 3rd Army under Patton. (*Chuckles.*) Touring Europe. Well, I enjoyed it. I like the war. Something new all the time. Come right down to it, I like killing people. Those people anyway. Rather shoot me some Germans than drive me a cab. I'll tell you that. (*She coughs. He looks in the rear view mirror.*) You ain't exactly dressed for Montana are you?

JENNIFER: You mean the cold?

DRIVER: How old are you?

JENNIFER: Sixteen last week.

DRIVER: And you don't even know what you got, do you?

JENNIFER: I beg your pardon?

DRIVER: Long drive. You want to sit up front?

JENNIFER: No thank you. (*A pause.*) It's pretty here.

DRIVER: Yeah. Hard always looks pretty from a distance. (*Jennifer coughs.*)

END OF SCENE 3

LILIAN: You must forgive me for making your father cry, Jen. I experiment with him sometimes as an infant might, turning him every which way to see if his stuffing's packed tight. You would be proud of him at the Captain's table in his "soup and fish." His is quite the most romantic moustache in first class…

Scene 4

The bentwoods are removed while Lilian speaks and when the lights restore we are in the front yard outside the old Victorian farm style ranch house. Dilly tries by jumping to peer into a window. She is aware of Jennifer, behind her, only when she is greeted.

JENNIFER: (*After watching for a moment.*) Hello.

DILLY: (*Startled.*) God Almighty!

JENNIFER: I'm sorry.

DILLY: You scared the piss right out of me. I mean it. You can scare a heart into stopping. You know that?

JENNIFER: I'm sorry.

DILLY: Sorry? You could be saying sorry over my almighty corpse.

JENNIFER: I'm sorry.

DILLY: Lord in a bucket! I know who you are! Cousin Jennifer is that you? What day is this? Lord, here I am talking to you like you were nobody at all. Jeez Louise! You want some of my Coca Cola? Well of course you don't that train's just got you tired as a snake. Well, golly! Let's see. Doc'll come tote your bags. (*She rings for him on a hanging triangle.*) Hired boy. He's a real deef-an-dumb but he knows when you ring this bell. Nobody knows how. Reverend Torvaldson says it's this or that to do with Indian blood. Well he's about half Indian and half horny. 'Course that's another story entirely. Well. Say, you ain't deef-an-dumb, are you? No, that's right, you keep sayin' "I'm sorry." Lord, you don't even know who I am do you? Well do you? I'm Dilly.

JENNIFER: I'm Jennifer.

DILLY: Well of course you are. Shoot, I said your name. Well put the bag down for hell's sake. Lord, I'm glad you're here! I got nuthin but boy neighbors and I wouldn't touch 'em with a ten foot pole. Head lice is about the best thing they got. (*Jennifer doesn't know what to say.*) You aren't slow are you? (*Jennifer shakes her head no.*) What on earth have you got on?

JENNIFER: This? My dress? For travel. Mother picked it out.

DILLY: Is it real silk? (*Jennifer nods yes.*) Are you pregnant? Well are you? (*Jennifer shakes her head no.*) No? Got the look. Real steady and smarty at the same time. You can tell me.

JENNIFER: I'm not.

DILLY: I don't know. You know how you get that way? (*Jennifer nods.*) Some old ranch woman Momma knows had her a baby and never knew it was comin'. 'Course she was a little bit stout, (*Indicating the house.*) We got company in there. Wears a white suit, boy makes your palms sweat. I drive him crazy. I do. Let's see. (*A tour by pointing.*) Mainhouse. Hire help. Corrals. Feed barns. 900 acres right to where you see that outcrop. Branding shed. Chicken pens. One cow, two cow, three cow, four cow. (*Laughs.*) Too many damn cows. Boys, I'm glad you're here. Do you swim? Ever done it in your birthday suit? We can. There's a quarry, 'bout a two mile walk. Can you high dive? I can. Like a damn chicken hawk. They say I do it better than any boy in the Scapegoat Mountains.

(*Doc appears at the back of the stage.*)

DILLY: Your parents are getting a divorce, aren't they?

JENNIFER: No. They're not.

DILLY: Mom said.

JENNIFER: They're not.

DILLY: Well, betcha they are anyway. Bet your traveling dress against Doc. (*Jennifer looks upstage at Doc who nods and smiles at her.*) He's mine and I'll bet him.

MARTA: (*From inside.*) Dolores? Who are you talking to out there?

DILLY: He knows how to kiss with the inside of his lips.

MARTA: Dolores?

DILLY: He's Assinboine, mixed, and he can walk hot coals when he's drunk.

(*Marta appears.*)

MARTA: Well, who have we here?

DILLY: Cousin Jennifer off the train, Mom. I just rang for Doc to get her bag. (*She signs to Doc who comes and picks up the bags, throwing a quick look at Jennifer and exiting after a sign from Marta.*)

MARTA: Well, for heaven's sake!

JENNIFER: Jennifer Landis, Mrs. McGregor.

MARTA: Heavens, you sweet thing, you were due on Wednesday's train! (*Moves down to embrace her.*) Oh, my goodness, my goodness. Are you exhausted? I last saw you in the fanciest perambulator man, woman or dog ever laid eyes on. Jiminy! Did you just get dropped here like a lost penny or what?

JENNIFER: The taxi driver let me off by the gate.

DILLY: (*A glance at her mother.*) Oh, wouldn't he!

MARTA: Jackson Trebb, who keeps long distance for owing your uncle money.

DILLY: Him and his worthless chickens.

MARTA: How is your mother, Jennifer?

JENNIFER: Very well, thank you. (*Handing over a wrapped package she carries.*) She sent you this.

MARTA: More bath bubbles, I suspect. Lilian always harbors suspicions about Montana. I've been embroidering something for her drum table but Lord knows when I'll finish. Is she at sea yet?

JENNIFER: On the Cunard for France.

MARTA: Well good, good, good. Your Daddy, too? Well, fine. Now why are we standing here in the dust? Dilly, run in and tell Pop and Mr. Esposito. Go, shoo. (*Dilly goes.*) Lord, those two men wouldn't break a conversation over their blessed chickens if the earth opened up at their feet. Aren't I dead glad you're here! Bless your sweet face.

JENNIFER: I'm glad to be invited.

MARTA: You'll share a room with Dilly. Heaven knows when she'll let you sleep. She's a full time talker but a good heart. (*Jennifer starts to cry.*) Oh. (*Holds her again.*) They'll be fine, your mother and father. Fine. Truly and truly. Don't cry. Shhhh.

CAIRN: (*Off.*) Sure the Morgan Grey *is* an ace cutter but they're pretty bad to run.

MARTA: I love your mother and I love you. Sea air works its magic. They just need to get away from practical things. Lord, I'm sure it just worries you to death.

ESPOSITO: (*As they enter.*) ...more protein you can give, sometimes the dog food, and strychnine the day of the fight, then they don't run.

CAIRN: I'll see no cockrel of mine doped.

ESPOSITO: This chicken is not interested in your moral universe.

CAIRN: Sure you can fight 'em...once, but then they molt and get bald and end bald as a doorknob...

DILLY: (*Interrupting.*) Cousin Jennifer, Pop. Cousin Jennifer here for the summer.

MARTA: And worn out and hungry and in a strange place. (*She touches Esposito lightly on the arm and Cairn notes the touch.*) Just look at the child. (*Cairn stands without speaking.*) Cairn?

CAIRN: Do those trains not have a schedule?

MARTA: Lilian and James had to leave on the Cunard.

CAIRN: Cunard? (*He glances at Marta and she shakes her head almost unnoticeaably to prevent him from going on. He looks back at Jennifer.*) Well, that's not a fit dress for horseback.

DILLY: (*Laughing.*) Pop.

MARTA: We might give the child tea before we throw her on horseback. (*Esposito laughs. Marta smiles at him.*) Well he does. Aren't we ever so glad she's come, Cairn? (*Cairn nods.*) This is Señor Esposito, Jennifer. Señor Esposito is in copper. He resides, ordinarily, in Guatemala. My sister Lilian's girl from clear back in Philadelphia. So.

JENNIFER: How do you do?

ESPOSITO: (*Takes her hand and gravely kisses it.*) It is a great pleasure to make a friend from Philadelphia. (*Dilly giggles.*)

MARTA: Dolores.

DILLY: Well, it tickles when he does that.

MARTA: Hush.

ESPOSITO: From your Philadelphia is Mr. Benjamin Franklin, yes? And also this was, at one time, the Capitol of your great country. Did you know this? Ah no, I am not without understanding of your Philadelphia.

DILLY: Don't know everything, though. Don't know my middle name.

ESPOSITO: Wallace, after the Scottish patriot.

DILLY: (*A furious look at her mother.*) You told him.

MARTA: Dilly.

ESPOSITO: (*To Jennifer.*) When you are rested we will speak again. Me e' mejorado por haberte conocido.

DILLY: (*Interrupting.*) Bet you don't know all the phobias, though.

MARTA: Dilly, don't you dare.

DILLY: (*Standing directly in front of Esposito.*) Do you?

ESPOSITO: (*Smiling.*) Phobias?

DILLY: Acrophobia – fear of heights, agoraphobia – fear of open places, ailurophobia – fear of cats, algophobia – fear of pain, androphobia – fear of men...

MARTA: Dilly, for heaven's sake. (*She reaches for her but Dilly dances away.*)

(*Doc appears upstage watching.*)

DILLY: Anthophobia – fear of flowers, apiphobia – fear of bees, antrophobia – fear of people...

MARTA: Cairn?

CAIRN: (*Shaking his head.*) Wish she knew her hymns half so well.

DILLY: Arachibutyrophobia – fear of peanut butter sticking to the roof of the mouth... (*Esposito laughs. She curtsies to him.*)

MARTA: Enough is enough, Dolores.

DILLY: Astraphobia – fear of storms, autophobia – fear of solitude, bacillophobia – fear of microbes, ballistophobia – fear of bullets, bathophobia – fear of depth... (*Cairn signs to Doc and goes back in the house.*) Belonephobia – fear of pins, botanophobia – fear of plants... (*Doc moves down behind Dilly.*) Ceranunophobia – fear of thunder, chromophobia – fear of certain colors, claustrophobia – fear of enclosed spaces... (*Doc grabs Dilly from behind around the waist, and picking her up, begins to carry her offstage.*) No. No! Clinophobia – fear of beds, put me down, let me go. (*She struggles frantically.*) Let me go. Let me go. Let me go. Let me go. Let me go.(*She is carried off. We hear this litany as they move off. Esposito laughs softly. He stops. Jennifer, Marta and Esposito look at each other. Esposito touches Jennifer's cheek. He tips his hat to Marta. He exits the other direction. The light fades.*)

END OF SCENE 4

LILIAN: It is quite the wrong idea I think, this vacuum packing of a marriage in a small enclosed space, bringing it to a boil, and then separating it like curds and whey into an upper and lower bunk. He flees me now, bolting after breakfast and marching around the deck with a dour Mr. Draper discussing his beloved amino acids and marshalling his "isoleucine, metrionine, and tryptophon" as if there weren't a single woman in the world.

Scene 5

Esposito sits on a benchwood, a drum table with a lamp on it beside him. He sits with his arms crossed over his chest holding his own lapels. Behind him stands Marta massaging his temples. In the bedroom Dilly and Jennifer, now friends through necessity, are trying on clothes and deep in surreptitious conversation.

MARTA: Do you like it here?

ESPOSITO: Yes, of course.

MARTA: Well enough to stay?

ESPOSITO: I like this Montana far better than any place which is not my country.

MARTA: When must you go?

ESPOSITO: Many minutes, many hours, many, many days.

MARTA: But gone by snowfall. It is very white and empty here in the winter.

DILLY: (*Having been whispering she now moves away from Jennifer and we can hear her speak.*) So finally I just grabbed his old hand and put it right on my breast...

JENNIFER: You didn't!

DILLY: (*Imitating her.*) "You didn't." I did.

MARTA: (*In the other room.*) I've made you something.

DILLY: It's not so easy to flirt with a deef-an-dumb. They won't take a hint.

MARTA: (*Handing him an embroidered handkerchief.*) For the summer heat.

DILLY: Well, after that it was Johnny-bar-the-door, I can tell you. (*Finishes putting on her mother's antique wedding gown which she has taken from her mother's drawer to play "dress up."*)

ESPOSITO: Ah. Muy hermosa. The cockrels. Yes, thank you. I have nothing so fine. (*He rubs his head.*)

MARTA: More?

ESPOSITO: Yes, if you would. (*She massages him again.*)

DILLY: There. Oh don't look so shocked. Girls here get bold or go snow crazy. There was some. Young widow down the road took to leaving a red blanket out on a line in the yard after the wash was in two winters back. When the wind was up it would flap

and move. She'd see it through the window. Made her feel like there was someone walking around, something alive out there, another person like. Everyday a wind blew she'd put out the red blanket and sit to her window. She told me watching that blanket in the wind was the only thing saved her going crazy. (*Indicating the veil.*) Am I on straight?

JENNIFER: (*Fixing it.*) Will your mother be angry we took it? It's so old.

DILLY: There is nothing to *do*. Besides what people don't know won't hurt 'em. Well? Think anybody will marry me?

JENNIFER: You look very nice.

DILLY: Well, they better. Cairn won't pay for my college.

JENNIFER: Why not?

DILLY: Got the first two nickels he ever made. Tryin' to marry me off to his old dried up, weatherbeaten, masturbatin' rancher friends killed off their first wives makin' 'em mend fence. God, Mama must have been pretty! He knew about Doc he'd fart fire. As if it mattered. That damn Indian just don't know when to quit. Always pretending to be doing something near where I am. It's funny. I got tired of him just like that. (*She snaps her fingers.*) If you got married how would you know it wouldn't happen?

JENNIFER: Wouldn't what?

DILLY: Hear a snap like that. (*She snaps her fingers.*) Wake up tired of him?

JENNIFER: I don't think most people do.

DILLY: Don't you?

JENNIFER: No.

DILLY: (*She snaps her fingers.*) You think Esposito's good looking?

JENNIFER: Good enough.

DILLY: He watches you.

JENNIFER: He watches you.

DILLY: Do you like me? No, do you? (*Jennifer nods yes.*) Would you give me something of yours if I wanted it?

JENNIFER: What thing?

DILLY: Just something.

JENNIFER: Say what?

DILLY: I don't know what. I just mean would you? (*They look at each other. Jennifer doesn't answer.*) You look different.

JENNIFER: I've never had on cowboy boots before.

DILLY: (*Snaps her fingers.*) Happened to your parents. (*Jennifer looks down.*) I'm sorry.

JENNIFER: Mother calls it a period of adjustment.

DILLY: Shirt has a tear. There's more in the chest.

JENNIFER: (*Opens the third drawer by mistake.*) Mother says that because we live and learn there are times when one or the other goes on ahead and then that one must wait or the other must hurry and catch up.

DILLY: Sure. That must be it. (*Cairn walks in other room, sees Marta and Esposito. Jennifer finds a beautifully embroidered slip and holds it up. Dilly again snaps her fingers.*) Happened to me, though. I don't want him to touch me.

JENNIFER: (*Astounded.*) What's this?

DILLY: From Mama. She does one every year for me.

JENNIFER: Goodness.

DILLY: For who she thinks I am.

MARTA: (*Suddenly aware of Cairn. Sees him. Speaks.*) Mr. Esposito had a migraine headache.

JENNIFER: (*About the slip.*) So much work that nobody would see.

ESPOSITO: She has quite exorcised it. Gone.

DILLY: Mama says underthings are what you know about yourself that no one else does.

ESPOSITO: This is a fine nurse, your wife. A wise man would fall ill from time to time.

JENNIFER: It's like gold. Does she ever make things for herself?

MARTA: (*To Cairn.*) I didn't know you were riding fence or I would have sent out for you.

DILLY: (*Hearing them outside the room.*) Shhhh.

ESPOSITO: Ah. My good friend…

CAIRN: Didn't know I had visitors.

DILLY: He's back.

ESPOSITO: (*Rises. Speaking to Marta.*) I thank you for this medical attention.

JENNIFER: Should we change? (*Dilly, listening, shakes her head "no."*)

ESPOSITO: I will show you now an amazement, something most extraordinary.

CAIRN: It's not my habit to neglect a guest.

ESPOSITO: (*Speaks to Cairn.*) For your delectation. (*He bows.*) My Rembrandt. (*He bows also to Marta and exits.*)

DILLY: Shhhh.

MARTA: He came an hour ago while I was at Miss Sawyer's. Doc let him in to wait for you. His head hurt him.

CAIRN: Didn't know he had headaches.

MARTA: Nor I. Very occasionally, he says.

CAIRN: Must be a lot of things he has from time to time...

MARTA: Cairn...

CAIRN: Traveling the world like he does. (*Jennifer mouths "Do they know we're here?"*)

DILLY: What? (*Jennifer mouths "Should we let them know we're here?"*)

DILLY: What is it? (*She has spoken too loudly. Cairn hears her.*)

CAIRN: Who is that?

DILLY: (*To Jennifer.*) Shhh.

CAIRN: Dolores?

JENNIFER: It's only us, Mr. McGregor. (*Dilly throws her a furious look.*)

MARTA: They're all right, Cairn.

CAIRN: May I see you, Dolores? (*A pause. The girls exchange a fearful pantomime.*)

MARTA: Answer your Father, Dilly.

DILLY: Yes, Papa.

CAIRN: I'd like you out here, Miss...

DILLY: I can't, Papa.

CAIRN: Within the next five seconds if you will.

DILLY: I'm half dressed, Papa.

CAIRN: Now! (*Dilly appears through the door. The veil is off but the gown is still on.*)

MARTA: Dilly.

DILLY: I'm sorry, Mama.

MARTA: It's so fragile, Dilly. That's why I keep it in the bureau.

DILLY: Yes, Mama.

CAIRN: And does your Mother allow you the run of her things?

DILLY: No, Papa.

CAIRN: This is correct, she does not. And were we being spied upon?

DILLY: No, Papa.

CAIRN: Then why might you be whispering?

DILLY: I was telling about Samuel and the one-way discer while you were making summer fallow.

MARTA: That's a hateful story.

CAIRN: Jennifer?

(*Jennifer enters.*)

JENNIFER: Yes, Mr. McGregor.

CAIRN: Might you have been listening to my conversation with my wife?

JENNIFER: We didn't mean to, Mr. McGregor.

DILLY: We were dressing up.

CAIRN: Have I not explained to you the principle of privacy?

DILLY: Yes, Papa.

CAIRN: You have the right to privacy, have you not, Jennifer?

MARTA: Don't frighten them, Cairn.

CAIRN: Have you not, Jennifer?

JENNIFER: Yes sir.

CAIRN: So do we all. God gave you a light side and a dark side and he give you privacy so you could keep your dark side quiet. Man don't keep his trash on the front side of his house does he? Does he, Dolores?

DILLY: No.

CAIRN: No. I strive, as my church teaches me, to bring you the best of myself, an' keep my doubts and failings right down out of your way. You find your privacy made public, why that's…that is the most painful moment in a person's life. You understand me?
(*Esposito enters carrying a cage by its handle. The cage is draped in red velour. Cairn notes his entrance.*)

CAIRN: Now. You have invaded your Mother's room and you were, both of you listening to a private conversation.
(*Simultaneously.*)

>   DILLY: No.

>   JENNIFER: Yes, sir.

CAIRN: (*Turning to Jennifer.*) And you a guest in my house. (*He shakes his head.*) Come to me, Dolores.

DILLY: Why?

CAIRN: That I may teach you the helplessness of private matters made public. (*Esposito starts to leave.*) Stay here.

MARTA: Don't humiliate us, Cairn.

CAIRN: No soul is humiliated by learning.

DILLY: She did it too.

CAIRN: Sometimes we must bear the burden for our friends. (*He sits. He beckons Dilly.*) Here. Pull up your dress.

MARTA: She is eighteen years old, Cairn.

CAIRN: Across my lap.

MARTA: I will not stand for this.

CAIRN: Nor will I. (*He strikes her six times. There is no sound or movement in the room other than this...afterwards a moment of shared embarrassment that includes Cairn. Dilly rises and smooths her dress. A pause. Esposito sets the cage down. He whips the covering off theatrically.*)

ESPOSITO: Mira! (*He lifts up the cage. In it is a two-year-old black fighting cock.*)

JENNIFER: It's beautiful.

END OF SCENE 5

LILIAN: At last the Val De Loire, the garden of France, and here I am content whatever his weather. How I wish you were here, Jen, mooching about the levees with me, gobbling lark paté and playing at Catherine de' Medici. But most of all chuckling, chortling, giggling. My kingdom for a laugh.

Scene 6

We are in the barn. Low, flickering light is provided by two kerosene lanterns. Diagonally across the stage from each other are two cages for game fowl hung from wires so they "float" about five feet in the air. In one of them is the black, or blood red, cockrel we have just seen Esposito bring into the living room. In the other is a white cock, the pride of Cairn's fighting stable. In the shadows, Doc hunkers down, eating his evening meal from a canteen lid which sits between his legs, watching the conversation between Cairn and Esposito. Esposito stands sideways between the cockrels, he drinks deeply from a fifth of whiskey. Cairn leans against the wall whittling with a knife taken from a hunting sheath at his waist. Both the conversation and the drinking have been in progress for some time.

ESPOSITO: So the gaff hit him in the lung, this one's brother...(*He points to the black cockrel.*) and he had been deep gaffed on the first fly, remember...so we were called to handle and while I thumbed him for bleeding someone calls out "he's dead, your chicken," and I say "not so dead as the other, my friend" and he says to me, "My car says he is dead" and I call, "What is this car?" and he says "Alpha Romeo" and I say, "Of this car I already have two." Everybody laughs. "But," I say, "But on the older one, one hubcap have I not, so I will bet my wife against your hubcap." (*Esposito laughs and drinks.*) This is how we pass the time in Guatemala.

CAIRN: Then?

ESPOSITO: My chicken killed him, but before I could pick him up he also died.

CAIRN: Nothing in this world gamer than a gamecock. I had an Arkansas Traveler got both feet cut off and fought ten minutes on his back before he went.

ESPOSITO: (*Nostalgic, impressed.*) Ah. (*He goes over to the white cockrel's cage.*) So this is the mayor of your village, eh?

CAIRN: Georgia Shawlneck. Started with them way back. Bought a trio off some barefoot kid at a Carolina Derby. Won 6 fights, that kid, took home $300.00. He may not be fast but when he cuts you, he'll cut you in half.

ESPOSITO: How many fights?

CAIRN: Eleven.

ESPOSITO: (*Appreciative.*) Ah. (*Turning back to his own gamecock.*) This one you don't see in your states of America. I breed.

CAIRN: Names?

ESPOSITO: It has no name. It is only mine.

CAIRN: Been pitted?

ESPOSITO: (*Shakes his head, no.*) But I told you of his brother. (*He turns back to the other cage.*) Let me see the Shawlback. (*Cairn tosses a coin which hits Doc to catch his attention. Cairn gestures for him to take the cock to Esposito. Doc takes it from the cage and hands it to Esposito. Cairn notices Doc's new boots.*)

CAIRN: Hey. (*Tosses another coin at Doc. He turns.*) Where'd you get the boots? (*Doc shakes his head as if not understanding. Cairn signs and speaks.*) The Boots. (*Doc signs that he saved for them. Cairn knowing they are too expensive looks at Esposito.*)

ESPOSITO: (*Smiles, pointing at Doc. Speaking to Cairn.*) He has the hands for this. (*Cairn nods.*) In Guatemala there are a hundred men who would employ him. (*Esposito ruffles Doc's hair.*)

CAIRN: I believe the boy works for me.

ESPOSITO: (*He shrugs his acquiescence. Speaks to Doc who is looking at him.*) Good hands and good boots. (*Doc smiles. Esposito inspects the cock.*) He feels good. (*Holds the cock up.*) And the bright eye.

CAIRN: 'Case you don't know what you got there, that's a hi-stakes cock.

ESPOSITO: Ah. You sell?

CAIRN: No.

ESPOSITO: Eggs?

CAIRN: No.

ESPOSITO: He sees my chicken.

CAIRN: I see he does. (*Gestures for Doc to take and cage the bird. He does.*)

ESPOSITO: I go back to Guatemala. We have stadium there for this. Air cooled. The velvet seats. Something you have not in your Montana. This respect you don't pay. I am finished here so I go back. Sin hogar no hay Corazon. Only your chickens my chickens do not kill. You like my string?

CAIRN: Sure?

ESPOSITO: Sure. Good Chickens. Listen, we fight these two, what do you think? Your mayor and my mayor they have an election. Why not? And we make hard stakes.

CAIRN: Such as?

ESPOSITO: Not money. The old way.

CAIRN: What then?

ESPOSITO: If him…(*He points to Cairn's cock.*) You take my string. Fifty, sixty chickens. I don't take them home.

CAIRN: And if I don't get 'em?

ESPOSITO: I wring their necks. A bad waste. But, I don't like to sell, I have here no other friend I might present. I can't take back. So if I make them dead at least they are still mine.

CAIRN: (*Pointing to Esposito's cock.*) And if it's him?

ESPOSITO: You will forgive your wife.

CAIRN: (*Walks over to him.*) What for?

ESPOSITO: Whatever you like. (*Cairn stares at him.*) You like this betting? You want my string? (*Cairn stares at him.*) Go ahead. I give you this too. Go ahead. (*Cairn slaps him.*) O.K., we bet.

END OF SCENE 6

LILIAN: Well, dearest, the battle was met in Loches, we cleared the dining room in a fury of recriminations that frosted the bowl of flowers and starched the white organdy curtain till they stood straight up like Grandmama's hair in a fright. I am called falsely delicate and willfully naive, and I volley with charges of disloyalty and being patronized to boot. Oh, dear. A second honeymoon this might be but only in Dante's book.

Scene 7

Jennifer and Marta sit on two sides of a rectangular embroidery frame. A table runner Marta has been working on is near completion. Marta has been teaching Jennifer to embroider. Each sits on one of the bentwood chairs.

MARTA: Well, no one had seen Black John in or about his cabin so Cairn and I took a ride over…let the needle touch the side of the thimble near the top…and naturally he was right as rain. Been out on one of his two week hunts and nothing would do but we must stay for a rabbit stew which Cairn hated because of the cat smell in that old cabin, but there we were. And all through dinner this little dog kept yap, yap, yapping at Cairn the whole time, yap, yap. So Cairn finally asks Black John what the dog was barking at, and the old codger says, "Not to worry, that dog takes on like that whenever someone's eating out of his dish!" (*Both Marta and Jennifer laugh.*) Careful there's no joining mark when a new thread starts…that's right. Well I wish I could make a life like my embroidery, don't you? I always think that, when I take out a row of stitches. Of course, two days after it's done and on the table no one looks at it. Ah, well. (*To Jennifer again.*) I'd finish with the "wheat ear" right to the edge. Carry it up and then slip the needle under the two straight stitches. (*Back to her own work.*) But I like the doing. I supply the neighbors. Whenever they hear I'm coming they have to pull them out of the closets to lie them out. (*Jennifer smiles. Marta glances at her own work.*) Well, isn't that nice? Pull tight, that cotton floss lies loose. (*Pats Jennifer's arm.*) Your mother never had head nor heart for hand work but you favor me, I think. When Lilian and I grew up she was always fixing her hair and I was always fixing the plumbing. (*An instruction to Jennifer.*) Use the small scissors. (*Back to her own work.*) You know what I think? It's the parts of the body runs people's lives. Now Lilian was always run by the eyes, and I was always run by my hands. She didn't like someone's or something's looks, why that was that. One time she was invited to a beau's home for dinner and she wouldn't sit to table because she didn't like the look of the chairs. Truly. Told me they were hateful and clumsy and probably mildewed and told them she had a sick headache. My, didn't your Grandpa paddle her when he heard! And he hit harder than Cairn. Parents. Well, we survive them mainly. With a few nicks and scratches. Whenever a parent gets broken the child thinks it's her fault. (*Looking at Jennifer's work.*) Good, good, good. Your father and mother may both come back from Paris to live together at 312 Dansinger Way or they may not. But you're almost past the time for you to cry over it. You belong to yourself now. You'll see. It's surprising but it's true.

JENNIFER: Do you love Mr. McGregor?

MARTA: Within limits. Within certain limits. We'll see. Not something to be cried over. Beginning or ending, I can't tell.

JENNIFER: Do you esteem Mr. Esposito?

MARTA: Mr. Esposito? Well, yes. We all do, don't we?

JENNIFER: Do you think him handsome?

MARTA: (*Smiling.*) Well, I think you quite impertinent. (*Looking at Jennifer's work. Referring to the embroidery they are working on.*) Here's something dead certain finished and that's a fact. The nice thing about embroidery is you can always tell when you're done. Will your Mother like it, do you think? (*Jennifer nods. Marta looks at the work.*) This seems so real to me sometimes that I forget to remember I'm in this world. And that's a mercy. (*Marta leans forward and kisses Jennifer on top of her head.*) Yes, I esteem Mr. Esposito, and so do you. It's all right. (*She watches as Jennifer resumes her work.*)

END OF SCENE 7

LILIAN: The storm is gone as quickly as it came and limps my sails. It gives one the malaise this working of things out. I recline and take the sun. Your father gnashes his teeth over the Renaissance and storms about the countryside like the black plague. My chateau is sumptuous, its facade pierced by large double-mullioned windows and crowned by towering dormers and sculptured canopies.

Scene 8

Lilian's letter beginning with "the storm is gone..." takes place simultaneously with the beginning of the following mime.
Esposito has gone for an afternoon walk and fallen asleep, his walking stick in his hand, one knee bent, his head pillowed on a stone. Jennifer and Dilly, out for a walk, see him. Dilly whispers to Jennifer. Jennifer shakes her head "no." Dilly whispers again and moves to Esposito and picks up his jacket which he has carefully folded beside him and puts it on. Over Jennifer's agonized but thrilled objections she removes his hat which covered his face, putting that on also. She takes off her shoes and slips her feet into his. Finally she approaches and carefully removes his walking stick from his hand. She tickles his feet. He sits up startled out of sleep.

DILLY: (*In Spanish.*) Hijo de Perra, mi presioso Callo esta muerto. Adoude encontrare' otto asi.
(*Marta enters carrying two buckets, one feed, one water. She watches. Rising, Esposito starts toward Dilly. She kicks her shoes at him, and flees with the hat and walking stick. He pursues her. Just when she is cornered, she tosses the walking stick to Jennifer who, surprised, catches it. Esposito turns away from Dilly to Jennifer. Jennifer tries to run by him but he catches her around the waist from behind and tickles her as she holds the walking stick out and away from his body where he cannot reach it. Being tickled she laughs and twists frantically in his grip until she lies on her back her arms extended over her head still holding the stick. He is on one knee above her. Dilly suddenly cries out.*)

DILLY: Stop it! (*Esposito turns to look at her.*) I'm sorry. (*The tableau holds for an instant and Blacks out.*)

END OF SCENE 8

Scene 9

Esposito again is seated at the table covered by the embroidery we saw Marta work on. On his lap, in a cherry wood box with a lined interior, are gaffs for cockfighting (the steel blades affixed before a fight.) Until Dilly enters the room, he sharpens them with a rhythmic, circular motion throughout the scene. In a second area, the barn, Jennifer sits crosslegged talking to the fighting cocks, who, this time, are invisible out over the audience heads.

JENNIFER: Nice boy, ch ch ch ch ch, strong boy, see where I am, look, ch ch ch. That's it. You see me. Bright eye, bright eye. ch ch ch. (*Dilly has entered behind her.*)

DILLY: What are you doin'?! (*Jennifer jumps.*) Like the barn now, huh? You first came you were scared of it.

JENNIFER: I like to watch them.

DILLY: Doc around? Esposito?
(*Jennifer shakes her head "no." Thunder is heard.*)

DILLY: Heat lightning. Sometimes you see so many strikes at the same time it looks like white hair on the mountains. (*Offers her a cigar from her blouse pocket.*) Cigar? Go on. Make a real man of you. (*Jennifer hesitates.*) Cairn won't know. They went for a ride on the rim so we wouldn't hear 'em fight. Your hair's messed up. (*She lights the cigars.*) You hang around down here you'll find what you're lookin' for. (*Jennifer coughs.*) Don't inhale. (*They smoke.*) Yeah. Look at 'em. You wish you were beautiful?

JENNIFER: Like the chickens?

DILLY: Yeah. How come you don't talk to me? (*Jennifer looks at the chickens. Dilly laughs.*) Makes a long summer. (*Looks up at the chickens.*) Claret, Morgan, Blue-Faced Hatch, Whitehackles, Ferris Ford Reds, Georgia Shawlneck. When I was twelve, Cairn gave me a trio of Black Roundheads. Flyers. Fought 'em with the neighbor kids without gaffs, just sharpened their spurs sharp as needles. I liked it, till they died.

JENNIFER: (*Pointing.*) Is he the best?

DILLY: Yeah. Pretty huh? Pop thinks he *is* that chicken. Really. When the Shawlneck fights Pop makes every motion the cock does, only small, little. You have to look to see it but it's there. Sometimes he'll come out here, watch the chicken. Watch, watch, till it's too dark to see. Yeah. He practices.

JENNIFER: Practices what?

DILLY: Chicken motions. (*Jennifer laughs.*) You can laugh? Thought maybe your face would break. Maybe you're like that story where the china doll comes to life…you know…walks into the painting and has adventures? (*Jennifer looks down.*) By the old rotted mill, saw Pop making chicken motions. (*Jennifer looks at her.*) Doc and I used to go out there. When you work a chicken, get him right to fight, you kind of throw him in the air backwards and he works his wings hard coming down. Makes 'em strong. Pop was doing that. What the chicken does. By the mill. He looked just like one. Gave me bumps. (*She watches Jennifer.*) Remember when I asked if you would give me something?

JENNIFER: Yes.

DILLY: Well there's something I want.

JENNIFER: What?

DILLY: You know.

JENNIFER: I don't know.

DILLY: You know what I want.

JENNIFER: I don't understand.

(*Doc has entered behind them and now drops his tool box. They startle.*)

DILLY: Lord in a bucket. (*Signing as she talks.*) Doc, damn you, sneakin' around, I told you to get off me. (*Doc signs back that he didn't come to see her. He has work to do.*)

DILLY: Bull. Tell it to the grizzlies.

JENNIFER: What does he say?

DILLY: Didn't know you were interested? (*Doc is signing to Dilly.*)

JENNIFER: What's that?

DILLY: Says he didn't think you could talk. You want to say hello?

JENNIFER: How?

DILLY: (*Shows her.*) This. (*Jennifer signs hello. Doc signs it back.*)

JENNIFER: He's been here two years?

DILLY: Working the cocks for Cairn. He's a chicken machine…aren't you? Feeds 'em, studs 'em, flies 'em, grooms 'em, worms 'em, handles 'em…

JENNIFER: What does he like the best? (*Dilly signs. Doc signs. Dilly laughs.*) What?

DILLY: He says he likes best to see the chickens die.

JENNIFER: Why? (*Dilly shows her how to sign it. Jennifer signs it. Doc, in answer, removes his shirt revealing that his torso and upper arms are covered by slash-scars. Jennifer recoils.*) Oh, no! (*Doc signs and Dilly translates for him to Jennifer.*)

DILLY: He says this…(*The scars.*) is what handling is. The gaffs are up to 3 inches long and sharp as a razor…sharper. The cocks get crazy when they see each other. They twist in your arms and cut you. You bring them up, let 'em peck, get 'em nuts. Take 'em back six feet. It's a dirt floor. Floodlights. Cut-judge signals you turn 'em loose. They fly and hit. Slash each other. Lot of times the gaffs get caught in their flesh. Then you catch 'em. Say your gaffs are in my rooster. Then it's my job to take them out. Slowly. Gently. No mistakes. Here is where a gaff goes through his hand when he does this. The other handler, his cousin, pulled it out. One time this guy thinks he dopes the chickens so later when he watches another fight, the guy trips him into the pit and he falls on the chickens and they cut him and cut him and cut him. His uncle has a pickle factory so his father takes him there and makes him lie with the pickles in the brine to stop the blood and seal the wound. (*Dilly laughs.*) He wouldn't eat pickles if he were you.

JENNIFER: How can he stand it?

DILLY: No, you. You say it. (*She shows Jennifer. Jennifer signs to Doc. Doc signs again.*) He says men have to work. (*The three stand silent for a moment. There is tension. Dilly backs up a step. Doc reaches out a hand to Jennifer. She doesn't move. He takes her wrist and pulls her slightly to him. She breaks his grip. He shakes his head, meaning she misunderstands him and reaches out to her. She backs away. He signs to Dilly.*) He wants to give you luck. (*Jennifer shakes her head.*) He says the chickens give him luck. He can give it to you. (*She nods encouragement to Jennifer.*) Ask him what he means, like this. (*She signs. Jennifer repeats it. Doc signs.*) When

they fight the cocks way, way back in the hills there are Indian women. Crow women. And the old women, very old, they want to touch the scars. Trace them. Because the Crow believe you can read how you will die in such scars. And if you are brave enough to read it gives you a wish. Not for yourself but you can wish for someone else but only if the cock that cuts you is dead. This is why he likes to see the chickens die. He says he can give you a wish. (*Jennifer turns to look at her. Dilly continues, gently encouraging.*) Go on. Why not? Touch him. It's nothing. Go ahead. Touch him. Let him. (*Jennifer turns back to Doc.*) Go on. (*He reaches out.*) Take it. Take it. (*Jennifer does.*) O.K. (*Dilly runs out and then walks into the room where Esposito has finished sharpening the gaffs and now examines the embroidery on the shawl. He looks up. Dilly stops.*)
(*As Dilly and Esposito play their scene, Jennifer kneels beside Doc and traces her fingertip lightly and slowly along his scars.*)

DILLY: Oh. I didn't know you were here.

ESPOSITO: Ah. I brought the gaffs so that your father might chose good ones for the fight. (*He opens the box and shows her.*) Like jewelry. They are Toledo steel from Spain. Beautiful. (*He closes the box.*) He is coming?

DILLY: They're driving on the rim.

ESPOSITO: Ah. (*A silence falls. Esposito touches the embroidery now on the table.*) Your mother did this?

DILLY: Yes.

ESPOSITO: An art. Your Mother's hands are from God. In my country, they would whisper your name in the villages if you could do this.

DILLY: There's more.

ESPOSITO: (*Pleasantly.*) Yes?

DILLY: Better than the shawl.

ESPOSITO: (*Nods graciously.*) Good. I would like this. (*Dilly unbuttons her blouse. Esposito sits still, legs crossed, relaxed, watching her. She takes it off. She unsnaps her skirt and lets it fall. Underneath is a chaste, full cotton slip. It is stunningly, intricately embroidered with tropical birds, mythological beasts and the sea. She stands with her arms at her sides.*)

DILLY: You're leaving.

ESPOSITO: Yes. (*A pause.*)

DILLY: (*Lightly tracing one of the designs on the slip.*) For my 18th birthday.

ESPOSITO: Ah.

DILLY: (*A slight pause.*) What shall I do?

ESPOSITO: Dance for me.

> (*Dilly begins slowly to dance. In the barn, Jennifer finishes tracing the scars. Doc begins to sign to her, complexly. She watches transfixed. There is no sound in either scene. The lights fade to a special on Cairn.*)

END OF SCENE 9

LILIAN: Oh, Jen, are there two things more different in this world than a man and woman in first acquaintance and the same a decade since? I believe we shall hire an interpreter, your father and me, and converse through this personage like Goths and Visigoths. Oh, for a new minted language! There is some hard place in men past understanding.

Scene 10

> *Cairn is restringing a barbed wire fence on his property. He has finished all but the top wire. Esposito has ridden out with him and now stands slightly behind Cairn, a rifle with which he has been hunting held relaxed under his arm. Cairn works and talks.*

CAIRN: These mountain boomers just walk right through a fence. I've tied cans to them but that about half works. You run stock in Guatemala?

ESPOSITO: No one can buy.

CAIRN: You're lucky. They break through, then they walk right back in. Don't know what they want.

ESPOSITO: Like the cocks.

CAIRN: Gamecock only wants one thing. Wants it hard. Can't get enough of it. Never. Gamecocks never bored, never petty, never lonely. They don't lie nor do they steal. A gamecock always knows its mind and a steer never has.

ESPOSITO: Or a man.

CAIRN: Oh, a man knows his mind. There's two times you'd better look out for a man, when he gets what he wants or when somebody else gets it. Hand me that cutter. (*Esposito does.*) A man who'd got as good as he'll get, had the prettiest woman he'll have, bought all the land he can handle is the most dangerous creature in the world. It's in that man to shed civilization like a snake. Feels like a cow when he wants to feel like a cock. (*Drives a splinter in his hand from the fence post.*) Ow. Shoot. (*Pulls out his knife, realizes he can't use it on the splinter.*) Broke the point right off this one. (*Esposito takes his own knife off his belt and holds it out to Cairn.*) Pretty fancy.

ESPOSITO: To blood the birds when we train. To see their macho.

CAIRN: (*Takes it. Works on the splinter.*) You know, there's some disagree with me, but I say a cockrel never feels the gaffs. Doesn't know when a lung's punctured or an eye's torn out. They are consumed with doing the one thing they were meant to do, thing they're never bored with, never done with, never done the best they could. (*Finished, he holds the knife out to Esposito.*)

ESPOSITO: Keep it. You have not such a knife.

CAIRN: (*Looking at the knife.*) You come to a chicken derby it's mainly old men. They're through with working, through with women, high up the mountain as they'll get they still love the cocks, and they still got a knife in their boot. (*He puts it in his belt sheath.*) Good cock always fights till he's dead. Otherwise you wipe out his whole line. Kill his mother. Kill his father, kill everything he comes out of. Long as a chicken's right, he's always got the one hunger that lasts forever…to kill you. (*Esposito smiles and nods. The lights change.*)

END OF SCENE 10

LILIAN: Hope once again. Springing down. Rather like the crazy clowns you can't knock down. There I was standing in the gardens of Villandry in my summer blue among vine arbors, citrus hedges and a wild profusion of dahlias and pink tulips, if not sunk in melancholy then most certainly tinged by it, when out of the labyrinth pops your father and sweeps me into his arms carrying an embroidered handkerchief in each hand for my inevitable tears...

Scene 11

It is 8 p.m. on the evening before Esposito's departure from Montana. It is generally understood but unspoken that the match between Cairn's and Esposito's champions will be fought at a site out in the foothills later on this evening. The McGregor family plus Esposito, Jennifer and Doc (in his church suit) are gathered in the parlor after dinner for family entertainment. The bentwood chairs are placed roughly in a semi-circle and all the assemblage, even the girls, are drinking champagne provided by Esposito. Marta, wearing the embroidered shawl as a cape and jingling an old tambourine is in the midst of a dramatic recitation.

MARTA:
> ... came a sudden stir in the ring of knives
> And a woman reached my side
> In the gruff patois of Apacheland
> "Stand back you dogs," she cried
> She was supple and lithe as a panther
> I saw two bright eyes gleam
> Through the mask one wore, and that silver voice
> Was I mad or in a dream
> "Stand back, Canaille, your Queen commands!"
> See! At me a knife-thrust sped
> But a woman throws herself between
> And she caught the blow instead!
> The police break in, of course too late
> Mad with grief I hold her head,
> "Bon Soir, mon ami, you know me, Yes?"
> Then a sigh – and Lizette was dead!
> La Reine des Apaches, La Reine des Apaches
> Save a wealth of love to myself bequeathed

With sin and crime is her memory wreathed
But a woman, if ever a woman breathed –
Was Lizette, La Reine des Apaches.
(*Great applause from the assembled, Esposito cries "Brava Bien hecho, muy Bien Hecho!"*)

DILLY: It was wonderful! Wasn't it wonderful? (*Embracing her mother.*) It was just wonderful.

ESPOSITO: So. And where did you learn this cautionary tale?

MARTA: Oh, we always recited as children. Lilian and I in Billings. Every Sunday for aunts, cousins and pets.

DILLY: Pop knows "The Shooting of Dan McGrew." Please!
"There's men that somehow just grip your eyes
And hold them hard like a spell
And such was he and he looked at me
Like a man who had lived in hell."
Please, Pop?

CAIRN: I've a mind only for the matches tonight.

MARTA: Oh, dear. The time. Well, it really should be Jennifer who provides our finale.

JENNIFER: (*Discomfited.*) Oh.

MARTA: She has such a lovely clear voice. She sings to me at our embroidery. Will you?

DILLY: But she doesn't want to.

MARTA: Hush.

DILLY: Do you?

MARTA: On this last evening?

ESPOSITO: (*Taking Jennifer gently by the hand and leading her into the circle.*) For her friend, yes? To wish the bon voyage. A small melody to carry with me back to Guatemala. For the long nights of the Sierra De Chama.

JENNIFER: I can't.

ESPOSITO: Ah. But why?

MARTA: Of course you can.

DILLY: (*Irritated.*) For heaven's sake, she said she doesn't want to!

MARTA: That's enough.

JENNIFER: I always forget.

MARTA: We have sheet music.

DILLY: That old stuff? Honestly, it was ancient when Grandma Alicia was a pup.

JENNIFER: (*An entreaty to Marta.*) Please?

ESPOSITO: A duet then? You will allow me to sing with you? (*Marta brings the sheet music.*)

CAIRN: Gettin' late.

ESPOSITO: Por favor, te pido disculpa. Soy un Via Jero? (*To Jennifer.*) You will do me this honor?

CAIRN: There's people waitin'.

ESPOSITO: (*To Jennifer.*) Debemos apurar. (*Looking through the old sheet music.*) This one? No. "I Don't See Your Name Stamped On Any Cigars." (*Jennifer laughs.*) No, I think not. "Where the Silvery Colorado Winds Its Way?" "The Millers Daughter," ah. Exactly. (*He hands it to Jennifer who smiles.*)

MARTA: What is it, Jennifer?

JENNIFER: Jennie Lee.

MARTA: Well, no wonder it's in Grandma Tates' things. She was a Jennifer too.

ESPOSITO: Good. Very good. To soothe the savage beast.

CAIRN: (*Rising.*) I'll get the birds in the car.

MARTA: Cairn, please. (*He sits again.*)

DILLY: It's after eight.

ESPOSITO: Senorita. (*A small bow.*)

MARTA: (*Dilly is whispering agitatedly in her ear.*) That's enough. (*To Esposito and Jennifer.*) Please.

ESPOSITO: (*Singing the first verse.*)
"I have come to take you home Jennie Lee
To the heart that's always yours, Jennie Lee
Tho' your life is one regret
I am sure I love you yet
I will help you to forget, Jennie Lee
To the quiet countryside, Jennie Lee
I will take you as my bride, Jennie Lee
Leave the city far behind
It has treated you unkind
And with me true love you'll find, Jennie Lee"

JENNIFER: (*Singing the second verse.*)
"We will seek that shady dell, James McPhee
Where our love we used to tell, James McPhee
By the quiet little stream
Where in love we used to dream

Life as dear to us will seem, James McPhee
Tho' the friends that you have known, James McPhee
Turned and left you here alone, James McPhee
There's a home where you can rest
In a village 'way out west
With the one who you love best, Jennie Lee"

ESPOSITO and JENNIFER: (*The chorus.*)
"Jennie Lee, sweet Jennie Lee
No fault with you I find
True love, sweetheart, is blind, Jennie Lee
Tho' false to me
You're my lovely sweetheart still
Jennie Lee"
(*Something in the song silences the room, there is no applause. Marta, tears in her eyes, rises.*)

MARTA: Excuse me. (*She leaves the room.*)

DILLY: (*She bends forward in front of Esposito and picks up the embroidered handkerchief Marta had given him which he dropped as he prepared to sing. She holds it out to him. Cairn watches.*) You dropped this.

CAIRN: (*Rising.*) It's time.

END OF SCENE 11

LILIAN: There really seems to be firm footing underneath, Jen. Isn't that wonderful and frightening? One feels a bit underdressed for a happy ending but perhaps these legendary beasts exist. We've drawn up new contracts of behavior and concern. We look at each other in the eye. We exist together again. Your father insists we return on the Ile de France on its first post-war sailing. He says it's "attractive symbolically." Old but new and all that. He likes the idea of it sliding backwards into familiar waters but all refitted. He says I may christen him with a champagne bottle if I feel it's absolutely necessary.

Scene 12

The stage is now bare. Stripped of furniture. Except for the bentwoods. The cock fight is concluded. The crowd earlier gathered, many on foot, many Indians, has departed. Those remaining: Marta, Jennifer, Dilly, Doc (who has handled for Cairn and whose bare arms show three or four fresh cuts) and the cab driver stand separately and silently watching. On the floor, downstage, Cairn's white cockrel lies bloodied and lifeless. Cairn, on one knee, runs a finger along the wounds of his dead champion. Esposito stands nearby holding his victorious cock. The cab driver, excited and nervous in the silence, talks compulsively.

TAXI DRIVER: Didn't even have to bill those birds. No way. Just set 'em six feet apart an' get outta the road. Devil take the hind most! Whew. Set them gaffs so deep, yessir so deep didn't seem like you could get 'em out with a pliers. Black un' ain't one of your flyers, or a slam-bang hit and misser but when he hits 'em, he hits 'em deep. (*Cairn takes Esposito's knife out of a holder on his belt and cuts the tape that held the gaffs on his chicken. Doc comes over and takes the cock out of Esposito's arms and cages him.*) Shook him in that second round, Cairn, but your chicken came back real good. Those Shawlnecks don't run do they? Yes, sir, they die standin' up. Took those last six, seven licks an' went to dying on his feet. Blew blood but he wouldn't fall over. (*Cairn rises and turns to look at Esposito who is wiping his brow with the handkerchief Marta gave him.*) Shawlneck'll take a lot a steel but that other – what kinda gamecock you call that? Real stinger, ain't he? Never saw a gaff like that though. Real short, straight gaff wasn't it? Puncture gaff, that what you call it? Mister? I'll buy me some of those gaffs, you got 'em handy. (*Cairn in one unbelievably quick move thrusts the knife into Esposito's belly at the same time Marta cries out.*)

MARTA: Cairn! (*Cairn backs off still holding the knife. Blood pours through Esposito's shirt.*)

ESPOSITO: Oh, my friend. Dios mio. See this. See this. (*Doc starts toward Esposito but Cairn backs him off with the knife.*)

MARTA: No! (*Cairn holds up his hand, telling her not to move.*)

ESPOSITO: Dios te salve, María! Llena eres de gracia. El Señor es contigo; bendita tu eres entra toda las mujeres, y bendito es el Fruto de tu vientre, Jesus. (*Dilly and Jennifer cling together.*)

DILLY: Oh Jesus, oh Jesus.

ESPOSITO: So much blood. (*Smiles at Cairn.*) Very much. (*To Jennifer and Dilly.*) Don't see this, little girls. (*Weakening.*) Santa Maria, madre de Dios, ruega por nosottos, pecadores, ahora yen la hora de nuestra muerte. Amen. (*Suddenly the pain seems to stop. Esposito recognizes its absence.*) Ah. (*He falls forward. Cairn turns and walks out without any sort of contact, still holding the knife. A frozen instant and then Jennifer runs to the fallen Esposito trying to turn him over to help in some way. Doc, knowing the magnitude of the wound, grabs her trying to pull her away. She turns on him in a frenzy, a hysteria of grief and they fight fiercely, she to be free of him and he to subdue. He finally throws her away from him and she stands, breathing hard, her hands covering her face. Marta goes to her and holds her. Doc kneels by Esposito and gently feels for his pulse. Then he turns and mouths words, signing but silent.*)

JENNIFER: What's he doing?

MARTA: He's singing a hymn.

END OF SCENE 12

Scene 13

Dilly stands in a spotlight on an empty stage.

DILLY: I still see his hands. They were everything. They appear on walls and float over the horizon. They were everything he was. He was like a child in another body. I wanted something from him but I can't remember what. Maybe to be turned inside out. Like I am. People shouldn't die before they get to disappoint you. Oh, shit…

END OF SCENE 13

Scene 14

The yard outside the ranch house. Glaring sun, Jennifer, in her traveling dress, stands by her suitcase, ready to leave. Marta hands her a reed woven basket. Dilly stands off to one side wearing a simple black dress.

MARTA: There's pork loin and you'll find a little packet of my herb mustard. And two apples. Early apples but good ones. And rhubarb pie. Enough to share if you find a friend.

JENNIFER: Thank you, Aunt Marta.

MARTA: Remember to sit on the side away from the afternoon sun. (*Jennifer nods.*) Give my very, very best to Lilian...tell her it was the best summer ever for my garden. Tell her I'm fine and that she's not to worry. Jennifer?

JENNIFER: Yes, Aunt Marta?

MARTA: You may tell your mother, or not tell her, anything you like. You are old enough now to have secrets, or old enough not to. That's something you must choose. I'm sorry.

JENNIFER: It's all right, Aunt Marta. (*Marta walks over and very gently kisses Jennifer on top of the head. Jennifer looks up at her and then down again. Marta holds out the piece of embroidery we saw Jennifer work on with her.*)

MARTA: Give her this from both of us. Dolores?

DILLY: Yes.

MARTA: Say goodbye to your cousin.

DILLY: Goodbye.

JENNIFER: Goodbye.

MARTA: (*Softly.*) Goodbye. (*Jennifer turns, picks up her suitcase and exits.*)

END OF SCENE 14

LILIAN: He wasn't there, my darling. Nowhere to be found at sailing. Not a note. Not anything. And so we've lost him. I don't know why. Captain Sundergaard was even kind enough to hold the ship for a time. Sometimes we lose things and it's not possible to understand. In any case, I stand to arrive on the 28th and you on the third. Oh, my darling. I intend to give the house a proper airing and have your pillows plumped by the time I see your sweet, sweet, silent questioning, necessary face. You know your father's been disappearing all of his life, if you remember. Bit by bit. Despite our best efforts. Like the cheshire cat or the poem we would say at bedtime of A.A. Milne's.

Scene 15

The four chairs once again represent the taxi. For the first time all the actors except Jennifer, Lilian and the driver have exited. The driver, in the front seat, is smoking. Jennifer sits somewhat tensely, looking down, her hands in her lap.

DRIVER: (*He lights a cigarette.*) Ol' Cairn he put him where the sun don't shine, didn't he? Look on ol' Guatemala's face was a damn study, I tell you! "Got my guts in my hands here, now how'd that happen?" (*Laughs.*) There's some damn marimba band playin' one coconut coon short tonight boy! (*Laughs.*) 'Scuse my French. Well, thief in the night, you ask me. No way. Didn't just blow blood over a couple damn chicken, huh uh. Had him his hand in the jam pot some way, you know what I mean? (*Laughs.*) Oughta put a big sign on the state line says, "Better keep it zipped up while you're in Montana!" (*Laughs.*)

JENNIFER: Put out your cigarette.

DRIVER: What say?

JENNIFER: Your cigarette. Put it out! (*Surprised by the confrontation he hesitates and then stubs it out.*) Thank you. And I would prefer it if you didn't speak to me.

(*The light shifts to a single spotlight on Lilian on the other side of the stage. As she speaks the stage is cleared and when she finishes it is empty of characters and furniture except for Jennifer, some distance from Lilian and carrying a small bouquet of flowers. Lillian recites an A. A. Milne poem. Jennifer and Lilian, now both dressed in black, look at each other for a long moment.)*

JENNIFER: Hello.

LILIAN: Hello, my darling. (*Jennifer starts to hold out the bouquet to her but then runs into her arms instead. The final image of the play is of these two women, moved and needful, wrapped tightly in each other's arms.*)

The End

Travelin' Show

ORIGINAL PRODUCTION

Travelin' Show premiered June 12, 1987 at Actors Theatre of Louis-ville and featured Chris Wineman.

TRAVELIN' SHOW

A bench in the town square of a southern hamlet. A man between the ages of 35 and 50 wearing a tractor cap and work clothes.

MAN: This here is a good town. Real nice. Real green. Got us a real honest to gosh town square. Civil War equestrian statue. Hardware store. Cafe. Town hall. Millicent Bagley boutique. State Farm Insurance. Lawn mower tune up and repair. Everything you might need. And nothin' you don't. Now that's the point. Cairo, Tennessee. You might say nothin' to do come dark. Far as I'm concerned that's what dark is for. That's why we got it. So your mind can be still.

   Last fall they drove in on this bus. Old school bus. Me and George Dale seen 'em. Taking our ease in the square. Bus had a bird in flames on one side. Woman makin' love to a swan on the other. Sign on the back. Leda Phoenix Hiball Theater and Ballet. Performance nightly. George he turns to me, says, "If that's not trouble there ain't no pork to a pig."

   That's right. Shouldn't be no pictures to the side of a bus. School bus is yellow an black. Period. Watched 'em real close. Five, six people on that bus but it wasn't no mystery which one was Leda Phoenix. Had her a purple dress got signs on it. Dyed red hair to her waist. White skin like she been where the sun don't shine. Worked like an ant. Doin' this, doin' that. Come night they lit her up. Whole side of that bus pull down make a stage. Seats off it set out front. Inside it got a mural like clouds in a sky. Lights on poles. Crazy. Some evenin's they done jugglin' an' unicycles, man dressed like Uncle Sam out on stilts. Some nights it was Kings, Queens, swordfights, God knows what. Some nights it was Leda Phoenix dancin' up on her toes to a tape cassette. Wearin' red stockin's an' some cotton candy kind of dress. Bout one night in four she did that.

People come to sit in them seats. Five, six, more. Ten, thirty, a hunnert. People runnin' down after chores sit in 'em so nobody else could. Brought lawn chairs. Brought blankets. Picnics, cardtables, top of they cars. Drove in from Cockertown, Bonneyville, who knows where. July the whole town run out of Coca Cola. There was people drinkin' 7 Up wouldn't drink 7 Up on a bet. Noisy. Felt like 'bout half a Mardi Gras. Wasn't right. Look. You gotta get your life to where it don't move around on ya. Settle into it. Let it rest where it is like some ol' yella hound. That's right. Get yourself over-stimulated you get yourself dissatisfied. Get dissatisfied, shoot, you halfway gone. You agitated. Don't know your own self. Leda Phoenix she got it goin'. Laid that agitation in gear. Like a vibration you couldn't stay out of. In the air.

Carl Heller's daughter Nita run off to dancin' school in Chicago. Whit Lindquist, seventy-six years old, drop his wife, moved down to the root cellar, started puttin' ships in bottles. Donny Lutes got to spittin' on police cars. Missy Crawford dyed red, white an' black stripes in her hair. It was ominous. An' ever night them crowds. Dancin', singin', playactin'. Leda Phoenix risin' like the moon over Cairo. Throwin' out her arms. Laughin'. People callin' her name. Throwin' flowers at her. Drinkin' pot wine outta mason jars. Gettin' later. Later. More 'til dawn. An' the town...I'm tellin' you, unrecognizable. Couldn't count on nuthin' bein' in the right place. Nobody doin' what they did yesterday. Didn't know what was likely to be said from minute to minute. Didn't nobody seem to know who they were. 'Cept me an' George. Sittin' on the bench. We wasn't laughin', you can count on that. We could see it comin'!

Last night of summer they wasn't no place left to stand, no place left to sit. People on roofs. People up in the trees like a flock of starlings. Waitin'. Waitin' on Leda Phoenix. Bus closed up. Quiet. Then this one light turned on an' here she come. Had a white cotton dress with her hair pinned up. Barefoot. Smilin'. Started playin' on a chinaberry pipe whistle. Real high. Little like runnin' your finger down the edge of some sharp knife. On an' on. When it was done she opened the front door of that bus and the old people got on. Pointed to the ladder and the children got up on top. Slapped that ol' bus, it started up. Went once around the square easy, them folks fell in behind, off they went. Last I saw they was north on 1147 headin' for the interstate. Left their picnics, pickups, jobs, houses, EZ boys. Gone.

Leda Phoenix she stood stock still in that white dress. Stood right there 'til there wasn't but a one-eyed dachshund in the square. Looks over at George an' me. Cups her hands over her mouth. Says, "Hell, boys, rest of it's yours, you can lock it up." Walks off. Gone.

You supposed to put your life where you can find it in the mornin'. 'Sposed to get it down reliable. You see that bus, you look out. Got the bird in flames one side, woman an' the swan on the other. You like it like it is, don't you listen to no chinaberry pipe. Get agitated. Take you on a trip you wasn't counting on. Get yourself gone.

Not George. Not me. We got it all now. Cairo, Tennessee. (*Blackout.*)

                    END OF PLAY

Vital Signs

ORIGINAL PRODUCTION

Vital Signs received a workshop production at Actors Theatre of Louisville from December 5 to 8, 1989. The cast included: Kymberly Dakin, V Craig Heidenreich, Debra Monk, Adale O'Brien, Paul Rogers, Lori Shearer and Pamela Stewart. The stage manager was Frazier W. Marsh.

Vital Signs received its professional premiere production at Actors Theatre of Louisville in the Humana Festival of New American Plays. It opened March 21, 1990 and played through March 31. The cast included: Kymberly Dakin, Randy Danson, V Craig Heidenreich, Adale O'Brien, Paul Rogers, Priscilla Shanks, Pamela Stewart and Myra Taylor. The stage manager was Frazier W. Marsh, the scenic designer was Paul Owen, the lighting designer was Victor En Yu Tan, the sound designer was Mark Hendren, props master was Mark Bissonnette, and the costume designer and dramaturg was Marcia Dixcy.

SETTING

The stage is empty except for three chairs. One is overstuffed, massive, providing sitting areas on the arms and back with a matching hassock in front of it. One is a rocking chair. One is a vinyl fifties kitchen chair. The surround is black.

DIRECTOR'S NOTE

Vital Signs is performed by six women and two men. Though the play is a series of monologues, there is constant interaction between its cast members. Some pieces are played directly to the audience members using them as characters. Some are played to other actors. Some are performed as internal monologues. In some pieces, such as "Nintendo Woman" and "Cocaine Hotline," non-speaking actors create the world of a video game arcade or office with mimed characters. Occasionally a piece has the element of a duologue with exchanged lines. Often other actors are onstage listening to another actor work. The more a director uses these means to provide variety and a sense of ensemble, the more powerful and funny the evening becomes.

The play uses only three chairs with no other scenery. The only prop is a tray of hor d'oeuvres. The costumes should be the actors' own rehearsal clothes. Lights shift to provide atmosphere, but there are no blackouts until the end of the act and the end of the evening.

Recorded music is useful behind certain pieces, such as "Encyclopedia Salesmen," "Truck Stop," "One Moment," and "Endings," but should not be overused. Flow is everything. The pieces should follow each other quickly, preventing, when possible, internal applause.

Characterization is important but should not give the impression of broad strokes or heavy use of dialect. The director will find that what gives this work its special flavor is the quick internal movement from comedy to something more painful, or vice versa, in a single two-minute piece.

The order has been determined to provide variety, help the pieces inform each other, and provide a movement toward a somewhat darker coloration by evening's end.

An appendix of four other pieces is provided as possible substitutions if cast composition would make them useful.

VITAL SIGNS

ACT ONE

BEGINNINGS

A woman sits on the back of the overstuffed chair with her feet on the seat. Also onstage are the characters for the two pieces to follow. They listen.

WOMAN: So, uh, invariably I'm uh, well, better at the uh...well I'm better at the start, at the beginning...or so I'm, well, generally told that uh, that I am...at the beginning...of...of...well I guess almost anything. Affairs...jobs, absolutely on jobs...trips, always better the first hour on trips...hors d'oeuvres, never want anything after the hors d'oeuvres...it's uh...well, I guess it's a, you know, a pattern...they usually tell me. So. See at the beginning I never, ever seem to know what I'm...It all seems very...full of possibilities...very romantic...very...and then when I'm still thinking that I find out I'm in the middle...well for me the middle is...well I experience flight syndrome... middle panic...middle muddle...and uh, characteristically the middle seems pointless...and of course no one likes being around someone feeling pointless so actually it's the end. But ah...strangely enough...well the end...I don't mind the end

because uh…well the end is that much closer to the beginning…
so uh…so I'm terrifically relieved…really…because I know I'll
shine in the beginning, which makes me more fun at the end.
Sort of. So honestly…to be fair…I…well. I try to, you know,
warn people that the beginning is in a way, well, the end. But it
doesn't help because well, and this, this is the uh bad part, I'm
usually attracted to linear thinkers who like to uh, move forward,
so we never stay in the beginning so it uh…it uh… doesn't work
out.

SUPREME LIGHT

A woman kneels beside a man sleeping on his back on the floor.

WOMAN: Hi, I've got sort of a moral dilemma, can I counsel with you? Our supreme light and pillar of universal enlightenment, he of the thousand eyes, Uraja Pradesh Mahavira, may he radiate forever, who has gathered the disciples of joy from every state and sixteen nations to build his temple in Butte, Montana, has received vibrations from on high that his German shepherd, Rusty, wishes to lie with me. No, really. I know this body is but the cup for the river that is always running and that pleasure is the gift of the material self for the delectation of the spirit of others but this kind of pisses me off. Look, I sold my Nash Rambler and rendered up the money. I made over the checking account and accepted the daughter of delighted poverty ring. I have sung the fifteen simplicities over and over on six months of latrine gift, and chanted with full heart while we hauled the four hundred tons of creek rock to build the Palace of World Peace and Erotic Meditations but this is where I draw the line.

MAN: Nine generations...

WOMAN: Sure, nine generations of supreme ones inhabit each micro-iota of my master's words but I was born in Trenton, New Jersey, and there is one doo-doo I don't step in.

MAN: Laura!

WOMAN: So I guess what I'm saying is this: I'm giving you my parabolic prayer rug and beads of the sixth union. I'm setting fire to my tent and bedroll. I ritually break the mantra thread that ties me to the universe to come and I'm blowing this joint, Larry. What I want is a Coors beer, some French fried onion rings, and the first Methodist church I can find. Rudyard Kipling was right about never-the-twain. Don't take up a religion your mother can't spell.

COCAINE HOTLINE

The entire company creates an office mime as background for Ms. Bottendorf.

MS. BOTTENDORF: Good morning, Cocaine Hotline, Ms. Bottendorf here to help you break the cycle of despair. Uh, huh. Uh, huh. Uh, huh. Well, I don't really see anything we can do if you're going to behave like that. (*She hangs up.*) Will somebody get me a Diet Pepsi for God's sake before I start screaming and trying to get my tongue into my Panasonic pencil sharpener. What kind of society is this!
(*Phone rings, she answers it.*)
     Good morning, Cocaine Hotline. Uh, huh. Uh, huh. Uh, huh. Uh, huh. Hold it right there. All right, Cornelia, you called for advice. I am giving you advice. Tell him you are flat out going to leave his ass. Uh, huh. Well, that's just too bad. Tell him when he wants help he can write you a letter. Tough Tootsie Rolls, Cornelia. You have to cut off the sex, cut off the money. Figure out the one thing he wants, Cornelia, and cut that mother off! If you do not act, and I mean before the sun sets, he's going to nosebleed his life all over your prairie-pattern quilts. Yes, well take it or leave it. I have three calls waiting. (*Hangs up. Stands up.*) I would like to say to all of you here at Cocaine Hotline that we are going down, going down with the ship, and we are out of Diet Pepsi, folks. No society can help itself without a constant supply of diet drinks that you can count on. I'm taking a john break. Let me know if the country buys the farm.

30 HOURS

One actress sits on the hassock and speaks to other actors on the stage.

ACTRESS: Everybody has about 30 hours of conversation, after that it's all reruns. Ordinarily, a person can do about twelve hours on their family, ten on their past, five on their divorce, three on their present and maybe forty-five minutes of personal philosophy. My theory is that almost anyone can be interesting for three dates which means you've usually been to bed with him before you discover he's a tape. The best I ever met rang in at 200 hours but it was all on Suzuki motorcycles which kept putting me to sleep. "Cranks were trued to blah, blah, blah...intake adapters blah, blah...carbs on the Honda/Webco 350 blah, blah, blah." It made me pray for an awkward silence. Every ten years we ought to be heard by a Board of Examiners who should tattoo a conversational rating to our foreheads. That way you could *get out* before it *ran out.* Ever try ten years of marriage on six hours of conversation? If it weren't for gossip, children or grocery shopping, ninety percent of all marriages would be conducted in silence. The only ones without a limit are deeply neurotic, desperately narcissistic, drop-dead alcoholic or have dangerous criminal minds. All in all, it's a bleak picture. (*Pause.*) Say something.

LOTTO

This actress enters from offstage and plays the piece with an audience member.

ACTRESS: I got the Lotto. I got it. I got all six numbers. Shhhh. I haven't showed this to nobody. Shhh. Here...you hold the ticket...help me check it out. Shoot, I looked a hundred times but Lord, I don't trust myself. (*Calls out the numbers.*) Six, three, one. They say it's $5.5 million in twenty-one installments. Lord in Heaven! I work down to the Hercules Cleaning Service. Well, it's a very rewarding thing to remove filth. People like you to do it. My husband, Joe, he's a retired insurance adjustor, and he does part-time lawn mower repair. We have a 1947 DeSoto. Original upholstery. That's our pride an' joy. They say that woman won ten million last year picked her up a bad nervous condition. She's in a peck of tax trouble and divorced her a husband she had thirty years. Joe and me we worked all these years to get our lives right. We're orderly in that way. I don't think they like you to clean or drive some old DeSoto with money like that. Seven, four, nine. Oh, my. My Momma, rest her soul, she always said, "If it ain't broke, don't fix it," "Don't trade the cow for a milk truck," things like that.
(*Pause.*)
Here, you keep it. You're more young and better situated for it. Put it in your purse. Shhhh. Go on. Do what I told you. Go on. And don't tell Joe. That's the way we are. He leaves the details to me.

COLD WAR

*This piece is played to other actors who find her political stance
slightly embarrassing.*

CATHY: Gee, really this...ummm...sort of...well, embarrassing
but...all right, straight out...I miss the Cold War. I do. I
liked...Oh, God...I liked being afraid of the Russians. At least it
made Reagan bearable, you know? Now, they're gosh, the two of
them, like artifacts, you know, like old newsreels, but they're still
playing in my theatre. It's like having to tell your President his fly
is open. Psss, George...get out of the tank, George...it's tacky to
ride around in a tank now, trust me. But with no Russians, boy,
who am I going to hate now? Myself probably. Boy, I used to say
to myself, Cathy, boy are you behaving like a jerk. You are really
screwed up. Boy, Cathy are you ever leading an unexamined life,
but...who cared, you know, because BOOM! Adios! Nuclear
winter.

Now I'm going to have to live with myself, you know?
Christ, who needs it? Instantaneously, no Lenin, no Marx, no
Communism. The first thing they wanted from us, buddy was a
McDonald's. A McDonald's. Think about it. You know what
that means. It means we're going to be up to our ass in styrofoam
cups and pop tops. One world, right? One big mouth is more
like it. One giant mouth, world tongue, universal craw snarfing
up everything in the refrigerator and then, then, boy, we'll start
in on each other *again,* only meaner and hungrier and drugged
up to our eyeballs until we're living in a pig wallow, cutting each
other's throats over potato peelings and calling it an inalienable
right.

Hey, remember the graffiti on the Berlin wall? "We came, we
saw, we did a little shopping." Sure shopping, they should have
shopping, but...I don't know...maybe I'm empathy dead. I'm
scared. It's stupid. I'm scared, O.K.? Don't look at me that way,
I'm a liberal. O.K., I'm wrong. Tell me what to think.

TRUCK

All the women sit or stand around the overstuffed chair. They are the truck stop's cafe employees. A male actor enters and takes their picture with a flash camera.

ACTRESS: Me? I waitressed at the only all-nude truck stop in West Virginia. It kinda caught on. We was all jaybird naked, cooks, cashiers, bus girls, the bunch of us. We'd flip to see who worked the tables near the front door in December. Guy pulls a twelve-cylinder, 456 horsepower Detroit Diesel into the lot. Slides into my booth in a white silk suit with a tie with a diamond stud. Says he's the one, the only, Reverend Billy Frost, got him a sixteen wheel ministry an' the home phone number of the Holy Ghost. "Good evenin' little lady," he says, "I take you to be in the Garden of Eden or tied to the spokes of the wheel of fire. Now I'll have me a decaf Cappuccino and a side order of small curd cottage cheese, an' when I leave, senorita, you're invited to ride." Slipped his silk coat over my shoulders, offered me his arm, walked me past the truckers to an all white rig, says "Resurrection Express" in letters of flame. "Climb up, little lady," he says, "leave the dust of the road behind you." His eyes were serene as a hawk on an updraft, so I did.

Sang hymns, shouted scripture, and screwed me seven times on the way to Laramie, Wyoming. Left me by the side of the road at this deep pan pizza parlor run by two Koreans. (*She approaches a male actor.*) Disappointed? Well, that's a real luxury in a life like mine, sailor. I got to generally trust any human being ain't armed or got blood on their shoes. Tell you what. Buy me a beer and give me a ride into Palm Springs, you can tell me *your* modus operandi.

ARBY'S

The actress sits speaking to several other women.

WOMAN: Honey, what the tight asses never teach you in school is when the end is. I'd known that I'd saved me about twelve years in two marriages. My second finally sat me down said, "Marjorie Ann, you been screwin' around on me for seven years, haven't slept with me in six months, haven't talked to me in ten days, now I filed for divorce this afternoon, I figured I better tell you so you'd notice when I'm gone."
(*Laughs.*)

I'm a good lookin' woman an' I have me some fun but I just don't have me a sense of conclusion. They say it ain't over 'til it's over? Hell, with me it ain't over 'till well over when it's over, an' sometimes it's not over 'til two overs over that. (*Laughs.*) I spent three days in Acapulco with a fella was an architect for Arby's Roast Beef. (*Pause. Male actor enters.*)

Hell, I thought those things just sprung up over night like mushrooms, didn't you? (*Laughs.*) He said when you have a structure you see when it fulfills itself and it's just naturally over.

MAN: Like a circle.

WOMAN: He said.

MAN: You draw a circle you know when it's finished.

WOMAN: Honey, I told him the trouble is you'd damn well know that before you started so what the hell's the fascination? Oh, I put me together some odd shapes in my life, darlin', but they never did look nothin' like Arby's Roast Beef! I start something' and then generally move on when somethin' shiny catches my eye, like a crow does. It's just one lopsided damn thing sittin' next to another lopsided damn thing, how I see it. Don't fit together any way you can make sense of, do they?

Third day with the architect we was waitin' for the elevator and outta nowhere he asked me to marry him! Honey, I was so God-damned surprised I said yes. (*Male actor exits.*) Elevator door opens, he steps in…Fell fourteen floors down an empty shaft. Now he lived, but the subject of marriage never came up again. (*Laughs.*)

Drawing the circle. Huh-uh, not my style, darlin'. Honey, I'll just scribble some good lookin' shit 'til I run out of paper. I don't want to see the structure 'til they turn out the lights.

BUSINESS WOMAN

The actress sits in a chair near the audience and plays the piece to an older male patron.

WOMAN: I don't feel there's a significant difference between us on this issue, Mr. Carlyle. I am willing to artificially depress our prices forcing you into a price war because it is my educated guess that our pockets are a little deeper and our markets a little better situated and we don't have the same need for fluidity and capital that a little bird tells me you do. There is, as I'm sure you're aware, a natural process of selection in business as my father used to say, "When it's time to go, it's time to go." Now in my opinion, you've had your innings and in a nice way, a very nice way, you've become a superfluous and even, though I don't like to say this, an inhibiting factor in an expanding market. Your options, Mr. Carlyle, are to sell or fold. It's Florida time, Mr. Carlyle, which can't be too unpleasant a prospect given the time you already spend on the links. Well, I've got a lunch and you've got a lunch so when you've run this by your people give me a call. Oh, one more thing. I greatly appreciate the fact that during all those years we worked together you were punctilious about treating me as an equal and colleague and not simply as your daughter. You can be assured in the changed circumstances that I will do the same for you. Sorry, have to run.

QUALITY TIME

Everyone exits except the actress who plays the piece alone on an imaginary playground.

WOMAN: Anna, Anna, honey, the slides's hot, honey, don't go down the slide without your bathing suit. No, no, no.

Billy, Billy! Get out from behind the swings! Further back, even further. You know what Mommy told you about swings.

Anna, Anna, some people don't like to see us without our bathing suits. Sick as that may be. Come get a towel from Mommy, sweetie.

Greg! Let go of her hair! Yes, I know it's your truck. No, she doesn't like it, Greg, she is screaming.

Little girl? Give him back the truck, darling, he's ruthless. It is his truck. Give him back the ...

Anna, not in the sand pile...yes I know we do that at home...Oh, my God, Anna...cover it up...put sand over it...with your foot...no, don't pick it up! Billy, make Anna put it down...Billy...not with the plastic bucket, Billy ...

Greg, stop it! She doesn't want to be in the tire. Good. No. She doesn't want to be on the see-saw. No sand fights, Billy. Greg, do not brush her off there. Because her mommy doesn't like it.

Anna, not in the fountain!

Billy, stop picking at it, it's a scab.

Do not hit foreign mommies, Greg. I'm sorry. I'm sorry. I'm sorry.

Billy! (*A pause. She watches the carnage.*)

Quality time.

IMPOTENCE

A woman sits on the overstuffed chair talking to another actress sitting on the hassock. In the middle of the piece a man enters and lies down on the floor. The performer moves to the man and lies down as if she were in bed with him.

WOMAN: The moving van pulls away. I monitor myself for a reaction. What? What am I feeling? In point of fact I'm ecstatic. The marriage is gone, he's gone, the furniture is gone, I feel great! Then I make a mistake and look in the mirror. Is anybody going to find *this* attractive? I get instantaneous depression. I'm ugly. Not to worry. My first week I have three dates. All right, two of them were married, but I'm still counting them as dates. I'm enthusiastic and sleep with all of them. It turns out they have one thing in common. They're all impotent. This is what they don't tell you when you get a divorce. Melly, what is going on? I worried available men would be ego-monsters dripping arrogance and command; they're not, they are sweet, vulnerable guys who have caught some kind of sexual flu. They're in agony, they weep, they rage, you have to take Kleenex to bed. I decide all men from 10 p.m. to 7 a.m. are living on an outpatient basis — poor babies! They must exist in this paroxysm of dread. Completely focused on what they can't control. Totally defined by an irrational muscle. Passionately believing it's all that matters. Found out despite the rest of their lives. One of them told me it was like cradling a corpse between his legs. And my job...my job is to fix it. Or else to console the inconsolable. And all of this...all of his pain, all of my responsibility, locked in a horrified panic reaction to the absence of six seconds of abandon. And this, Melly, this is my dream of sexual freedom. Gosh, it makes me long for the security of a bad marriage.

Nintendo Woman

The entire company supports the speaker by creating an imaginary arcade. This is a very physically active piece.

WOMAN: Blast that sucker, Earth Girl...wo-wo-wo-wo-wo-boom... Nintendo woman...hit it yattata-yattata-yattata smash...mobile unit, tank crusher fifteen degrees right...Shawham! Got that bitch-mother, yes! You lookin' at the one, the only, the arcade Goddess of East St. Louis, fella. Eat green slime space station drone! I stayed eight straight hours on Karma-Blaster for one quarter, man. I saved the princess of the moon of Jupiter nine times on Planet Warrior left-handed, seven times right-handed, two times with my teeth, an' once with my genitalia. Missile one, missile two, all side turrets now! Hey, players, Kerrack! Look me over, stick monkeys. Do I reign supreme? Step on up if you're cool to my heat. State your name and pick your game, suckers. This is the *real*, jockeys, an' out there, out the arcade, is the no program, unbeatable, featureless, creatureless slough of despond. Don't go out there, babies! In here it's a quarter a game. But out there it's without price. No control! Whack! You have no control! Slam! We got Rocket-Tank, Black Asteroid, Slime People, Cobra Carrier, Lost Worlds of the Snake Robots. Stay with me. Stay safe, players, It's spoiled out there, on tilt, out of order, computers down. Let it go. Let it be, babies! Quarters all around. Sha-bam! Play it up!

IGUANA

An actress and actor sit on the floor with their backs against the overstuffed chair and their feet on the hassock as if they were in bed.

ACTRESS: I had me a pet iguana. Silver, green. Tied a red bow on him 'cause he moved fast. Kept in the shadows. Bought him at an outdoor art fair. Halloween present. My brother's wife wouldn't have him in the house. I didn't mind. Fed him a regular line of flies. He was voracious. I started datin' this guard dog trainer was a Viet Nam vet. Real nice and reserved. Met him out to the fairgrounds at the Fish and Game show. Had forearms big as my waist. Wore a shoulder holster. Even in bed. We'd put on Grateful Dead tapes, drink piña coladas, fool around all day. Sat bolt upright in the Pullman bed. "Oh, oh," he says, "Incoming," he yells. Pulls a .45. "Infiltrators!" His eyes was all pupil. Nostrils flared. "You ain't cuttin' off my balls." Starts firin'. I flattened back on the head board. Used up the clip. There was holes in the trailer and iguana on every flat surface in the room. "I think you got him," I said. "Fucking Cong," he says. Fell back, slept fourteen hours. I never tried to replace the iguana. There are just certain things you shouldn't own because of the way the world is. Certain things you shouldn't do either, but I'm not gettin' into that.

I Love You

An actress sits on the floor and pulls a man down to lie in her lap. The piece ends in a kiss. They freeze.

ACTRESS: I love you. Always before I've had to love on speculation. I could call it by its name but I knew it had a shelf life. Sort of the top of something that I knew was on the way down. Saying "I love you" was just pointing out your position on a loop. It was how you described a high point. Someone was beautiful and I loved that. Someone cut through the bullshit and I loved that. Someone made me, thank God, forget myself and I loved that. But never, never was I crazy enough to turn myself over to it. As soon as I said it, I made damn sure I had it on a leash and I knew it died from repetition. The bottom line for me were the couples in restaurants who never say a word while they eat. I knew it all was reduced eventually to silence. Until you made it safe for me. No matter what happens, you always pay attention. Imagine that. To most people, paying attention is merely part of the acquisition. You pay attention so I can take myself seriously so I can take you seriously, so I pay attention. It's a miracle. I love you.

Fried Chicken

The actress sits in a vinyl chair, or is already there. She speaks dully and without emotion.

ACTRESS: So he asked where his dinner was and I said it was almost midnight. He grabbed me by the hair and said get him food. I said get it himself. He hit me in the face with the heel of his hand and I could feel my nose break. He pulled me into the kitchen and I fought. He turned on the stove and forced my hand down onto the burner. Get me a beer he said, so I did. He said food so I put my hand in a sandwich bag full of ice and started to fry him some chicken. He told me wash, he didn't want blood in the eats. I said fuck you under my breath and he threw the beer. It hit me in the breast. He put me on the floor and said if it was a fuck I wanted, well a fuck I'd get. He ripped my clothes and did it to me from behind. Then he told me to bring him the chicken. I gave it to him. He ate and went into the TV room and watched a game. He fell asleep. I got the grill starter and poured it over him and lit it. He slapped at himself like there was mosquitoes and then sat up straight and asked was something burning? Then he ran right through the glass sliding porch door and died on the patio. I changed the channel and watched *Hawaii Five-O* but it was a repeat. Then I called you. My hand hurts. Oh my Jesus.

HOR D'OEUVRES

A genial, cheerful woman in a white server's jacket enters with an hors d'oeuvres tray and passes them out to the audience during her speech.

WOMAN: I been circulating hors d'oeuvres at white people's parties for a good many years. I like 'em. White people I mean. The hors d'oeuvres vary. It's kinda general callin' them "white people." So I'll just call 'em Tiffany and William, all right? Tiffany and William they're a little handicapped but they're still functional. Now I got a limited perspective but they can definitely eat hors d'oeuvres and call you by your first name. Tiffany and William they got problems, but shoot, we all do. Main problem is a sense of humor. They never laugh when they see a whole bunch of white people eating hors d'oeuvres and a bunch of black people servin' 'em. I laugh all the time. Tiffany likes it, she likes to see me happy. William, well I always call him Mr. Barnes, he always says to me, "Good evenin' Lona, how are you doin'?" An' I always say, "Fine and dandy but for my back problems, Mr. Barnes." An' he always says, "Well, Lona, we're not getting any younger." Then he smiles an' takes two bacon-wrapped chicken livers an' claps me on the back. Tiffany, she always pat me and ask how my little girl is an' I say "Henry doin' fine," an' she pat me some more an' say she got some dresses from her little girl if I want. Tiffany, she always passes on the bacon-wrapped chicken livers.

They sort of pre-occupied too. I go by 'em on the street six, seven times a year but they don't see me. Oh, maybe if I had my hors d'oeuvres.

Yes, I like white people. Umm. Tiffany and William. They so happy runnin' things, an' dressin' nice, an' shootin' game, playin' tennis an' eatin' hors d'oeuvres. Poor things. I think they're a little...well, you know...not quite right. Well, we can't fix everything in this old world. I know that. We just got to feed 'em an' be nice to 'em, hope they have the best time they can. They kind of a lesson really. Can't everybody be black. (*She exits.*)

TRICK SHOT

An actress alone on stage.

ACTRESS: They call me 20-20. I'm a trick shot artist. I can pepper a copper plate three foot by three foot, draw you a portrait of any American president with forty-eight shots. Fifty-four for Roosevelt 'cause of the cigar. I can shoot off the wick on a candle or put six holes in a Dr. Pepper before it strikes the earth. I fell in love with a Lebanese rope dancer called Mademoiselle Sofie at the Louisiana State Fair, and she with me, an' we hit out in tandem. She was a long drink of water with eyes like plums and hair that just touched her ankles. Taught her a few easy shots like the silver dollar throw 'cause there's a moment it don't rise or fall so you're just pluggin' a stationary object, but mainly she was the "holder." Held apricots, long stem roses, and a glass ballerina I shot cupped in the palm of her hand. We done country fairs down through the asshole of the south 'til it got too chill to shoot. In a Motel Six in Tupelo, Mississippi, I caught her in a single bed with an animal trainer just out of jail runnin' a mangy chimp and pekinese basketball act. Next day I blew off her right hand holdin' the ace of spades at a thousand booth flea market. Now I didn't mean to do it, but it was hell to explain in the circumstances. I guess it always gets down to travelin' alone, don't it? Love being the fickle pursuit it is, there ain't a whole lot of people wantin' a short-term romance with anybody's as good a shot as I am. It's a hopeless damn thing tryin' to mix a full-time career with a long-term relationship. You know when her hand hit the ground it held on to the card? Surprised the hell out of me. Funny how the best things you do in this life you couldn't do twice if you tried.
(*The lights dim to black.*)

ACT TWO
CHORALE

The entire company is onstage. As the lights come up they applaud as if at an awards celebration. The actress holds up her hands for silence. She speaks.

ACTRESS: I would like to thank my father Augustus (*More applause.*)

Lee for running off with the music teacher and leaving a note on the ice box and being heard from subsequently on major holidays and showing up late and leaving early at selected funerals. (*More applause.*)

I would like to thank Uncle Charlie for explaining that men were always hot for it and would tell you anything to get it and to watch out all the time and be alone with them as little as possible. (*More applause.*)

I would like to thank Luke BeJart for finally getting me out of my clothes without saying anything at all and then going off to the University of Maryland and becoming a Trappist monk.

I would like to thank my first husband Jackie for being kind and patient and nurturing and understanding and ultimately gay.

I would like to thank the fourteen men I slept with in 1981 for the yeast infections, non-specific urethritis, the abortion, the week in St. Croix, the terrible blank verse and considerable satisfaction.

I would like to thank Carl the lawyer for my child Jeremy even though it wasn't right for him to get a divorce given his wife's dependency and history of depression, and the fact that she wouldn't give him the house.

I would like to thank my second husband Allen and his teenage children Joyce, Danielle and Tim for doing the best they could until it became obvious that the majority of us didn't like each other and some of us didn't flush the toilet.

I would like to thank Matvey the Czechoslovakian emigre plumber with the haunted eyes and high cheekbones for being interested even if I can't sleep with him right now and for bringing me that hand carved, hand painted box and the wonderful recording of the Male Chorus.

I'm in good shape now. Really. Thanks. Did I leave anyone out?

(*Lights cross-fade. The attention immediately shifts to a woman sitting in the rocker. She addresses both the cast and the audience.*)

SKINS

ACTRESS: Skin players, stick, ooo-ee yes uh-huh. Mamie Le Smile, now, Mamie Le Smile, ooo-eee. She had a bitchin' left hand and speedo speed, she did. She could sling a riff so sweet, wouldn't nobody jam, for fear they weren't up to it. The best lady drummer, no kiddin', that's flat. She was, she was, oh yes. Had six, she did, six brothers yes. They was two sax, two bass, one mortician and a real bad mental went down in an armed robbery at the Cut-Rate, corner of Marshall and Lagoon. Kansas City was her town and renown. She sit in at the One Note, flog them men drummers clean outta the room. Catch-you-later, so long, piss off! You wanted some weed, some seed, a sawbuck, or some late night blues, oh she was the one, she was. Did the road for two years with Basie, but she was a car sick so she cashed it in. Had her picture in *Life* magazine, half sweat an' half smile, dicen' them sticks so quick they was gone from the photo. Whoosh! Hell, she could make a blur look like a back beat, yes. Sure, she playin' weekends when she was eighty years old an' stone bone blind did Mamie Le Smile. Eighty-third birthday led the whole bar outside singin' "Cajun Lady," yells "fuck it," steps out in front of the 10th Street bus. Bam! Sure she died but she was survived by a thirty-six hundred dollar dent set a record on that particular model. Word got out it started leakin' drummers, rainin' drummers, deluged with drummers, oh yes. Scootch Gissel took him a cab from Chicago, driver tossed him the keys, say "You bought it my man, you in the taxi business." Stick men by thumb, stick men by limos, bikin', hikin', pullin' their sets in red Flyer wagons. They was triplin' the price on hotel rooms. Funeral day, yes took an hour seventeen minutes for those headlights to pass her bar. After that they laid out three hundred sets in the Pick Pac parkin' lot, played them a 30 minute riff off "After You've Gone" you could hear in L.A. stood up an yelled "Fuck It" and drank themselves away by the light of the moon. Mamie Le Smile. Hell, I bet she'd screwed two thirds of 'em. She had a bitchin' left hand an' she always left a drink in the bottle. God bless her tart ass. Bottoms up. (*She mimes downing a drink.*)

ENCYCLOPEDIA SALESMAN

With the full cast still onstage listening, the actress addresses the audience.

ACTRESS: Oh, I love those boys who sell encyclopedias with their bright eyes and souls! Always dressed so nice, every bit as good as the Mormon missionaries, if you ask me. You will never see a grease spot on their ties, it is completely unheard of and that's a fact. Oh, they come to do the mind honor and they dress to fit. I'm on all the lists: Encyclopedia Britannica, World Book, Compton's, House of Knowledge, Facts Illustrated, all of them. I always try to fix them a nice little something, maybe a quiche and some vegetable juice, nothing heavy. Then I sit right down in the hallway, with my heart pounding so I can catch the doorbell on the first ring.

There is such a lovely formality to it all that it reminds me of the days when there was such a thing as society. And the graces. I pull back the wing chairs in the living room so he can spread out his full color charts and graphs and maps and samples and I curl up on the sofa with my tea and the conversation just buoys us up and carries us along as if we were sitting with our harps in the clouds. We usually start out with the Brazilian Rain forest and work our way right through stars and stellar populations to Yiddish literature and the Haskala traditions and sometimes dark will fall without our noticing and the ideas they will actually perfume the air. Oh, if there's a life of the mind now, it's in encyclopedia sales. And those boys, those dear boys, it's quite usual after you've given them the check for them to kiss your hand when they leave, and smile and smile until your heart nearly breaks.

JAY

This piece begins with the actress sitting but early on she rises, moves the hassock stage right of the armchair with her foot and ends sitting on it.

ACTRESS: See, my vocation is giving pleasure. People are mainly scared of people. I read where most people only have two or three friends in a whole life, plus a couple of marriages. I was the high school mascot for the North Broderick Bears an' I saw right off I was more popular as a bear than a person. There was always somebody wantin' to pet me, play with me, tryin' to look up my nose hole, see who I really was. Right then I knew I was meant for it. Went on to be the Virginia Tech Hokie, sort of a turkey kind of thing, which was good as it gave me bird experience. Later on I kind of free-lanced as a fresh water shrimp, and a year down at Disneyland as Daisy Duck, but that was generally too heavy a drug scene. My big break came at the National Baseball Card Show in Miami, where I did day work as the Toronto Blue Jay. Well, I wasn't on the floor an hour before I got real attracted to the St. Louis Cardinal. Talk about your chemistry! We started rubbin' up to each other, whew, got so hot we snuck off to the broom closet. Guy heard something going on, opened the door, saw two giant birds in among the cleaning fluids screwin' like they was an endangered species. Well, there were these little flaps. That guy laughed so hard he started to choke an' I had to do the Humperdink maneuver on him to save his life. Turned out he was marketing manager for the Jays, so he got me on to work the fans. I'm not out in public as a human more than eight, ten hours a month. Humans these days don't have a sense of mystery. They're pretty much what they are which is why they love me. Shoot, I wouldn't ever come out I didn't have to. Oh, I'm into it. I go sky diving for the full effect. It's a real shame it's come down to where you have to leave your own species for a good life. That's just about the end of the road I guess.
(*The full cast exits except for the actress doing "Graceland" who puts on a pair of glasses and moves up behind the armchair.*)

GRACELAND

A young woman on and off mike at the Graceland Reception Center.

YOUNG WOMAN: Good morning and welcome to Graceland, a division of Elvis Presley Enterprises. If you are buying tickets for the homes, grounds, or attractions...is this thing on? Hello?...homes, grounds, or attractions, please follow the blue line between the blue ropes. What's that? I'm in the middle of an announcement, sir...are you looking for the Elvis recreational bus or the automobile museum? Combo ticket one for all attractions is available for $15.95. That includes...sir, you in the "I got bombed at the Strategic Air Command Visitors Center" tractor hat, we would prefer you did that in your bedroom with a woman, ostensibly your wife. Sir, Combo 2 includes the automobile museum but not the bus. No, sir, there is no combo that includes the Lisa Marie jet airplane but not the auto museum. Because I say so. I am not at liberty to say why. Because that is what Elvis wants you to see on Combo 2. I do not appreciate being called four-eyes, sir, when all I have is astigmatism. Get outta my face, sucker. Sir, I cannot let you in, in any case, wearing a Mick Jagger Altamont jacket. Because, sir, Elvis Presley died for your sins, and Mick Jagger is the Anti-Christ. Mick Jagger never recorded a Christmas song in his life, or served in the Army, or knew his gospel. He represents the foreign, bi-sexual annihilation of the rock-and-roll dream and he don't set a foot in this sanctuary with you or without you! Next! (*She exits.*)

FATHER'S CIRCLE

The actress enters talking and sits in the rocker. She is alone onstage.

ACTRESS: My father wasn't in my life exactly. If you drew a circle around a life he would be sitting just outside with his feet on the line, reading a book. Once, out of nowhere, like coming into focus...I was twelve, I think...he stood up from the chair and took me on the ferry to Coney Island. It was like a date. I wore my black and white skirt with the rust blouse and two bows in my hair. I never wore bows but I wanted to look like a daughter. We went to the aquarium and saw Ookie, the gentleman walrus. It was a triumph. The keeper asked me to pet him. "Give him a kiss," he said. "Ookie likes the ladies." He had a papery feeling against my lips. My father laughed and clapped his hands. Actually clapped his hands. And then he took my arm and I remember looking at passersby to see if they knew we were a father and daughter. On the ferry ride back, we sat side by side and sang "Daisy, Daisy" very low so no one else could hear it and each had a Baby Ruth. Then we were home, and he stepped back outside the circle and picked up the book. I don't think he came inside again. Maybe he did, but I don't remember it. (*She remains sitting, an actor and actress move on from different entrances and confront each other. From time to time he tries briefly to interrupt her.*)

ABORTION LAWYER

WOMAN: Suitable? No, actually that doesn't seem "suitable" to me. It is, and I'm sorry to say this, particularly coming from you, Brent, unacceptable after I've done all the bloody prep and legwork on this case, to tell me now, at this point, the Attorney General's office doesn't want *me* to prosecute it.

MAN: You know why—

WOMAN: And no, I don't think we get a "reverse spin" with a male attorney sticking it to abortion bombers and yes I do have an emotional view of the perpetrators and emphatically yes it makes me noticeably angry and they make me angry and you make me angry. Excuse me. Just hold on and I'll get this down to a rational level. Breathe in, breathe out. O.K.

Brent, you say my sex, no matter what I say, *is* an issue here. All right, granted for the sake of argument. Then it's good, it's an issue. Because without a female attorney it looks like the gender most affected either doesn't care or can't fight its own battles or isn't competent. They should know when they bomb medical facilities necessary to my freedom and well-being and then stand on a cross and wrap themselves in the flag that the cases will be fiercely prosecuted by the gender that has the most at stake. I am not only protected *by* legal process from these thugs, I *am* legal process and I will nail their self-righteous hides to the wall! (*Two other actresses enter and stand watching.*) Now I intend to do two things: I intend to prosecute this case and I intend to eat lunch. You can't do anything about number one and you are cordially invited to number two, my treat. How about it? (*She hits him fairly strongly on the shoulder for emphasis and exits.*)

SURPRISE

One of the two actresses who entered during the last speech sits on the hassock and speaks to the other who leans over a chair.

ACTRESS: What replaces surprise? There used to be surprises every day. The first time I asked a man to go to bed with me and he did. Finding out, suddenly, in college that I could do the work. Eating a brussel sprout and not minding. Realizing I actually had friends. Right through my thirties there were always surprises. Now I seem to see it all coming. Last week my brother-in-law stole change off my dresser. As soon as I knew it, I knew that I already knew he was capable of it. I suppose what happens is that you identify patterns. That in some larger sense you're always just playing percentage baseball. What surprises me is that I don't mind. What surprises me is that I have no nostalgia for surprises. What I guess interests me is why I'm getting such pleasure from a world I can second guess? We should be devastated, don't you think? I see pictures of Neptune, I see magnifications of aphids, I get mugged in a department store elevator but it's just more of what was already there. What I think is it's a theological/ biological preparation for non-existence. I think I'm being prepared to leave. If the body releases chemicals that make pain more bearable then maybe it gives us a tolerance for repetition to make parting more bearable. That would be nice, don't you think? Otherwise we'd always want to stay. Maybe that's why we don't mind. Maybe that's why I'm not looking for any surprises. (*The speaker moves the hassock back in front of the chair and exits. The actress listening moves up and sits in the armchair. A male actor leans against the wall above her, bored and irritated as Duke Pharsee.*)

DUKE PHARSEE

Slapping herself and fanning herself simultaneously.

ACTRESS: You in there, Duke Pharsee? You in there with the window open? I hope you know what you're doing in there? You are letting mosquitoes roar in that open window come eat me alive like some road kill on the Hiawatha Bypass. You like a mosquito youself, Duke Pharsee. Eternally dressed in your yellow and black high school B-team letter jacket, suckin' up my money on food, on magazine subscriptions like some Asian tiger mosquito got into the country in a shipment of used tires down to Houston or Galveston or some humid place like that. You the same kind of immigrant to my country with the agenda of siphoning off my life blood through the agency of my unchecked sexual attraction. It is my opinion that the itch precedes the bite and even attracts it. Don't think I don't recognize you as the parasite you are because I do. Just because I prefer love to be a minor irritation and not a preoccupation leaves me precisely at the mercy of small-time hustlers like you. Now slam shut that window, throw down my *Cosmopolitan* magazine, get your little stinger in here an' let's see if we can pass the time before the good shows come on the T.V.

(*She throws a leg over the chair arm and puts her hands behind her head. Holds a beat. She then rises as the actress doing the next piece enters, and she and the man assist the woman delicately as she sits on the hassock.*)

No Personality

ACTRESS: They tested me twice on account of their dumbfoundedness the first time. And those results they came down the same way both times. Within a fraction of a point, so they told me. "How'd I do?" I'd say and they'd get this startled look and they'd say, "Well, Miss Latonia, we're pleased to say it's conclusive and definite, you don't have a personality." And I don't. I'd imagine there's a lot of us here and there. More than you think. It's hard to spot. You might be one. Now, if it turns out you are, don't feel bad. The head doctor he told me not to worry, it was kind of like being a punctuation mark. "There has to be a rest period between ideas and you're it. Look around you," he said, "there's a lot of people doing things and saying things, and things just go from bad to worse. They need you." Well, I'd never looked at it in that light, and I've tried not to get a swelled head over it. You may be stuck with a personality but that doesn't mean I can't respect you as a human being. (*She rises and moves downstage.*) The thing is that those that have a personality stew in it. They are sort of like telling the same joke to everybody. Whereas you and me are more free-floating, more restful to the passerby. More like watching water. The way things are, maybe we're the coming thing. (*She sits in the vinyl chair. Another actress enters and speaks to the empty rocker. This speech is one long build to a crescendo.*)

Nightmare Daughter

ACTRESS: This isn't fat, mother, this is bloom. The bloom on the rose. This is the radiance you read about in your two hundred romance novels a week. Don't look down on the carpet. I'm not on the carpet, mother. I'm here in the kitchen near the *refrigerator.* You caught me, sheriff! Two in the morning but you sniffed me out. I'm the Sara Lee bandido. The Che Guevara of Haagen-Dazs ice cream. By day my name is Nutra-Slim but come sunset, I rip the calorie counter from my heart, I trample grapefruit and carrot sticks and celery under my Nike Air Cross-Trainers and I expand. I fill with cholesterol like a deranged zeppelin. I inhale cheesecake, I eat the graham crackers box and all. Bits of packaged ham and pepperoni flake my disordered hair. My fangs drip butter almond swirl. And with my eyes rolled back in my head I crash through the wall into your pristine, chintz, unendurably perfect bedroom and I fling myself on you screaming, "This is me, mother. This is your nightmare daughter, you patronizing, priggish, punishing, unforgiving cancer of my life."

(*She holds for two beats and sits in the chair she has been speaking to. Another actress moves on talking and sits in the armchair. She never rises during this speech.*)

BEES

ACTRESS: They ain't no honey climbers I know of anywhere outside
Tennessee. *Fadin' out.* Back of the hills they long on that fresh,
wild honey up on the cliffs for hard doctorin' an' love potions,
but there ain't many will go up to get it. Ol' Grandpa did the
high hangin' 'til his hands went stiff an' he couldn't hold rope.
My brother, John Vale, took up, but he got his eyes stung out by
a bee swarm covered his face like a black mask. Leaves me. See,
how you do is seek out the swarms on the high cliff walls. A
swarm will run fifteen feet across on a million bees. Got to drop
down to 'em on a hemp twist ladder far as it takes. Sister Lilah,
she hand climbs from below, sets a fire down of 'em, smokes that
swarm off the comb. When they fly it's like the sun risin' 'cause
there's that golden honeyhouse where it was black with bees. I
come down the hemp twist ladder, carve slabs from the comb, let
it fall to a willow wove basket, lower it down to the ground. Air
around your head's got bees in it like ash from a fire. I'm to
where I can take thirty, forty stings an' not hurt, nor swell, nor
cry out. Only way they don't swarm ya's if you're right with Jesus
an' cool as a stone. Johnny Vale he was doing' it on nerve 'cause
he stole an' fornicated. Bee stung him on the nipple an' he took
the name in vain. Lessen' fifteen seconds there was a thousand
bees on his face exploded his eyes like a grape. Thousand bees
together they's like a radio receiver for your heart. They know
your sin's in your sweat. They can sense in your rhythm if you're
ready for judgment. They know if there's guile or there's honey
in the cells of your mind. See, Jesus is the order that holds off the
Apocalypse. If he ain't in the bloodstream, life eats you alive.
(*An actress already onstage lies erotically on the stage floor in front of
the armchair. Everyone else exits.*)

ONE MOMENT

ACTRESS: God, you're beautiful. You must really work out. I've been watching you...from across the street...with binoculars. Wow, this is embarrassing. I mean, not every minute. Not every night. Only if there's nothing on television. Then this afternoon... boom...there you are with my doorman. Incredible. And now here we are. Oh God that...that feels...euphoric. God, I would never have thought of doing that with that. Listen, before we make love would you mind filling out this form? It's sort of a sexual history and...I don't know...sort of ground rules. I'll get you a copy of mine. The whole thing won't take more than half an hour. Yes, yes touch me. The phone's right there in case you have to call people for details. God, I want you. The thing I hate most is the man wearing a prophylactic for oral sex. The first time I saw a man with a rubber on his tongue I just about died laughing. Listen this is hard to say but if your history seems dicey I have a clear plastic shower curtain I could put over you and we could just kind of hold each other...you know, after a milk bleach bath, or we could just do visual sex or a phone date, I mean if the surgical gloves put you off? Look, I hate this, but would you mind if I checked your gums? Here, you can look at mine. I know, let's light the candles. (*The lights go down to a single pool of light on her.*) There. Intimacy.

STOLEN LIVES

Two men move on and sit on the arms of the armchair. Two women enter and stand back to back behind it. In this piece all lines in parentheses are spoken by Carl.

JAY: Me and my brother Carl (yo!) we took up with the DiMathis sisters in a time warp back in '78 ('79), '78, when we were sellin' cleanin' fluid door to door (see this spot on my tie?). They were two agoraphobics over two hundred pounds (dressed). Livin' their lives in every detail like Bette Davis. (It's true.) Invited us in on Friday, February 15, 1978 …
(*Whenever the women speak they do Bette Davis imitations.*)

FLORENCE: Come on in, boys.

JAY: And when we walked out of there six weeks later it took seven damn years to get functional (or paroled). Florence DiMathis …

FLORENCE: Don't stare at me, honey, unless you mean it.

JAY: …preferred to live in the movie *Now Voyager* as a New England spinster who blossoms into a fashionable woman of poise and charm …

FLORENCE: Let's not ask for the moon when we have the stars.

JAY: Whereas Alexis DiMathis (hoo-boy!) preferred *The Bride Came C.O.D.* (A temperamental oil heiress elopes with a Hollywood bandleader.)

ALEXIS: Hello, baby. You miss me?

JAY: There was two kinds of scenes they liked (scenes where we died) an' scenes where they died. In between we'd eat gourmet an' be chained to the bed for bouts of untamed sensuality (an' Shiatsu massage). It was a pretty good life. (Beat loadin' trucks for UPS.) The problem was *A Stolen Life* (1946 Warner Bros.) where Bette played identical twin sisters. Kate Bosworth (kindly and introspective) and the vivacious but thoroughly bitchy and unprincipled (Patricia). See, they both wanted to play Kate (cause she ended up with Glenn Ford). Me. (Well, you were older.) March 28, an' the DiMathis sisters was doin' their mornin' toilette (kinda wedged in) an' this pink water started runnin' out from under the bathroom door (oh-oh). "What's goin' on there, girls" (he yelled). An' the door slams open an'

Alexis leans on the jamb in an off-the shoulder black negligee (an' she says ...)

ALEXIS: Rafe darling. Patricia has been killed in a boating accident. I've been living her life. Can you ever forgive me? (Florence, she was in the tub face down.)

JAY: Shit. (Shit.) Hell we called the police in about one split second. (Freaked out.) Freaked out. (Shit.) They come squealin' up. Alexis starts yellin' ...

ALEXIS: My beautiful sister! Animals! Let them rot in hell!

JAY: (And when the cops hustle us out) She winks, see?

ALEXIS: Drifters! Murderers! Scum of the earth.

JAY: We served seven years in Tehatchapi (Maximum Security). Alexis, she would visit in a black veil and give us gloxinia.

ALEXIS: My heart is a hell, and you are my jailors.

JAY: (Don't ever get involved with Bette Davis, brothers.) She don't play straight parts.

SPIDERMAN

All performers from the last piece exit. Two women enter. One sits on the armchair back and another on the seat. A third actress enters and speaks.

ACTRESS: I seen things. Uh, huh! There's stuff goes on, stuff! Sure there's crap too. Flying saucers, crap like that. Every night there's fifteen, twenty thousand husbands out doing what they shouldn't, lose track of time, gets to be 3 in the a.m....You think a couple of them don't go home tell their wives they was kidnapped by little orange men in a glowing cigar-shaped object? Uh, huh. On the contrary you got the bonafide unexplainable. Me. A common person. Butter my toast like the pope, right? Right. Listen, I'm on my honeymoon. Indianapolis, the Holiday Inn, honeymoon suite. He wants mirrors on the ceiling...like I want an aerial view. Sixteenth floor. Fire! Fire! Open the door, we got your proverbial wall of flame. Great. The last thing I'll remember will be the missionary position in a mirror. We go out on the balcony. This big. Inferno time. Can we jump? No. Can we go back in? No. I turn to my husband, I say, "Hey, at least we came before we went." Tears run down his cheeks. I look down, a guy is climbing the side of the building. No ropes. What is he wearing? You got it. Blue and red. It's Spiderman. I'm not pulling your chain, man. I got saved on my honeymoon in the famous Indianapolis Holiday Inn fire by a super hero. Uh, huh. You think I'm kidding, right? He has me on his shoulders and my husband by the belt, we go straight down the outside glass. I say, "Hey, Spidey, where's your pal Superman?" He says, "Superman has no dick. He's in therapy." Stuff. I seen stuff. You want to know something else? My marriage broke up, I date him. You want to know something else? I'm pregnant. Weird hormonal chemistry, you know? Sometimes filament spins out of my body. I'm beginning to climb. (*Her eyes fill with tears.*) I'm beginning to climb. (*She sits.*)

Roller Coaster

The actress speaking and the actress above her on the chair back sometimes move in unison to create the roller coaster.

ACTRESS: The gargoyle. It had four 360-degree loop-de-loops and a first fall that could put your heart in your forehead! What a beauty! It had incline roll drops, one left, one right that felt like they went on to Chicago and a slow draw up at 90 degrees that stood the hair on your toes on end! Me and Sis waited two damn hours to get on that machine an' when we jumped on, it took off. There was a gent there, I yelled, "Hey, man, the roll bars," an' he looked startled but we were on the incline and I yelled down, "She's not in, Goddamnit. Throw the switch. Shut it down!" I could see somebody start to run but we crested the top an' it took off. "Grab the rail. Left hand. Now me. Not there, the belt. The belt! Let me get an arm behind...up...move forward... behind you. I got it. I got you. Hold on. Hold fucking on. Oh my God. Oh my Jesus. Stop this son of a bitch!" We hit the loops. One, two, I saw Sis bite through her lip. Three, four, and her hand on the rail moved to her face and swinging out of the fourth loop she went out of the car in this rising arc making a shy little high-pitched noise and I wrench around and she was lying out sideways in the air and she saw me and she waved. Like you were supposed to wave when you left people. Like she lived in the air and she'd never come down. Like it was the wildest best part of the ride. Like she was still alive.

(The speaker exits leaving the actress who began the evening sitting as she first did on the armchair back in a special.)

ENDINGS

ACTRESS: I sat in the chair by the bed watching him sleep until I ached from sitting and then went out to the tool shed where I had hidden the suitcase and put it by the door of the car and stood without knowing what to do next in the yard listening to the trucks go by on the freeway down below. He was so good about beginnings and endings and summing things up and knowing what must be done and explaining why it was the way it was now and I'd never seemed to have a talent for it. I owed him a good solid ending that he could carry around with him and trot out on occasions and gatherings but for the life of me I couldn't think of one and it was a serious, hopeless failing and couldn't be forgiven. I thought of so many things that had happened and then more things and more things, but I couldn't make an explanation of them so I went back in and lay down beside him because if you can't explain endings, then you probably don't deserve one. And he shifted and touched me lightly and that was familiar, and the shadows in the room were familiar, and the beginnings of the birds were familiar. And as I fell asleep I thought, well, that's all right, it's going on then. It's going on. (*The lights dim slowly.*)

CURTAIN CALL.

APPENDIX

The author includes the following pieces for possible substitutions if casting or context would be improved by them.

Hams

ACTRESS: Before they put the highway through, well, I looked out over actual living grass. There was a cypress row and past that, scrub woods, wild flowers. I bought the house because of what was across the street. Nothing. Nothing was across the street. Dusk time I'd sit on my porch...listen, never mind. Now I have trucks, more trucks. All right, life changes. Then they put up the billboard. I've got six windows in front. Out each window I see a cartoon Shakespeare three stories high with a lampshade on his head carving a ham the size of my Volkswagen, and in day-glo letters it reads, "Ham It Up." Daybreak, noontime, late night... "Ham It Up." I buy a chainsaw. I buy Army fatigues. August 12, one a.m., I cut that mother down. Ecowarrior! August 17th, it's back, it's bigger, it has stadium lights. Three canned hams tap-dancing in top hats with canes and three stories high on countersunk steel pillars it says "Pearls Among Swine." I sleep no more. I buy climbing gear. Attach chains to the top. Rent a 16-wheeler. Pop that clutch and I topple that son-of-a-bitch like Ozymandias! And I dance, and dance, and drink myself insensate, and sleep eighteen hours. When I regain consciousness, they're putting up the new sign. It's a sliced ham with wings and a halo, playing a harp. "Pig Heaven." There is a moment in life when you know what you will become. When you fully understand that there is only process, only struggle and that heroism is not the single reflexive blow, it is the power of repetition without hope. And when you know that, you must not hesitate, you must not vacillate, you must not ruminate, you must sell out! After that, believe me, the world moves on and the prices go down.

PASSING THE TIME

ACTRESS: Are you…you're going to think I'm crazy…Are you passing
the time? Sometimes I think…never mind. A voice tells me that
I'm "passing the time." A key meeting, for instance, the
presentation to the client, wild adrenaline, jobs on the line, it
sells. People are ecstatic, they're like hugging and…look it's a
triumph and…well, I hear this cool laconic humorous voice
saying, "Well, that's passing the time."

I've had it happen when I'm making love. I've heard it when
I take flowers out to Mother's cemetery. I bought a new car. Hey,
that's a big thing, that's a twelve thousand dollar thing. I'm
driving it off the lot, and I hear this whisper in my ear, "Say, this
is passing the time." Things I love to do, people I want to be
with, moments I've been waiting for, "Well, that's passing the
time."

As if the real thing, the real, real thing, the thing that isn't
"passing the time" is always where I'm not. And I can't seem to
make the simple, clear gesture, say the authentic thing, just for
God's sake be here. Just *be* here. I'm living just…just a little *off,*
you know just infinitesimally wrong. Missing my life by inches.
Passing the time.

Healin'

ACTRESS: Healin' don't ordinarily git born on you as is much supposed. More than usual it's just passed along. Aunt Jesse Colt she give it to me. Told me I was an ugly child, so I needed talents. Said, "Here, girl," an' she cupped a hand over each of my eyes and blew that gift in between the fingers. My healin' gifts is three. I can heal burns, cure the babies' yella thrash, an' draw out the dog day blues. Women gits them blues in the heart of the heat. Just lie about, good for nothin', cryin' over who knows what, bein' miserable an' pissin all over their men. Man gets somethin' of the kind, but you can't heal on it, he got to drink it out. Now I'll sit down by a woman, read her Ezekiel, chapter seventeen, verse six. Parch me some red pepper at the fire. Powder it, cook it in a tea, add bayberry, two tablespoons white corn liquor, and sing what I please. She don't see a man for three days she'll cure. You don't want such blues there's three avoidances. Don't get married 'til forty, don't travel more'n fifty miles from where you're born, and don't lie with no red-headed man plays the banjo in a public place. Them three I know from personal experience. They're just incurable. Any other way you get 'em, you send for me. I got travelin' gifts.

SOUNDS YOU MAKE

ACTRESS: There's a very particular sound I associate with you. Just the smallest exhalation of breath. So light sometimes it's just on the edge of being heard. But you mean me to hear it. It's not spontaneous or surprised. It's meant to wound. It's meant to delicately remind me of my unreason. It intimates something soiled and hopelessly emotional. That you by all rights should disdain or reject in me but at the same time it makes you unassailably good because all you do is make the sound and that resigned, fluttering palms up gesture and stay reasonably silent in the face of what, if you did speak, you might call my *provocations*. And every time you do it, I feel vaguely ashamed because *I* haven't been good, *I* haven't been accepting or forgiving or forebearing. I've had the immense bad taste to feel something when you didn't instigate it, or ask for it or, worse yet, simply weren't in the mood for it. And the worst of it is that it's so painfully clear how much you enjoy what you're feeling about me and how you want me to hear you feeling it. So that I realize that now what used to be my pleasure in your company has become this longing to never, never, never hear you make that sound again. Never. Never.

SOFTBALL

A game of fast-pitch softball. A pitcher. She throws one.

PITCHER: God, I hate softball. Two more outs I got my three hundred sixty-third no-hitter. (*She pitches.*)

Two more games we got our eighteenth straight world championship. Kind of takes the thrill out it. (*She pitches.*)

Another damn strikeout. Last July I fell asleep in the middle of an inning on a three-two count. (*She pitches.*)

I'm a damn immortal for $600 a week playing for a solid pack tuna company I wouldn't feed to my cat. (*She pitches.*)

I had this record in the Bigs I would own a state. Bonuses! Don't talk to me about bonuses. Every time I strike out twenty, I get a free cheese pizza. Toppings is extra. (*She pitches.*)

God I hate this batter. Guy doing the stats says 80% of my career strikeouts is blondes with natural curl. (*She pitches.*)

Ball? My ass that was a ball, ump. You're calling a strike zone about as big as her tits. I take that back. Her tits was the strike zone, we'd a had a twenty-seven straight walks here. (*She pitches.*)

We win. Whoopee. Time for the old shower, if there was a shower. Sometimes I bring water to the park in a ziplock bag. Go back to my motel, switch on the light bulb, see half those blondes I struck out on the pornography channel…have me some cold nachos and a warm 7-Up. Self satisfaction! That's what I got. I got a world of self satisfaction. Women's sports.

END OF PLAY

Cementville

ORIGINAL PRODUCTION

Cementville, produced by the Actors Theatre of Louisville, premiered at the 15th Annual Humana Festival of New American Plays, March 1991. It was directed by Jon Jory. The cast (in order of appearance) was:

Dwayne Pardee	Jim Petersmith
Tiger	Suzanna Hay
Nola	Corliss Preston
Dani	Annette Helde
Netty	Adale O'Brien
Lessa	Kimberley LaMarque
Bigman	Fred Major
Mother Crocker	Sally Parrish
Dottie	Peggity Price
Dolly	Cynthia Carle
Miss Harmon	Jessica Jory
One-Eye Deneauve	Bob Burrus
Kid	Lex Monson
Eddie	Tom Stechschulte

CHARACTERS

DWAYNE PARDEE, a wolf in wimp's clothing, 45
TIGER, at the end of a long rope, 35
NOLA, all the shrewd innocence of youth, 22
DANI, a tough talking frog in a small pond, 35
NETTY, mothers everything that moves, 40
BIGMAN, promoter, wrestler, hustler, fool, 40
LESSA, athlete in a cul-de-sac, 32
MOTHER, don't tread on me, 50
DOTTIE, wild beauty and bad karma, 28
DOLLY, sex and madness reconciled, 26
ONE-EYE DENEAUVE, country nightmares, 45
MISS HARMON, a little terrified order in chaos, 17
EDDIE, the Frankenstein monster, 42
KID, a boxer with a world view, 70

PLACE
The play takes place in the locker room of a boxing arena in Cementville, Tennessee.

TIME
The time is the present.

CEMENTVILLE

ACT ONE

An empty, run-down locker room in an unused boxing arena in a small industrial city in Tennessee. Peeling plaster, water stains. Portions of the ceiling bubble ominously. One door with a twist lock leads in from an outside hallway. One door leads into a shower room the delicate would avoid. One door stands open revealing a broom closet partially filled with rotten, rolled up Venetian blinds and a decaying mop and bucket. Along the walls of the room stand lockers of two distinct periods. A ceiling fixture with three naked bulbs provides most of the illumination. Above the lockers there are posters ranging back to the 1950s naming fighters an aficionado might recognize. Some, mold has obliterated, some have inexplicably survived. The floor is littered with beer cans, Coke cups, newspapers and nasty drek. Several lockers stand open, revealing their own distressing mess. A small man in his forties walks past the door. A moment. He returns and stands framed in the doorway looking in.

DWAYNE: Geez. (*Enters and stares around him.*) Geez, I don't know...
   (*A woman's voice is heard in the outside hall.*)
TIGER'S VOICE: Anybody home?
   (*Dwayne starts out the door, realizes he is trapped, moves into the broom closet and closes himself in. Tiger appears in the doorway. She*

wears a tank top and jeans with an Elvis Presley jacket that reads "Taking Care of Business" on the back. She carries a flight bag, a cat-carrying case and a beer. She has a rolled up comic in her back pocket. She is around thirty-five. She surveys the room.)

TIGER: Son-of-a-bitch! (*She kicks a can.*) Hey, kid! (*Turns on light.*) Jeee-sus.

(*A young Girl enters. She wears shorts and a heavy metal T-shirt. She carries a push broom. She is seventeen or eighteen.*)

NOLA: Yo.

TIGER: We supposed to dress in here?

NOLA: He said.

TIGER: We supposed to do it standin' up? (*Walking into the shower room.*)

NOLA: Huh?

TIGER: Benches.

NOLA: Right.

TIGER: You got benches?

NOLA: To sit down.

TIGER: Yeah.

NOLA: I don't know.

TIGER: (*Half pleased.*) There's a dead rat in the shower room.

NOLA: Showers don't work anyway.

TIGER: You seen a big man in a suit?

NOLA: On the pay phone two hours.

TIGER: Damn.

NOLA: Real agitated.

TIGER: Every time there's a man on a phone my life gets screwed up. You know was it a parole officer?

NOLA: No ma'am. (*Indicating the cat case.*) What's that?

TIGER: Family.

NOLA: (*Bending to look in.*) Kitty, kitty.

TIGER: It's a Chihuahua. French kisses better than a man. You got a cigarette?

NOLA: Sure. (*Offers one.*)

TIGER: They use this crap hole for anything?

NOLA: Not since Jesus was a pup.

TIGER: Yeah? Look, go find the big man and tell him I don't dress standin' up. And get me a beer. Make that a six-pack.

NOLA: You the one on the poster?

TIGER: No, I ain't on the poster.

(*Another woman enters. She is in her late twenties and prettier in a worn way. She wears a sweater and a beret. She carries a container of fast food, a Pepsi, french fries and a half-eaten burrito.*)

TIGER: She's on the poster.

DANI: (*Looking at the room.*) Are you kiddin' me?

TIGER: What's your name, kid?

NOLA: Nola.

TIGER: Nola, Tarzana Queen of the Jungle. Tarzana, Nola.

NOLA: Hey.

DANI: I'm not doing this.

TIGER: (*Experimentally opening lockers.*) Yeah?

DANI: I got a cleanliness clause.

TIGER: Rubbers. There's used rubbers in this locker.

DANI: Great.

TIGER: Well, I'm glad somebody was havin' fun.

NOLA: I was gonna, you know, sweep up, you know, but, whoa, he's got me hoppin'.

(*No one speaks, She starts to leave.*)

NOLA: Six-pack.

DANI: Nola.

NOLA: Yo.

DANI: I'm Dani. You want my autograph?

NOLA: Yeah.

DANI: Clean this up.

NOLA: Yes ma'am. Soon as I…

DANI: Now.

NOLA: The big man, he…

DANI: I'm paid to hurt people, you understand.

(*A moment. Nola sweeps.*)

DANI: Tiger. You are drivin' me nuts.

TIGER: I like lookin' in lockers.

DANI: How's that rat doin'?

TIGER: Chihuahua. Bes' goddamn roommate I ever had.

DANI: Bigman says you bring her in here he's gonna eat her.

TIGER: Be the last bite he ever takes. She don't like that Motel 6. Got a nosebleed. (*She takes her out.*)

DANI: You get any sleep?

TIGER: Not a hell of a lot.

DANI: Eighth graders. They oughta electrocute 'em, not put 'em in a motel. Where's Bigman?

TIGER: On a pay phone.

DANI: Where's his brother, Eddie the asshole?

TIGER: Cruiserweight Champion of America?

DANI: Ain't that a bitch? Crowd loves them cruiserweights. I gotta see a gynecologist.

TIGER: Oughta cut down to two room-clerks a week.

NOLA: Want me to wipe out some lockers?

DANI: Yeah. (*To Tiger.*) Where else am I gonna find a man by the time the bus gets in?

TIGER: Forget it.

DANI: I like to stay in working order.

TIGER: (*Short laugh.*) I'd rather rust.

DANI: There's a dead rat in the showers.

NOLA: Showers don't work anyway.

DANI: Great. You want the other half of this cardboard burrito?

TIGER: (*Takes it.*) Sure. What town are we in? (*Puts her dog back in the cat case.*)

DANI: Deepest Tennessee.

TIGER: No, really, what town?

DANI: Hey, Tiger, I really *don't* know. What town were we in yesterday?

NOLA: Cementville. You're in Cementville, Tennessee.
(*Dani and Tiger snort.*)

DANI: I'm in Cementville, Tennessee, with the All American Wrestling Federation Shower of Stars Tour. (*To Tiger.*) You got aspirin?

NOLA: How many stars?

TIGER: What was that, kid? (*Getting the aspirin.*)

NOLA: How many stars we in for tonight?

DANI: Well, kid, that's somethin' the rubes never know. You got five bucks?

TIGER: Hey.

DANI: This a *fan,* Tiger. What separates the fans from the rubes is inside dope. You a fan, Nola?

NOLA: Yes ma'am.

DANI: You got five bucks?

NOLA: I got twenty bucks.

TIGER: Don't let her hustle you.

DANI: Five bucks I answer three questions. (*Takes the aspirin without water.*)

TIGER: I'm going for the big man. (*Stops by Nola. Gives money.*) This is for the beer. The buck's a tip. Keep an eye on that case. (*She exits.*)

DANI: She got a steel plate in her head.

NOLA: No.

DANI: Yeah. I fucked Tom Cruise.

NOLA: Yeah?

DANI: Yeah.

(*Nola pulls out her money, peels off a five, holds it out. Dani takes it.*)

DANI: O.K. The question was how many stars? You got a cigarette?

NOLA: Sure.

DANI: Cementville, Tennessee, huh?

(*Nola nods.*)

DANI: You ever heard of Madison Square Garden?

(*Nola shakes her head "no."*)

DANI: Well, I played there and now I'm playin' here.

NOLA: Wow!

DANI: O.K., we got the main event, right? Irish Bob McCarthy vs. Stosha "The Wild Man" Oronovsky.

NOLA: Whew!

DANI: That's Bigman doin' the Irish an his brother Eddie the asshole doin' the Ruskie. They fought for the championship eighty-three times this year.

NOLA: (*Shocked.*) Brothers?

DANI: Yeah.

NOLA: Irish Bob?

DANI: Well, he ain't Irish and he ain't Bob, an he owes me four weeks salary, the scumbag. Anyway, there's those two plus me, Tiger, Netty and Angelessa. O.K. We open up with me wrestlin' Tiger. Then Netty wrestles Angelessa. Then Tiger wrestles Angelessa masked. On like that 'til the combinations run out. Girls do tag team, then Bigman an the asshole do the Cruiserweight Championship, an we grab some showers an go out an get wasted.

NOLA: (*A pause.*) Just six stars?

DANI: Yeah, right.

NOLA: Doin' the whole thing?

DANI: Six, yeah.

NOLA: Who's the woman in the iron mask?

DANI: Sometimes Angelessa, sometimes me.

NOLA: Shoot. She was my favorite an she ain't even a person.

DANI: It's a bitch, ain't it? You got one more question for the five bucks.

NOLA AND DANI: How can I get started in professional wrestling?

DANI: One: it's major shit work for bad pay. Two: gives you foot fungus. Three: wrestlers got an attitude an bad knees. Now get the hell out of here, I'm tired of you.

NOLA: O.K.

(*As She starts to leave, Netty, a motherly woman in her forties, enters with Angelessa, a powerful black wrestler in her late twenties dressed in a sweatsuit with a college name and "Property of the Athletic Dept." emblazoned on it. She is carrying a large duffel bag. She wears a Walkman.*)

NETTY: Oh my God, did we have a good, good, good, good dinner. Country cookin'. Green beans, darlin', so much good bacon fat they kep' on slippin' out of my mouth onto the floor. Hi, Dani. (*To Nola.*) Who's this pretty thing?

NOLA: Hey.

DANI: Helpin' clean up this pigsty.

NETTY: (*Cheerful.*) Ooooooo, it's nasty, isn't it. What's your name, darlin'?

NOLA: Nola.

NETTY: Uh-huh, that's a pretty name. You straight or gay, honey?

NOLA: Huh?

NETTY: Boys or girls?

(*Nola stares at her nonplused.*)

NETTY: Well, never mind, you'll get it figured out. You seen Eddie?

DANI: Haven't seen him.

NETTY: Well, I'm worried about that vicious ol' fart. No answer in his room.

DANI: Forgot to brush his teeth an died of the smell.

NETTY: Oh, now. He's our meal ticket an we got to worry over him. (*To Nola.*) Darlin', you gonna get us a bench to sit down on? I'm a big ol' fat lady, I got to have me a bench. Y'all want some Black

Jack chewin' gum? Angelessa? (*To Dani.*) Angelessa ain't talkin', she's in a depression.

DANI: She's always in a depression.

NETTY: Oh, she is not. (*To Nola.*) Scoot. Shoo. You help us out now, O.K.?

(*Nola exits. Netty speaks loudly because of Lessa's walkman.*)

DANI: What happened to your eye?

LESSA: Somebody messed with me.

NETTY: You smile, the ol' world smiles with you.

LESSA: I got two hundred aggravated reasons to kill people. You smile.

DANI: (*Pushing Lessa's duffel bag with her foot.*) Goin' somewhere?

LESSA: Get your foot off my bag.

DANI: You cop a fade, you owe me fifteen bucks.

NETTY: You know, you got me thinkin' now...what if the asshole O.D.'s in his room? I mean, he's a freebaser, right? Wasn't he freebasin'? He was. Shoot. That just about gets me worried.

DANI: Bigman said he was clean.

NETTY: Well, they're brothers, honey. They got to speak well of each other.

(*Nola enters dragging two benches.*)

NETTY: You are a dreamboat, sweetie. That's a real nice bench. Have yourself some Black Jack Gum, it's refreshin'.

(*Nola takes a piece.*)

NETTY: (*To Nola.*) You seen the costume trunks, darlin'? (*To Dani.*) Didn't I just see them in the hall?

(*Lessa nods, Netty speaks to Nola.*)

NETTY: You wanta drag those trunks on in here, honey? See, I'm a fat lady an I got a bad back.

(*Nola goes to do her bidding. Tiger re-enters.*)

NETTY: Tiger, which way I go for the coin telephone?

TIGER: Bigman's on it.

NETTY: Only one?

TIGER: Only one I saw.

NETTY: You seen the asshole?

TIGER: Not since I screwed him.

NETTY: You did not?

TIGER: Two years ago.

NETTY: You saw him on the bus last night.

TIGER: I see him, but I don' *see* him. You know what I mean?

(*Nola drags a costume trunk into the room. Lessa takes off her Walkman. Tiger reads her comic.*)

NETTY: Well, nobody has seen him and that's what I'm talking about. You think I should get Bigman?

LESSA: (*Gets down to do stretching exercises.*) He usually on time.

DANI: Oooooo, you gettin' on that floor?

TIGER: There's bad shit on that floor, Lessa.

LESSA: I got to stretch.

DANI: Well, I'm not stretchin' on that floor.

LESSA: You never did.

DANI: Now don't get on my back, Lessa. I got infected ovaries. (*Dani lights up a cigarette.*)

NETTY: Well, you poor thing.

(*Nola drags in a second trunk.*)

Ain't that nice? You know we gonna be in bed without a vibrator the asshole don't show up.

TIGER: (*A crooked grin.*) Nice talk, Mama.

NETTY: Them fans wanna see them Champion Cruiserweights.

TIGER: (*To Nola.*) Wanna pull that thing over here? (*Tiger gets their first aid kit, a red fishing tackle box, out of the trunk.*)

NETTY: The rubes be wantin' their money back, we be in bed without a vibrator.

LESSA: Don't call 'em rubes.

NETTY: The fans…

LESSA: That's right.

DANI: They're rubes.

LESSA: Fans!

NETTY: Now you two, be nice.

NOLA: 'Scuse me.

NETTY: What's that, darlin'?

NOLA: (*To Tiger.*) I'm goin' for the beer.

LESSA: (*From the floor.*) No rat dogs or alcohol in the dressin' room.

TIGER: The dog goes where I go. I'm in Cementville, Tennessee. I got bad ribs, dog's got a nosebleed, I ain't been paid an I'm gettin' a six-pack. (*Tiger takes a large pill bottle out of the first aid box and swallows several, dry.*)

DANI: (*To Lessa.*) How come you carryin' your bag?

LESSA: Thought I'd let you do my laundry.

NETTY: See now, we're gettin' bad tempered 'cause of this money thing. I knew it.

DANI: Damn straight.

NETTY: So, I think Bigman...

DANI: I say we get cash before the show.

LESSA: An don't call it a show.

DANI: Lessa, you a real pain in the ass when you're depressed.

LESSA: I'm an athlete. I don't do a show.

DANI: O.K. I say we get cash before we do tonight's Olympics.

TIGER: He ain't gonna pay us before the show.

DANI: Well, if the asshole overdosed he ain't gonna pay us afterwards.

NETTY: Now, I think y'all ought to have a stick of Black Jack Gum...

DANI: I'm just tired of his kickin' our butts all over the lot.

LESSA: Kept you off the street for three year.

DANI: I told you I don't like that.

NETTY: Well now, Bigman, he got various traits...

TIGER: No kiddin'.

NETTY: There's good an bad...

DANI: I'm talkin' about...

NETTY: ...Take into consideration...

DANI: Paychecks!

NETTY: ...Nobody here...

DANI: Lessa?

NETTY: ...Starvin' to death.

DANI: Four weeks, right Lessa?
(*Lessa doesn't answer.*)
Four weeks, right?
(*Lessa keeps warming up.*)
You didn't get a paycheck, right?

LESSA: I'm into my warm-up, O.K.? Gettin' my game face together, you dig? I like to keep my mind in the ring.

DANI: You better not have got a paycheck, Lessa. I don't care what Olympics you was in, you better not a got a paycheck.

LESSA: I had a paycheck, you'd be lookin' at air.

NETTY: All I'm sayin' is I'm worried about Eddie.

TIGER: Eddie?

DANI: The asshole.

TIGER: His name's Eddie?

DANI: I thought you screwed him?

TIGER: Yeah, I screwed him but I always called him asshole.

LESSA: (*A grin.*) You kiddin'?

TIGER: Seemed to energize him.

(*They laugh.*)

NETTY: 'Cause if he's hurt or sick or somethin', well…

TIGER AND LESSA: "We're just in bed without a vibrator."

(*They laugh.*)

DANI: O.K., but I got financial obligations.

LESSA: Still payin' your pimp?

(*Dani turns, infuriated. Tiger steps between Dani and Lessa.*)

TIGER: Enough, O.K. Jesus, I hate women.

NETTY: Must be a full moon, I swear. (*Netty goes about taping a mirror to the front of the locker she has chosen.*)

TIGER: Let's just get the card on an get us out of this pisshole.

DANI: Easy for you to say.

TIGER: (*Points to the dog.*) Gotta get her to a vet an get me some orthopedics, O.K.? An that sure as hell ain't here.

NOLA: (*Enters.*) Six-pack. Had to go a distance.

TIGER: (*To Lessa and Dani.*) Everybody cool?

NOLA: Wasn't hardly nuthin' open. Corona, O.K.?

TIGER: Corona? Damn. That ain't that Japanese stuff, is it?

NETTY: Oooooo, Corona, that's good.

TIGER: 'Cause they put sugar in that shit, it's nasty.

NETTY: Noooo, honey, ol' Mexico. Yes ma'am. I had some good times on that beer.

(*Tiger uncaps the beer with her teeth.*)

DANI: Now we got to hear about the Jai Lai player's wife.

NETTY: She had three breasts, and they were perfectly formed.

(*Bigman enters. he wears a green polyester suit. He looks like a wrestler.*)

BIGMAN: (*Taking over as is his want.*) O.K., ladies, we got to have a little pow-wow here.

NETTY: You havin' a hard day, honey? (*She pats his shoulder.*)

BIGMAN: (*Seeing the case. To Tiger.*) You got that frog-dog in here?

NETTY: (*To Nola.*) You want to get us some washin' water, darlin'?

BIGMAN: Goddamit, Tiger, hand it over.

TIGER: (*Low, eyes burning.*) You would regret touchin' this dog.

BIGMAN: (*Draws back.*) Hotel called, Tiger. Seems you forgot to pay a check in the coffee shop.

TIGER: The milk was sour, the roast beef was green, and the toast was wet.

BIGMAN: We got to be good citizens, dammit.

TIGER: I ate that sandwich, I'd be a dead citizen.

BIGMAN: Pay the friggin' bill, all right?

DANI: What she 'sposed to pay for it with?

BIGMAN: Look, I got a lot of problems, I don't wanta hear this minute shit.

DANI: Don't sweat the small stuff, right?

BIGMAN: Yeah, I...

DANI: Get to the heart of the problem.

BIGMAN: Tell me about it.

DANI: Paychecks.

(*Bigman, as if by reflex, hits her with his open hand across the head, not on the face but above the ear.*)

TIGER: (*Knowing what's coming, leans her head against a locker.*) Damn.

DANI: You hit me, Bigman.

BIGMAN: No, I didn't.

DANI: You hit me in the head.

BIGMAN: (*To the rest.*) Sit down and listen up.

DANI: Nobody crosses that line. I don't take that from no fuckin' nobody. You hear me?

LESSA: Chill out.

DANI: (*To Lessa.*) Butt out.

(*Tiger sings a couple of snatches of "Me and My Shadow."*)

BIGMAN: Hey.

DANI: Hey, what?

BIGMAN: I didn't hit you.

DANI: Yeah?

BIGMAN: (*To the others.*) You hear this?

DANI: (*To the others.*) He hit me.

BIGMAN: You ever have a coach, Dani?

DANI: Get outta here.

BIGMAN: Football? Basketball? Any contact sport?

DANI: What the hell does that have to do with...

BIGMAN: You ever played a fuckin' sport you'd know what a coach was.

DANI: You hit me!

BIGMAN: I cuffed you.

DANI: Yeah, so?

BIGMAN: So the cuff is how the coach gets the athlete's attention. The cuff says wake up you are being communicated with with information.

DANI: The information is…

BIGMAN: Hold it…

DANI: You owe me four weeks' salary.

(*He cuffs her again. She goes after him and after a brief scuffle is subdued and held by Tiger and Netty.*)

DANI: Touch me again I'll tear your hand off.

BIGMAN: I got no time for this.

LESSA: Can I ask you a question?

BIGMAN: In a minute. Dani, Dani, your problem is inappropriate behavior. Like you don't pee in a blender.

DANI: (*To Tiger and Netty.*) Let go of me.

BIGMAN: An athlete lives physical, focused, physical. Your sprinter…

DANI: Off me!

BIGMAN: Your sprinter, short distance, waiting for the start, Chicago could fall down they don't hear it. You want to communicate mentally with an athlete…(*He touches her shoulder.*)

DANI: Don't touch me…

BIGMAN: …You gotta cuff 'em. That's all I'm sayin'. It's like an alarm bell, an idea is coming. (*He notices his suit.*) Look at that? You got oil or some crap on my jacket. For *this* I *should* hit you. Jeez. Looka this! I cuff you like a coach. I never hit you. Is that clear? (*Dani walks over and hits the locker.*)

BIGMAN: Is that clear?

(*She hits it again.*)

BIGMAN: Is that clear?

DANI: Yeah, it's clear.

BIGMAN: Good!

(*Nola enters with bucket of water.*)

BIGMAN: (*To Lessa.*) What's your question?

LESSA: We gonna wrestle?

BIGMAN: O.K., listen up. What is that, beer?

(*No reaction.*)

BIGMAN: Is that a beer I see before me? What's my position on beer in the dressing room?

LESSA: No beer.

BIGMAN: That's right. Whose beer is this?

TIGER: My beer.

BIGMAN: O.K., I'm makin' an exception; gimme a beer.
(*Tiger tosses him one.*)

NETTY: (*Patting her.*) You doin' real good.
(*Nola exits.*)

BIGMAN: What is this, Bulgarian beer? Jeeminy. You don't buy
American and you piss about the country goin' down the tubes.
(*He takes a hit.*) Not bad.

NETTY: (*To Dani.*) Forget it.

DANI: (*Calmer, but still pissed.*) You forget it.

BIGMAN: O.K., you got your ears on? Hey, Lessa.
(*She still stretches.*)

BIGMAN: Lessa. Jeez. Take a break, O.K.? (*More beer.*) O.K., you're all
like family. You know that. You tour with me, you're family.

NETTY: O.K.

BIGMAN: O.K., right. We got a situation here.
(*Nola starts pulling in a dressing room unit with two mirrors
surrounded by lights. It rolls.*)

BIGMAN: Hey! You?

NOLA: Yo.

BIGMAN: Not now.

NOLA: You said.

BIGMAN: Not now. Read my lips.
(*Nola pulls it back out.*)

BIGMAN: O.K., we got a situation. Now, we're in…where are we?

TIGER: Tennessee.

BIGMAN: I know we're in Tennessee. What am I, a moron? O.K.,
where in Tennessee?

TIGER: Cementville.

BIGMAN: O.K., Cementville. A good wrestlin' town. They had
Wednesday night fights here…years, O.K., a town promoted by
Bill Walla, O.K.? He don't take care of business, I get us the date.
The strong survive, right?

NETTY: That's right.

BIGMAN: Right. O.K. We do big, or even we do good, I get his other
Tennessee dates. See the picture? Maybe next year we take all his
dates get rich. You followin' me? O.K. We got a situation. My

brother. (*He takes off his hat.*) An all-star. A man put six years in the big time…World Wrestling Federation…A man puts butts in the seats, a draw, in other words. A headliner…

(*Dani has put up her hand.*)

BIGMAN: What?

DANI: I gotta go potty.

BIGMAN: No.

DANI: No?

BIGMAN: Later.

DANI: Later what? I gotta go.

BIGMAN: Dani. The Gettysburg Address, Pearl Harbor there are times you don't go potty.

LESSA: Bigman?

BIGMAN: Yeah, what?

LESSA: They got no fights in here Wednesday nights.

BIGMAN: So?

LESSA: You said…

BIGMAN: I said in the town. Hertzburger Arena.

DANI: Yeah? So why aren't we there?

BIGMAN: 'Cause they bumped Billy Walla for a fuckin' ice show.

DANI: So you book the Hilton here?

BIGMAN: Hey, this is a famous fight joint. Jake Lamotta, Ezzard Charles.

DANI: So what are they, cavemen?

BIGMAN: Willie Pep, Kid Gavilan, Archie Moore. This here is a place for worship. Gods, I'm not exaggeratin', gods have spilled blood here.

DANI: (*Wrinklin' her nose.*) And apparently piss.

(*Tiger laughs.*)

BIGMAN: Knock that off. Hey, Dani. (*He ticks the following off on his fingers.*) Who the hell were you? Who the hell are you? And who the fuck are you gonna be when I dump you?

(*There is silence in the room.*)

BIGMAN: We make the date work, next time we're in the Hertzburger Arena. (*He looks at his watch.*) What am I talking here? I'm bleedin' time here. My brother…(*He pauses, a strange look on his face.*) My brother is indisposed.

NETTY: I knew it.

LESSA: Damn shame.

DANI: Whatsa matter he can't fight drunk?
> (*In one move, Bigman reaches down and puts Dani up against the lockers. Women scatter.*)

TIGER: Whoa!

NETTY: Bigman!
> (*There is a frozen moment. Then, strangely, Bigman puts both fists to his forehead and sobs.*)

BIGMAN: Oh man. Oh man.

NETTY: Hey, baby…

TIGER: O.K., Dani?

BIGMAN: That man…

NETTY: Come on, honey.

BIGMAN: Oh man.

NETTY: Sit down, darlin'…

TIGER: Take a load off, Bigman.

BIGMAN: It's O.K.

NETTY: Take a hit on the beer.

TIGER: You want a shot?

BIGMAN: Gimme room…back off.

TIGER: (*To Lessa.*) Inside my bag there, half pint…

LESSA: Not me.

TIGER: (*To Netty.*) Wild Turkey.

NETTY: One-half pint.

BIGMAN: I'm O.K., get the hell off me. (*He stands up.*)

LESSA: (*To Dani.*) You O.K.?

NETTY: There.

TIGER: (*Bringing him the almost empty half pint.*) Try this.

BIGMAN: I'm in fuckin' AA, Tiger.

TIGER: You was drinkin' beer.

BIGMAN: Beer ain't booze. You don't hand a half pint to a man in AA.

TIGER: My mistake. (*Takes bottle.*)

BIGMAN: Have a little Goddamned consideration.

NETTY: Well, she's sorry. She is. Now you sit down an drink your beer.

BIGMAN: This ain't booze. They give this to nursin' mothers.

NOLA: (*Enters dragging the makeup mirrors.*) Comin' through.

BIGMAN: Hey!

NOLA: Yeah?

BIGMAN: I said when I said.

NOLA: You said fifteen minutes.

BIGMAN: What are you? Hearin' things? Take it out in the hall. Smoke a joint. I'll call you.

(*Nola drags the mirrors back out.*)

BIGMAN: (*Getting emotional again.*) Jesus, Eddie, I don't know...

NETTY: Easy, big fella.

BIGMAN: My own brother...

NETTY: He's not dead is he, darlin'?

BIGMAN: Some bitch...I got one hundred bucks...no questions ...anybody knows who was in his room last night.

(*Silence. Lessa turns back to her locker.*)

BIGMAN: Lessa?

DANI: Some escort whore.

BIGMAN: You saw?

DANI: A local. Blond wig.

BIGMAN: Where?

DANI: Saw her in the hallway, from the back.

BIGMAN: Yeah?

DANI: So?

BIGMAN: With him?

DANI: Yeah, he was tanked.

BIGMAN: I find her, she's dead. I find her I cut off her tits. I pull her inside out by her tongue. This is Eddie, my brother. Blood of my blood. (*He pounds his chest.*) I'm very full.

NETTY: Of course you are.

BIGMAN: I got feelings up to here.

DANI: O.K.

NETTY: Strong feelin's.

BIGMAN: Yeah.

(*A pause.*)

TIGER: We cancel?

BIGMAN: No, we don't cancel! Whatta ya mean cancel? I'm like Jackie-Fuckin'-Kennedy. I'm a professional.

LESSA: Let me wrestle you.

BIGMAN: Get outta here.

LESSA: Bikini. I'll do it in a bikini.

BIGMAN: Get outta here.

LESSA: I'll do it straight.

(*A pause.*)

BIGMAN: Straight?

LESSA: Real.

BIGMAN: Real? What are you, a brain transplant?

LESSA: I bench press 300. I'm an Olympic athlete.

DANI: Yeah, 19th in the shot put.

LESSA: (*To Dani.*) Yeah, well, I was there. Where were you?

BIGMAN: Ladies, demeanor, O.K.?

DANI: I just saved your ass, Lessa…

BIGMAN: Hey! O.K. Lessa. Number one, "real" looks like nuthin'. You seen "real" wrestlin'? The fans would rather watch paint dry. You know who comes to watch "real"? Mothers, mothers come to watch. And while they watch they knit. You're fuckin' screwy, O.K.? Number two, I win, who cares, you win, listen, you think two thousand morons in tractor hats wanna see a black chick ice the Cruiserweight contender? What, is this whole business lost on you? I got a brother in the hospital, unconscious. I don't have time for this.

TIGER: So we cancel, right?

BIGMAN: What'd I tell you?

NETTY: You said no.

BIGMAN: What is a promoter?

DANI: Don't ask.

BIGMAN: I'm serious. C'mon. What's a promoter?

TIGER: A guy with front money?

BIGMAN: No.

NETTY: Makes arrangements?

BIGMAN: No.

DANI: Fucks other people with promises?

BIGMAN: He's like a farmer…

TIGER: Get outta here.

BIGMAN: From piss he makes peaches.

NETTY: This is a nice thought.

BIGMAN: Thank you. No Eddie. This is like a huge, monster problem. Do we fold? No. I got responsibilities to my girls. I'm like your father.

DANI: Hand me that other beer, will ya?

BIGMAN: I get on the phone, I get a replacement.

TIGER: Yeah?

BIGMAN: But not on a plateau, you know? I see in the problem an opportunity. I make a big move and get a big payoff. So who, who do I get?

DANI: Gorgeous fuckin' George comes back from the dead.

BIGMAN: The Knockout Sisters.

NETTY: You're kiddin'?

TIGER: The blondes?

BIGMAN: *60 Minutes.* Connie Chung Saturday Night. Presenters on the goddamned Grammies!

TIGER: (*To Bigman.*) The blondes with tits?

(*Bigman nods, a long pause.*)

LESSA: They are coming here?

BIGMAN: Bingo.

(*Pause.*)

LESSA: Didn't they get picked up in a drug raid screwin' the L.A. mayor?

BIGMAN: Yeah, briefly, but *People* magazine, *National Enquirer...*

DANI: Banned from wrestlin' for life?

BIGMAN: Hey, people forgive.

LESSA: They got film on them doin' crack.

BIGMAN: So?

DANI: *Screw Magazine* has them on the cover makin' a sandwich with the mayor.

BIGMAN: It's publicity.

LESSA: They barred for life.

BIGMAN: From W.W.F., from A.W.P. These are giants, these are corporations. I'm an independent.

TIGER: Hey, Bigman, they are in the slammer.

BIGMAN: Nah.

TIGER: Get your money out man, they are doing time.

BIGMAN: (*Unfolding a newspaper.*) What does this say?

NETTY: "The Knockout Sisters, free at last and home with Mama."

BIGMAN: Cairo, Tennessee. The mother lives in Cairo, Tennessee. So, I'm a genius or I'm a genius? Peaches from piss, right?

(*The women pass the paper around.*)

TIGER: You pulled that off?

BIGMAN: One phone call. Twenty-five cents.

DANI: Get outta here?

BIGMAN: (*To Dani.*) Tell me I'm good.

DANI: You're an animal.

BIGMAN: Tell me I'm good.

    (*A pause.*)

DANI: You're good.

BIGMAN: You betcher ass. I am *good.*

TIGER: They travelin' with us?

BIGMAN: (*Nods yes.*) We treat 'em right.

DANI: What're you payin' em?

BIGMAN: O.K., I got a lot to do.

DANI: I don't get a check tonight, Bigman, I'm walkin'.

LESSA: I'm gettin' a check *and* I'm walkin'.

BIGMAN: Ladies, don't promise nuthin' you can't deliver. O.K. I'm
    makin' out a card. The sisters supposed to drive up here in ten
    minutes. First two prelims same as always. Get dressed. (*Starts for
    the door. Turns. Exuberantly throws his fist in the air.*) Yes! (*Does a
    little end-zone dance. Spikes his hat.*) Touchdown! (*Picks it up.*)
    You wanta see a promoter, ladies? Bigman, he says, he does, it's
    done. Believe it! (*He exits.*)

    (*There is a pause.*)

TIGER: (*To Lessa.*) How much support wrap you got?

LESSA: Six-foot roll.

TIGER: I'll buy it off you.

LESSA: You can have it.

    (*The women begin to put necessaries from their bags into lockers.*)

DANI: He's got to pay 'em what?

NETTY: Mucho dinero.

DANI: Man, it boils me!

LESSA: They get paid, we get paid.

NOLA: (*Enters with makeup tables.*) Comin' through.

TIGER: (*Pulling a comic book out of her bag to read.*) You seen their act?

DANI: Nothin', their act is nothin'.

LESSA: No moves, no skills.

NETTY: Y'all foolin' yourselves.

LESSA: Yeah?

NETTY: They got "it."

LESSA: They a couple crack-head whores. I'm embarrassed to be in the
    same locker room with 'em.

DANI: Stand around…

LESSA: Stan' around. Lie around. Hell, I hear they was doin' some
    Danish sex show and Man Mountain Montgomery zipped up his

fly and discovered 'em. You know what their finishin' hold is? The Va-Va-Voom – it's a bump-and-grind makes their opponents faint.

(*Nola plugs in makeup table lights.*)

TIGER: What the hell is that?

NOLA: Dressin' table.

DANI: Where'd you get it?

NOLA: Rosemary Clooney's dressin' room.

TIGER: Say what?

NOLA: There's this room, see. Little room. Got about two inches of water on the floor an the lights don't work. Got a poster for Rosemary Clooney on the door an dead roses inside.

NETTY: Rosemary Clooney?

TIGER: Ol' time country singer, died when her plane hit a mountain.

LESSA: Yeah, right.

DANI: Some real singer played this dump?

NOLA: She looked real pretty on the poster.

TIGER: Started out singin' back-up for Chubby Checker.

NETTY: Oh, that one.

DANI: Well, who you think ol' Rosemary's dressin' table is for?

LESSA: He's givin' those bitches a dressin' table?

NETTY: Now y'all listen here now…

DANI: I don't…

NETTY: Dani…

DANI: Want to damn well…

NETTY: Mark my…

DANI: Hear it.

NETTY: I'm just an old Alabama waitress now but I'm makin' more wrasslin' three nights a week…

TIGER: When we're lucky…

NETTY: …than I did slingin' hash in seven, and I ain't the only one.

DANI: (*To Tiger.*) She's goin' now.

NETTY: Owe ol' Bigman for gettin' into show business…

TIGER: Jesus.

NETTY: …an havin' us a better life, praise the Lord. (*A moment.*) Just thought I'd speak up. People who ain't stayin' should get goin', and people who are stayin' should get dressed.

(*A pause.*)

NOLA: I saw 'em on television.

NETTY: (*To the wrestlers.*) Them girls is an *attraction*. Now let's *get down*. (*She begins to tape herself up for the fight.*)

NOLA: There's a tall one an a short one an the short one is mean an sneaky an, you know, hateful, an the tall one smiles an does, like, you know, dance steps an fluffs out her hair an has a pet tarantula.

DANI: (*Cold.*) Sounds great.

NOLA: An they're sexy as all hell with kinda Cher costumes, an they come on to the fans who go like boogaloo and love 'em.

LESSA: What's your name, girl?

NOLA: Nola.

LESSA: O.K., Nola, shut the fuck up.

NOLA: Sorry.

NETTY: Got me a bruise shape of an elephant.

LESSA: Hey, Netty, I'm a professional, you know? I got pride in my work. I do hard, dangerous stuff. I don't get hurt an nobody in the ring with me gets hurt. Now you put a couple showgirls in with me they gonna spend a lotta time on their ass. They screw with my timing I'm gonna take 'em out.

DANI: Well, I don't really think you got a problem.

LESSA: Yeah, why is that?

DANI: 'Cause you ain't gonna be in the ring with 'em.

LESSA: They gonna fight Bigman for the Cruiserweight championship?

DANI: It's Tiger and me do the semi-final so it's Tiger and me move up.

LESSA: Tiger ain't got the moves, she on the injured list, plus they gonna be lookin' for bad guys, O.K.? An' you our little heroine.

DANI: Get it, I make fifty more a week. I'm on the poster. I got top girl's billing an do the top girl's fight.

LESSA: Yeah, well, you watch how it goes down.

DANI: I got the *contract!*

NETTY: (*To Tiger.*) How you feelin', honey?

TIGER: I feel like shit.

LESSA: All bets is off around here, you mark my words.

TIGER: Stifferen' hell an got about a third mobility.

DANI: You better pull in your horns, Lessa. You gonna need a friend with Bigman.

LESSA: What's that sposed to mean?

DANI: You know just what I mean, baby. Go on, tell me you don't.

LESSA: Screw you. (*Puts her Walkman back on.*)

DANI: Yeah, right. (*Goes to trunk.*) You want your stuff, Netty?

NETTY: I want romance.

> (*Dani hands her a costume from the trunk. Netty starts to dress as "Pajama Mama."*)

DANI: Romance on the road. You want to suit up, Tiger?

TIGER: I want good drugs, a beach, an a hunnert comic books.

> (*Dani hands her a costume. Tiger begins to dress as "Bloody Mary" — a red leotard with metal studding.*)

DANI: (*Tapes a mirror to her locker.*) I want to win me a cruise vacation an marry any Arab we ain't shot. (*To Nola.*) Whatta you want, kid?

NOLA: I want to wrestle.

DANI: Yeah, it's a fuckin' paradise to be in wrestlin', kid. Travel opportunities, glamorous companions, luxurious surroundings, big money an the opportunity to meet crack-heads who went down on the mayor of L.A. (*She ruffles Nola's hair. Dani begins to dress as Tarzana, Queen of the Jungle.*)

NETTY: (*To Nola.*) I done twenty-six different jobs.

DANI: Oh man…

NETTY: I done dry cleanin', road work, cannin' line, store clerk, bartender,

> (*Simultaneously.*)

> NETTY: typewriter repair, phone company, resolin', slaughterhouse, garbageman, dock loader…hotel maid, post office, fire fightin'…fast food, shirt factory, sewer sweep.

> LESSA: Which trunk is my stuff in?

> TIGER: Over there.

NETTY: 'Bout as close to a movie star I'm gettin'.

NOLA: I know the holds…

> (*Lessa begins to dress as "Black Lightning," a super hero outfit with a lightning logo across the front.*)

NETTY: Uh-huh. That's good, honey.

NOLA: Backbreaker, pretzel, rope loop, double camel. I know all the holds.

NETTY: Well, sure, the holds is your basic…but you got your showmanship an your crowd work, see…(*Netty has finished dressing in a voluminous pair of striped men's pajamas.*)

NOLA: Boy, look at that! What you call that?

NETTY: Pajama Mama.

TIGER, DANI, LESSA: She puts 'em to sleep!

(*Tiger begins to lace on boots.*)

NETTY: Say, you want to come up to the hotel after the show…

DANI: She'll show you a few holds ain't on your list.

NETTY: Now, that ain't nice.

DANI: True though.

NETTY: I don't work your side of the street, you oughta give me room.

DANI: Hell, there's enough hotel clerks for everybody. (*She starts to do her makeup.*)

NOLA: Sure.

NETTY: What's that, honey?

NOLA: I'd like to.

NETTY: Uh-huh.

NOLA: Get a few tips.

NETTY: Uh-huh. Well, O.K. then.

DANI: (*To Netty but half amused.*) Surgeon General oughta stick a message on your pussy.

NETTY: Now just knock that off.

(*Lessa, with her basic fight costume on, kneels briefly and bows her head. Netty begins to lace on boots.*)

DANI: Will you stop prayin', Lessa, I can't stand that!

LESSA: (*Rising and looking in the Knockout Sisters' mirror.*) How we supposed to do if the bitches got the only mirror?

TIGER: What the hell happened to Eddie? (*A pause.*) We talkin' about this, we talkin' about that, how come the man ain't wrestlin'? (*No answer.*) Yeah, sure he's an asshole, but he's *our* asshole.

NETTY: Well, you know Eddie…

TIGER: Yeah, I know Eddie…probably dropped some laced meth.

NETTY: Well, now, Eddie'd been saying he was clean.

DANI: Maybe you heard somethin', huh, Lessa?

(*No response.*)

NETTY: He's been havin' that little numbness in his left hand.

TIGER: I seen Eddie wrestle real hurt. I seen him wrestle through a hamstring.

NETTY: Heart trouble?

TIGER: Bigman would have said.

LESSA: Somebody bit his dick off.

DANI: Yeah, sure.

LESSA: I'm tellin' you.

DANI: Bullshit.

LESSA: O.K. They didn't bite his dick off.

TIGER: You kiddin' or what?

LESSA: Two AM. There's this screamin', Eddie's on the floor outside his room…

NETTY: Who would do a thing like that?

DANI: I would but you'd probably get food poisoning.

(*Tiger gives her the thumbs up sign.*)

NETTY: (*To Lessa.*) He was naked in the hallway?

LESSA: Pretty ugly, thrashing around, yellin'. I called the paramedics. Did a tourniquet.

NETTY: (*Horrified.*) You did a tourniquet?

LESSA: Used some dental floss. Shut down the blood but he fainted.

TIGER: Jesus!

LESSA: You said he was with some whore, huh, Dani?

DANI: Yeah, he was with some whore.

NETTY: I told that man, I told him stop messin' with strange all the time. God, how much got bit off?

LESSA: I forgot my ruler, O.K.?

NETTY: Shoot *I'd* service him he wasn't so mean.

TIGER: Jesus, Netty!

NETTY: Well, that poor man didn't have a thing in the world but that dick and now it's bit off.

TIGER: Maybe they can sew it back on. They tell you now you get a finger cut off in a lawn mower you wrap it up in a Kleenex bring it down to the hospital.

DANI: They wrap his dick in a Kleenex, Lessa?

LESSA: Put it in a sandwich bag.

NETTY: Now there's some men you can picture without a dick but poor Eddie just isn't one of 'em.

TIGER: He didn't pay her, or what?

LESSA: Or worse.

DANI: Life's just funny in't? Here you're the one hates his ass an you're the one there to help.

NOLA: You think he can come back an wrestle without a dick?

DANI: His dick didn't work when he had it.

NETTY: Now no speakin' ill of the man when he's bad off.

DANI: I'd speak ill of him on the best day he ever had. He's a schizoid scumbag. And there isn't anybody in here...except her...(*Points at Nola.*) doesn't know it personal.

TIGER: Well, whoever done it put us in a hell of a fix. Now that's straight.

LESSA: Whoever done it probably had a damn good reason. An that's straight.

TIGER: (*Pulling out a tin of gourmet dog food and an opener. As she talks, she feeds her dog.*) This tour folds, we a bunch a worn out ol' bitches on the street. An if the word is some one of us chomped his member they'd hire the Hells Angels before they'd hire us. I got no skills, an armed robbery conviction, an a sick dog. Now let's kiss ass an wrestle.

NETTY: On the money. (*A moment.*) Now Eddie did say it was a whore, right?

TIGER: Far as we hear Eddie ain't said shit, an Eddie won't say shit, he'll just kill somebody.
(*There is a crash behind the door between the lockers – the Women turn.*)

DANI: You hear that? That's rats. We in this dressing room with rats!

NETTY: Now take it easy, honey...

DANI: No way. Nooooooooo way.
(*Lessa opens the door. A small man in his early forties wearing jeans, a work shirt and Vietnamese Tiger jacket is revealed nervously clutching a thick autograph book.*)

DWAYNE: How you doin'?

TIGER: Son of a bitch.

DANI: You scruffy little maggot what you doin' in here?

LESSA: Step outta there, cracker.

DWAYNE: Yes ma'am. Yes ma'am. Dwayne Arthur Pardee. How you doin'?

LESSA: How'm I doin'? What're you doin'? You in the broom closet, Dwayne whatsit.

DANI: You in there lookin' for Rosemary Clooney, or what?

TIGER: (*Pulling him up in her face by the shirt front.*) You in there lookin' for poontang, Dwayne?

LESSA: You in there chokin' the turkey?

DWAYNE: No ma'am.

LESSA: No ma'am what?

DWAYNE: I ain't chokin' the turkey.

NETTY: Well, you been in there a hell of a long time, honey.

DWAYNE: Yes Ma'am.

NETTY: (*Moving Tiger away from him.*) Well, you wanta tell Momma why you in there?

DWAYNE: Yes ma'am. See, I'm an autograph professional.

DANI: You a professional nutcase.

NETTY: (*To Dani.*) Now hush now. (*To Dwayne.*) You been there a couple hours waitin' for our autograph?

DWAYNE: Well...see...I was in, you know...an umm...an this uh big fellow he uh...uh...

NETTY: Kinda put you out?

DWAYNE: He did. He did. So I...you know...

NETTY: Come on back in?

DWAYNE: I did. I did. An he uh...an he uh...

NETTY: Kinda put you back out?

TIGER: Netty, get him outta here.

NETTY: This is a fan, O.K.? This is a wrestlin' fan.

DANI: He's a fuckin' pervert.

DWAYNE: No ma'am, I'm an autograph professional. I got...I got every famous person...everyone been in Cementville since...see here...(*Opens the autograph book.*) 1972. Cass Elliott. Ol' Mama Cass. Year before she died. God bless her. See 1972. Gene Hackman. The Four Preps. Well, three of 'em. See this here this is American heroes, see, the American way right here, right here in Cementville. O.J. Simpson. See? Irene Ryan, you know, Beverly Hillbillies. Tony Boyle, United Mine Workers. See this here is goin' in a time capsule. Anita Bryant, God bless her. See here. This is my life work.

NETTY: Well, good on you.

DANI: Get him outta here.

NETTY: Now you want us to sign your book, honey, huh?

DWAYNE: Yes ma'am. I do. Yes ma'am, yes ma'am.

NETTY: Now Dwayne, you wasn't watchin' us get dressed through a crack 'er somethin' and jerkin' off in there, was you?

DWAYNE: No ma'am. No ma'am. I wouldn't do that.

NETTY: 'Cause then we'd have to kill you, Dwayne.

DWAYNE: Well, you know, the big fella...

NETTY: You was hidin' from the big fella?

DWAYNE: Yes ma'am, I wasn't...well, what you said.

NETTY: O.K., we'll sign your book then. (*She takes it.*)

DWAYNE: God bless you. You just an American Beauty Rose in my book. You American heroes, God bless yer pure hearts. You gonna be in the time capsule. You gonna be there when Jesus Christ walks again.

(*During his speech, the women, even Nola, sign his book.*)

DWAYNE: You the mothers of America. Umm, one to a page, ma'am. You the heart, the red heart of us men folks. You the arms that swing the cradle. You on a pedestal, a way high pedestal to Dwayne Pardee. Yes sir. You a hot lunch when the men's in the fields. Yes sir, you may be prostitutes an wrasslers but you mean home to me.

NETTY: O.K., Dwayne, we about got this together now.

DWAYNE: You cut from the cloth of Jesus Christ's momma. Yes ma'am. An I'm talkin' for the mens now. Speakin' for your daddies.

TIGER: (*The last to sign.*) O.K., Dwayne.

DWAYNE: For your husbands and sons an I say to you: Get you home an get me some dinner, bitch...

DANI: (*Head in her hands.*) Oh man...

DWAYNE: ...Goin' to town in yer red lipstick, paradin' yourself like Jezebel with a tambourine, bringin' down the temple with your lascivious hips...

LESSA: (*Moving towards him.*) Let's take a walk, dude.

DWAYNE: (*Grabbing Tiger from behind.*) Touch me, Loretta...

(*She gives a sharp cry because of her ribs.*)

DWAYNE: Touch me, rub me, take me to heaven!

(*Lessa grabs him by the hair. He lets go. She throws a hammerlock on him and turns him to the door.*)

LESSA: Walk.

DWAYNE: My book...gimme my book...

LESSA: (*Taking him out the door.*) Move it.

DWAYNE: I'm a...ouch! ...autograph professional...you hurtin' my arm...

LESSA: I'm breakin' your arm...

(*And they are gone.*)

TIGER: ...the damn ribs.

DANI: You O.K., Tiger?

TIGER: Don't touch me.

NETTY: Stand up.

TIGER: Hold on...

NETTY: Stand up, it's better, honey.

TIGER: Son-of-a-bitch...ow...leggo...damn...mother-brother-son-of-a-bitch kiss my ass dammit...

(*Tiger's furious tirade finally reduces the rest to laughter.*)

TIGER: Hate this damn wrasslin'...ow...got up like some kinda...stupid...Goddamn ribs...shoulda torn off that autograph bastard's balls, hung 'em on a rear view like Goddamn cashmere dice...itchin' all over, fleas, head lice...get the Goddamn bubonic plague in this Goddamn shit hole...get the athletes foot...what the hell are you laughin' at, you cross-eyed, knock-kneed, piss-ant, putrid, dick-lickin', flat-chested, slung-assed nowhere broads! (*She starts laughing too.*) Don't make me laugh!

DANI: You aren't mad, are you, Tiger?

(*More laughter.*)

TIGER: Hell, no, I'm happy!

NOLA: He left his book. (*Holds up the autograph book.*)

DANI: Gimme that thing.

NOLA: Well, but it's...

DANI: (*Taking it from her.*) I said hand it over. (*Rips out handfuls of pages, walks to door and flings them down the hall.*) Pervert!

TIGER: Son of a bitch.

DANI: You know they got celebrity insurance now. All these nutzoids trying to shoot movie stars. (*Finishing her makeup.*)

TIGER: We ain't movie stars.

DANI: You tellin' me.

NOLA: You think he was kind of crazy?

DANI: Yeah. An he ain't the worst. We the entertainment for fuckups. When you go crazy tryin' to live this life they send you over here for Wednesday night wrestlin'.

NOLA: (*Looking at the ripped-out pages.*) Who's Eugene McCarthy?

NETTY: (*To Tiger.*) Can you get up, honey?

TIGER: Yeah, I can, but not yet.

(*Lessa re-enters.*)

NETTY: (*To Lessa.*) O.K.?

LESSA: Yeah.

DANI: (*To Lessa.*) So?

LESSA: Said I was his Ethiopian Queen, said come over to his place he had musk oil.

DANI: What'd you do with him?

LESSA: Put him in the dumpster.

NETTY: How long you think he was in the broom closet?

LESSA: I think he grew there like a fuckin' mushroom.

NETTY: Talkin' the good book...

LESSA: An' humpin' parking meters. Yeah, I was married to a preacher once.

NETTY: Well, now, I didn't know that.

LESSA: It ain't your job to know, is it?

TIGER: (*To Netty.*) Give me a hand up.

LESSA: 'Bout the last thing I need me is a soulmate.

DANI: No problem.

> (*Simultaneously.*)

>> LESSA: Zip my head.

>> RING ANNOUNCER: (*Offstage at a distance. Ring Bell.*) Ladies and gentlemen, the all-American Wrestling Federation presents its Shower of Stars Tour.

> (*Netty pulls Tiger up.*)

BIGMAN: (*Enters.*) All right, lemme have your attention. (*Calls out to the hall.*) Come on in here, Mother.

(*Mother Crocker, a rough looking woman in her late fifties in a black church dress with a strand of pearls. She smokes a cigarillo. She enters and appraises the room and its inhabitants.*)

BIGMAN: This here is Mother Crocker, Mama and Manager for the Knockout Sisters...step in, Mother...she'd like to give us a little ground plan on how it's gonna come down tonight. Mother Crocker, I'd like to welcome you to the American Wrestling Federation. We got the finest up an coming girls in the sport. An I'd like to personally express my thoughts on the job you done makin' the Knockout Sisters a world-wide attraction. You done a great job. O.K., let 'er rip.

MOTHER: Pretty run-down lookin' bunch.

BIGMAN: Yeah, but wait 'til you see 'em in action!

MOTHER: Y'all are dead meat. You're a two-bit tour playin' morgue dates and you got never-was, never-will-be talent on the way down. I wouldn't be caught dead puttin' my top attraction down this pisshole but I got me a public relations problem. See, we messed up, got ourselves into politics, put a crimp in our image. Now we got to lay low, stay in shape an make a few bucks. On the upside we probably goin' to get a film deal out of that mess, we're negotiatin'. The Knockout Sisters is A-One, U.S. prime horseflesh. While we're slummin' with you girls, you're going to have ace crowds an make the only decent money you ever made in your miserable lives. While we're together your sports pimp here...(*Indicating Bigman.*)...gets me coffee. You understand? I say fuck a sheep, he fucks a sheep, is that clear?

BIGMAN: (*A big smile.*) She got a great sense of humor, doesn't she?

MOTHER: Now think this over. How do you think a couple small-town girls became the fourth biggest wrestling attraction in the United States of America in two years? (*She pauses.*) That's right. Mobbed up. Just like Sinatra. You capice? Now this wrestlin' wears out an attraction, which is why we segue into film. But meanwhile, meanwhile don't bruise the meat. You understand me? You injure, deface or otherwise crumb up the dollar value on my attraction you're going to hear some fucking Sicilian. Got it? Dottie, Dolly, get in here.

(*The Knockout Sisters, one tall, one short, both attractive in a hard way with platinum hair, little bare-shouldered mauve dresses and spike heels, enter.*)

MOTHER: Say hello to the little people.

DOTTIE: I'm Dottie.

DOLLY: I'm Dolly.

MOTHER: Who are you?

DOTTIE AND DOLLY: We're the Knockout Sisters.

MOTHER: (*To the room.*) Remember what I said.

(*Blackout.*)

END OF ACT ONE

ACT TWO

The fights are on. The first prelim is over. Dani is changing from her Tarzana costume to her Texas Gold outfit, featuring gold sequins, gold cape and a gold cowboy hat. Tiger is still basically in her Bloody Mary outfit. Netty and Angelessa are upstairs working. The Knockout Sisters in a little lavender dressing kimonos are heavily into their glamour makeup trip. Mother is out watching the fights, and Bigman is ranking out Dani and Tiger for the quality of their work. Dottie has decorated her locker with scarves, photos, dried flowers, and Eastern wisdom.

BIGMAN: I got seven hundred rubes out there laughin' their asses off while you pattycake.

DANI: Hey, I can't touch her ribs or put her on the floor, or if I get her on the floor she can't get off the floor, so what am I supposed to do?

DOTTIE: (*Stretching and preparing.*) Money, money, money, money, money, money, money...

(*Simultaneously.*)

> BIGMAN: An athlete eats pain for lunch, Tiger.
>
> TIGER: Dammit, where's that whiskey?
>
> DOTTIE: Money, money, money, money, money, money, money, money, money, money, money, money.

BIGMAN: (*To Dottie.*) What the hell is that?

DOTTIE: It's my warm-up.

DANI: You got seven hundred rubes, huh?

BIGMAN: Yeah, six hundred, six fifty.

DANI: Three hundred, countin' people with a brain twice.

DOTTIE: See, life is a series of circles. One circle inside the next, inside the next.

BIGMAN: (*Trying to be polite.*) Circles, uh-huh. (*To Tiger.*) Got to get the rubes *hot,* Tiger. Get 'em wild and riled. They not *smokin',* they get pissed.

(*Simultaneously.*)

> TIGER: I don't know, Bigman.
>
> BIGMAN: Put 'em on the edge. Keep 'em on the edge.

DOTTIE: Each one of us has a circle. See on that circle...
  (*To Bigman.*) Excuse me, I am talkin' to you.

BIGMAN: You got a circle. We got a circle. Everybody got a circle.

DOTTIE: You got two choices—get enlightened or die.

BIGMAN: Sounds real good. (*To Tiger.*) You got to go back out there
  with Lessa...

DOTTIE: Excuse me...

BIGMAN: An *turn it on.* They gonna be walkin' out!

DOTTIE: Excuse me.

BIGMAN: What!?

DOTTIE: Now I don't like that tone. Did you hear that tone, Dolly?

DOLLY: Yeah.

DOTTIE: Sometimes a tone such as that causes me to hyperventilate,
  and then I jus' have to go home.

BIGMAN: Listen.

DOTTIE: Yeah.

BIGMAN: Now I'm sorry...

DOTTIE: You're sorry what?

BIGMAN: Sorry Miss Crocker.

DOLLY: That's right, pig snot.

NOLA: (*Enters with a bottle in a paper bag. To Dani.*) Shoot. I am
  sorry. It's kinda, well, you know, boarded up around here. Shut
  down. No liquor store, no nothin'. I went...finally there was,
  you know, this guy, you know, in a doorway, I bought this from
  him. (*She pulls out a Smirnoff bottle about a third full of brownish
  liquid.*)

TIGER: What the hell is that?

NOLA: Said the vodka wasn't no taste so...

DANI: That is one suspicious color.

NOLA: So he kinda flavored it with sherry.

TIGER: Hell with it. (*Takes a hit.*)

DOTTIE: Now that is disgusting.

TIGER: Yeah, it's vodka and sherry.

DANI: Nasty.

DOLLY: I don't work with drunks.

TIGER: Lady, I'm numb or I'm gone. (*A long drink.*)

DOTTIE: So that each one of us has a circle. Like this...(*Makes a circle
  in the air.*) A path. Call it fate. Call it what you will.

DANI: I call it bullshit.

DOTTIE: I want this woman out of the dressing room.

BIGMAN: For Christ sake, Dani, shut up. (*To Dottie.*) O.K., a circle.

DOTTIE: Yes.

BIGMAN: Of fate.

DOTTIE: Yes.

NOLA: (*To Tiger.*) I had to give him the ten. 'Cause he was like a bum
– like he couldn't make change.

DOTTIE: An Dolly an me, see, we are in the circle of sex goddesses.

TIGER: I gotta get dressed, doctor my dog. (*Tiger continues dressing as
Pocahontas.*)

BIGMAN: Jesus!

DOTTIE: (*Snaps Bigman with a towel.*) I am expressin' myself.

BIGMAN: (*Suppressing growing anger.*) Sex goddesses.

DOTTIE: Nefertiti, Mary Magdalene, Marilyn, Madonna and us!

BIGMAN: (*Red in the face.*) Nefertiti.

DOTTIE: That's right. We gonna get good karma, give good head, get
us ace parts in the horror flicks.

DOLLY: We gonna be dismembered in a close-up the size of this
fuckin' room. You watch for it!

DANI: (*In the presence of some kind of madness.*) This is *real* interestin'.
(*Pulling on cowboy boots.*)
(*Simultaneously.*)

> RING ANNOUNCER: (*Bell sounds.*) The winner, in 17 minutes,
> the pleasingly fat queen of the mat…Pajama Mama!
> (*Bell sounds.*)
>
> DOTTIE: We carryin' forward, along the circle, the wisdom of
> the forbearers…
>
> DANI: And their tits, too. Right?

DOTTIE: That too.

DANI: It's very mystical.

DOTTIE: It is. You worked with Kad Ra Mas?

DANI: I'm like on the waiting list.

DOTTIE: "Know and embody your circle." He said that.
(*From above, there is the sound of the crowd stamping their feet.
Some plaster dust drops down.*)

BIGMAN: (*Looks up.*) What the hell the girls doin' up there?

DOLLY: (*Slapping herself in the head as she looks in the mirror.*) This
don't look right!

DOTTIE: Money, money, money, money, money, money, money.

DANI: Shut up.

DOTTIE: (*Immediately completely focused on her.*) Lace up my shoe.

DANI: You got granola for brains, bitch.

BIGMAN: (*Seeing Dolly rise meaningfully from her table.*) Lace up her shoe.

DANI: You lace up her shoe.

BIGMAN: Don't screw with me, Dani. Lace up her shoe!

(*Dani laces up Dottie's shoe.*)

DOTTIE: See some of us *are* desire, and some of us *serve* desire.

DANI: And some of us have our heads up our ass.

(*Bigman immediately kicks her in the behind with the flat side of his shoe.*)

DANI: Ow.

BIGMAN: You havin' a hard time understandin' me? You got a mouth ought to be washed out with soap.

DANI: I'll think it over.

(*Bigman turns away, She immediately kicks him. He turns.*)

DANI: I thought it over.

TIGER: (*To Bigman.*) Go easy.

(*At this moment Lessa re-enters, she is* hot. *Netty follows. You can hear crowd disorder in the background.*)

LESSA: Hey, Bigman! They got some guy out there shootin' crap at me...who knows...a blow pipe. Hit me with a rock or ball bearing or some low-down shit...

NETTY: Jesus, Bigman.

BIGMAN: (*To Tiger and Dani.*) You see what you got started out there?

LESSA: Coulda put my eye out...

BIGMAN: And?

LESSA: An I went out after him.

BIGMAN: Outta the ring?

LESSA: I'm tellin' you I went out after him so nobody else has to tell you, an I'll go out after him again...

(*Simultaneously.*)

> LESSA: If I ever see him anywhere near ringside the rest of the night...
>
> BIGMAN: I got one, only one rule, you don't go into the crowd under no circumstances no matter what.

NETTY: Got a bunch of animals out there, Bigman.

BIGMAN: Stay *in* the ring!

LESSA: Grabbed me out in the crowd started feelin' me up!

BIGMAN: …Got no business leavin' the ring!!

> (*Suddenly there is a gunshot. Everyone turns. It is Dolly sitting at her dressing table holding a 9mm pistol.*)

DOLLY: Y'all are makin' a lot of noise. I like it real quiet when I'm puttin' on my lipstick.

DOTTIE: You can smear lipstick.

DOLLY: Ordinarily we got a little room to ourselves. But if we got to be in the barnyard with the hogs, then we like to make it clear who's the head hog.

DOTTIE: See beauty is serene. I wonder could anybody go get me a little plain water in this cup?

NOLA: I'll get it.

DOTTIE: You are so sweet.

NOLA: Could I ask where's your tarantula?

DOTTIE: (*Touching her arm.*) I set it free.

TIGER: You want a hit, Lessa?

LESSA: (*Pointing at Dolly. To Bigman.*) You putting up with this crap?

> (*Nola exits passing Mother who enters carrying a program. Lessa begins to change to "The Mercenary," dressed in jungle fatigues with a bandolier of ammunition.*)

MOTHER: We got dissatisfied customers, goddammit!

NETTY: Oh, oh.

MOTHER: What we got here is some piss poor *no control*. You got nut-bustin' males in a room, you got to dominate 'em!

BIGMAN: I am in knowledge of this.

LESSA: Nobody, noooooobody shoots shit at me when I'm workin'.

MOTHER: (*To Bigman.*) One rule only, keep the dogs on a leash.

BIGMAN: What I'm gonna do…

MOTHER: …is toss 'em raw meat.

LESSA: (*Emphatic but to herself.*) Nobody!

MOTHER: Who's on next?

BIGMAN: Tiger goin' on Lessa bein' "The Mercenary."

MOTHER: Well, that's real smart!

BIGMAN: I believe so.

MOTHER: (*Slapping him sharply.*) That oughta set off a riot, get us all killed.

TIGER: Hey, we do this every night.

> (*Nola reenters with Coke cup of water for Dottie.*)

BIGMAN: They ain't gonna…

MOTHER: You think you're in goddamn Minneapolis?

    (*Crowd roars.*)

MOTHER: You probably got Klan out there, probably got skinheads, neo-fuckin' Nazis, general all purpose defectives, got you a nice mix.

LESSA: You got you a nice mix.

MOTHER: What's your name, honey?

LESSA: What's your name?

MOTHER: My name is Sara Mae Louellen Crocker, originally from the Crocker auto repair Crockers before I saw Fantasy Entertainment was the growth industry of the 90's.

LESSA: Angelessa.

MOTHER: You wanta get hurt?

LESSA: I done my job in fifteen states.

MOTHER: Well, Lessa, you can either bleach yourself white or buy yourself some permanent rest in Cementville, Tennessee. These people pay good money to see people they don't like get beat up by people they do like *inside* the ropes. They don't like smart people, they don't like rich people, they don't like Arabs, they don't like Jews, and they don't like you. So they come down here to drink beer and yell shit at you an then everybody goes home happy. Fantasy Entertainment. Well you broke the rules an went *outside the ropes*…you went an got real an now you're fucked.

    (*Crowd roars. Dani chuckles.*)

MOTHER: (*Hands Lessa a ten.*) Go back to the hotel buy yourself some skin cream an a magazine and let me get this straightened out.

    (*Big Crowd roar.*)

BIGMAN: O.K., get us some wrestlers.

MOTHER: Shut up.

BIGMAN: Shut up?

MOTHER: This crowd won't sit through much more, they want my girls.

BIGMAN: Shut up?

DOLLY: This eye shadow, Mama?

MOTHER: Needs more.

DOLLY: (*Angry with herself.*) I keep on gettin' it wrong!

DOTTIE: I'm gettin' a headache, Mama.

BIGMAN: This is *my* friggin tour! Now…

MOTHER: (*To Bigman.*) Send 'em out naked.

BIGMAN: (*Appalled.*) Do what?

MOTHER: Send some of your talent out naked, get the rubes' minds on their cocks. We're not workin' while their blood's up. I got inve*stors*. I got invest*ments*.

BIGMAN: I can't send my girls out naked!

MOTHER: Why not?

BIGMAN: Why not Why not? This is America, that's why not!

MOTHER: (*To the Knockout Sisters.*) Pack it up and move it out. We're goin' home.

BIGMAN: We got a verbal contract!

MOTHER: Dream on, sucker!

BIGMAN: Those rubes'll get nuts.

DOTTIE: (*Passing him.*) You got her upset now.

BIGMAN: Give me five minutes…

DOLLY: You think we need this? We did a fuckin' hairspray commercial.

DANI: You got any balls, Bigman?

BIGMAN: Give me one miserable minute here…

DOTTIE: You couldn't peddle this act to a dog show.

TIGER: Watch it!

BIGMAN: (*Grabbing Dolly's purse off the makeup table.*) Okay, ladies, let's see what we got here… (*He dumps the contents on the ground.*)

DOLLY: Hey, dickwad…

BIGMAN: (*Snatching something up.*) Oh, yes.

DOLLY: Hey!

BIGMAN: Seems to be… (*Taking it out of her reach.*) Uh-uh. Seems to be white powder…

DOLLY: You dumped my personal items…

BIGMAN: In a little bitty glacine bag.

DOLLY: …out my bag.

MOTHER: Bigman…

BIGMAN: Might be say an illegal substance…

MOTHER: You got both feet in your mouth…

BIGMAN: …be a real no-no seein' you're one day outta the joint.

(*Dolly slams trunk lid closed.*)

MOTHER: Gettin' Dolly excited…

BIGMAN: See just who is *head hog!*

DOTTIE: What you are holdin', sir, is a personal memento.

BIGMAN: What I'm holdin', bitch, is a trip back inside. (*To the wrestlers.*) You girls ever seen this shit before?

TIGER: (*Seeing Dolly pull out the pistol.*) Watch it!

DOLLY: (*Moving toward him with her pistol.*) *You* ever seen this shit before? (*Dolly jams the gun against Bigman's nostrils.*)

DANI: O.K., O.K., we're messin' around while the rubes is trashin' the joint.

(*Lessa laughs.*)

BIGMAN: You think this is funny?

LESSA: Uh-huh.

DOLLY: Let's see you eat it.

BIGMAN: I ain't eatin' this.

MOTHER: Dolly, you are so unstable, honey.

DOLLY: Eat it.

DOTTIE: You want him to eat your precious memento?

NETTY: You think maybe we could get past the gun part?

DOLLY: Eat it!

TIGER: She's got fucked up eyes, Bigman.

NOLA: I could get us all some Coca Colas.

DOLLY: I been in a snuff film, pig snot. It was widely distributed.

DOTTIE: Money, money, money, money, money, money.

DOLLY: One, two...

(*Crowd roars.*)

BIGMAN: (*Tosses the powder back, immediately chokes and spits it out.*) Choking...

NETTY: Pound him.

(*Dani and Nola whack him on the back.*)

DANI: Spit it out. Get rid of it.

(*Dolly has gone back to the makeup table lowering the pistol.*)

NETTY: Whack him some more.

BIGMAN: Sand.

NETTY: Say what, honey?

MOTHER: You a little accident-prone, Bigman.

BIGMAN: That shit was sand. What the hell you carryin' sand around for in a little bag?

DOTTIE: May I share with him, Dolly?

DOLLY: You share with him.

DOTTIE: On July 16, 1985...

BIGMAN: (*To Nola.*) Get me some water.

DOTTIE: I was at Daytona Beach with Dolly's husband Earl. Now the sky was real pure teal blue…

BIGMAN: (*To Mother.*) We need wrestlin', for God's sake, what are we doin'?

DOTTIE: …just that single instant between day and dusk when time is suspended…

(*A young woman, perhaps sixteen, in an Andy Frane usher's uniform with a thin line of blood coursing across her face from a cut in her hairline, appears in the doorway. She smiles.*)

MISS HARMON: Mr. Vague?

BIGMAN: Holy Jesus.

MISS HARMON: Paging Mr. Vague, please?

BIGMAN: What?

MISS HARMON: Mr. Vague?

BIGMAN: Vag.

MISS HARMON: Mr. Vag? Oh boy, oh boy, Mr. Vag.

NETTY: You're bleeding, honey.

MISS HARMON: (*Oblivious.*) Uh-huh.

DOTTIE: Ooooo, I hate that.

MISS HARMON: Mr. Vag, Mr. McClendon, the referee, he said, oh boy, here I wrote it down…we better get him some wrasslers pretty pronto, because that crowd, it's ugly, it's a real ugly crowd. It is. So, oh boy, that's the whole thing, the whole message. From Mr. McClendon. 'Cause they're about to shit a brick, Mr. Vag, they really are. So perhaps I could…I could bring him your perspective.

BIGMAN: Godammit, I'm just tryin' to make a living!

MISS HARMON: (*Writing.*) …Make a living.

BIGMAN: I got my brother in the hospital with his dick cut off!!

MISS HARMON: …Cut off.

BIGMAN: I got the Knockout Sisters from Screw Magazine feedin' me sand and the Cosa Nostra tellin' me to send my stable out naked an I got tanked up rubes trashin' uninsured property I'm gonna be responsible for…

MISS HARMON: Rubes?

BIGMAN: Now you tell me what the hell to do!?

(*Irate crowd sound.*)

MISS HARMON: Well, I'm not sure, but they're throwing chairs.

NETTY: We ought to think this over, Bigman.

MOTHER: (*Steps forward. Wipes blood off the girl with her handkerchief.*) You tell him there is wrestlers comin'. Go on. Go on.

MISS HARMON: I will. Yes Ma'am. Y'all, oh boy, y'all have a nice day, ya hear.
(*Big Crowd sound. She disappears. A moment.*)

DOTTIE: (*Serenely.*) An I looked at Earl split by the horizon, with his history of impotence problems, standing there kind of give out, and I said, "Earl, I am Dolly and Dolly is me, we are the circle, we are the earth for you." An I lay down on the dusky beach and took him inside me and he cried out, "Dolly, Dolly, I'm home, Dolly." An then he had a heart attack and dropped dead.

DOLLY: Pretty much the way it always went.

DOTTIE: So I took some of that white sand from under his head and brought it home to Dolly as a memento which you have swallowed.

DOLLY: You hurt my heart.

TIGER: You got you some live ones, Bigman.

BIGMAN: I'm in charge here!

MOTHER: (*To Bigman.*) You want to know what to do?

BIGMAN: No!
(*Big crowd sound. A moment. He paces.*)

BIGMAN: O.K., maybe.

NOLA: (*Entering.*) I got the water.

BIGMAN: (*Knocking the cup out of her hand.*) I never asked for any damn water.

NETTY: Biggie...

MOTHER: You get the Indian... (*Pointing at Dani.*) An the cowboy... (*Pointing at Tiger.*) Out there in their underwear.

BIGMAN: I said that, I said underwear.

MOTHER: (*To Dottie.*) Hold it! We still got those garter belts?

DOTTIE: Oh, I'm just a little pack rat.

MOTHER: You announce you a specialty bout...what did we call it that one time?

DOLLY: Bra wars.

DANI: Forget it.

DOLLY: You the Virgin Mary, huh?

DANI: I fuck but I don't tease.

MOTHER: Extra fifty dollars?

DANI: You can't find a whore for fifty dollars.

MOTHER: A c-note?

   (*She tosses it on the floor. Lessa reaches for it. Dani picks it up.*)

DOLLY: Hard to find a *good* whore for a *hundred* dollars.

   (*She hands Dani two garter belts and stockings. Dani now changes from "Texas Gold" down to underwear, garter belt, stockings, and a sheer cover-up Dottie hands her.*)

DANI: (*Mildly.*) You don't know what a whore is, babe. You livin' in blonde world. We just aren't playin' off the same sheet of music, toots. See, I'd rather be a hundred-dollar whore than a thousand-dollar blank. (*She walks away.*)

BIGMAN: (*Turning to Tiger.*) Tiger.

TIGER: You saw the bout. I been leanin' on this locker 'cause I can't get off it.

BIGMAN: O.K., Netty.

MOTHER: Those boys aren't lookin' for no ugly fat people in a G-string.

   (*He turns to Lessa.*)

NOLA: I can wrestle.

MOTHER: Yeah?

NOLA: I can wrestle good.

MOTHER: How old are you?

NOLA: Nineteen.

MOTHER: Where you worked?

NOLA: The Whale.

MOTHER: Where?

NOLA: It's an independent gas station with skateboard service.

MOTHER: Wrestled. Where have you wrestled?

NOLA: No place. Since I was twelve I saw all the bouts in three hundred miles. Thursday nights I practice with Jadine.

BIGMAN: Jadine who?

NOLA: My cousin. She weighs one ninety.

MOTHER: What kind of underwear you got on?

NOLA: Black with a red heart.

MOTHER: You're in the ring...

NOLA: Yeah.

MOTHER: She takes you down with a flying leg scissors...

NOLA: Yeah?

MOTHER: You do what?

NOLA: Counter with the grapevine, slip into a chicken wing and drop the heck out of her with a Carolina slam.

MOTHER: (*Holds out bills.*) Thirty bucks.

NOLA: I'm in? I'm in the bouts?

NETTY: You wanta do this, honey?

  (*Crowd roar.*)

NOLA: I wanta wrassle. I wanta wrassle my ass off.

LESSA: Your mama oughta *whip* your ass.

NOLA: My mama already whips my ass. She whips my ass with a coat hanger.

BIGMAN: You do a good job there might be somethin' temporary on the tour.

NOLA: (*Beside herself.*) On the tour?

BIGMAN: See me up in my hotel room after the bouts? Number's ten-0-six.

NOLA: (*Looks at Netty.*) O.K., I'll be there. (*Leaps in the air, arm and fist extended.*) I am in! Yes! Get down!

BIGMAN: Right, that's settled.

NOLA: (*To Mother.*) What's my name?

MOTHER: Frenchy.

NOLA: All right!

  (*Nola begins to undress. She gets ready to go out in her underwear plus garter belt, stockings and sheer cover-up handed to her by Dottie.*)

TIGER: (*To Nola.*) Have a hit.

  (*Nola takes one.*)

LESSA: (*To Bigman.*) I got to have my money.

NOLA: Yes!

MOTHER: Let's get us some wrestlers in the ring.

  (*There is a flurry of activity as Nola and Dani get ready.*)

MOTHER: O.K., main event...

BIGMAN: Yes ma'am, now what we're gonna do is...

MOTHER: Shut up.

BIGMAN: I'm just saying...

MOTHER: Shut up. You tried to leverage me, now you're warm piss. You wanta wake up in your water bed with a fresh cut horse's head, you keep talkin'.

DOLLY: That was a good movie. (*Angry.*) I could *be* in that movie!

MOTHER: (*Pointing at Nola and Dani.*) I want the same two...

LESSA: Wait a minute…

MOTHER: …in the main event.

DANI: (*Gives Lessa the finger.*) Hey, Lessa?

NETTY: (*Points at Nola.*) Now, Frenchy gonna be tired, and she's
green.

(*The Usher appears again in the doorway. A thin man in a black
suit, white shirt, black string tie with a haunted face and a burr
haircut has her by the hair.*)

MISS HARMON: Mr. Vag, there is a gentleman to see you, Mr. Vag.

THE MAN: How y'all doin'?

BIGMAN: Get your hands off my staff.

(*The Man flicks open a switchblade in his free hand.*)

MISS HARMON: Oh, no.

THE MAN: I'm Mr. One-Eye Deneauve down from Lecher County,
Kentucky for the wrasslin'.

MOTHER: (*Moves up beside Bigman.*) Hello, One-Eye.

THE MAN: I drove a distance to see me some gut-pumpin', butt-
bumpin', airborne wild pussy in a good family entertainment
type show. See I hump two-hundred pound cartons all week so
I'm seekin' an action attraction an I got squat zip right to this
point.

MOTHER: I'm Mother Crocker, One-Eye, you probably seen me on
the T.V.

THE MAN: Yes ma'am.

MOTHER: Seems like you got some sweet child by the hair there.

THE MAN: Could be. Now we don't get us some fine tits an see us
some body fluids on the mat pretty quick, we gonna have to
come down here cut out your pumpin' heart an eat that
sumbitch like a nacho.

MOTHER: (*Walks up to within two inches of the man's face.*) One-Eye,
we got some fine tits comin' up, an y'all aren't a hunnert percent
satisfied you can have any woman in this room in a heart-shaped
bed with mirrors on the ceiling all expenses paid an no questions
asked, but you cut the girl here you gonna be one dead fuck.
How's that sound?

THE MAN: You got a deal. (*He releases Miss Harmon. He winks and
clicks his tongue, looking at Dottie.*) You a fine woman, Mama. I'll
check on back. (*He's gone.*)

MISS HARMON: (*Nervous but determined.*) I could have handled the situation. I got personnel training.

(*The crowd begins stamping and clapping.*)

DANI: Why do I do this?

MOTHER: You want to stay down here?

MISS HARMON: Well, they need me in B Section non-reserved.

(*There is a burst of screaming from above.*)

MISS HARMON: Oh, boy... (*She exits, closing the door behind her. People exhale.*)

DOTTIE: I'm not fuckin' him. I got standards.

LESSA: (*Steps forward.*) Lemme do the main. I got the know-how. I got the experience. I can handle your girls like they was marked fragile. I'm not goin' out in the crowd again. I will...I will apologize to...to the crowd. I'm a professional athlete, that's all I am and I need this work. I can make your girls look good. I can take punishment. If I have to do it I can take a straight punch. I uh...I know how to take orders, do what I'm told. I'm askin' for the fight.

MOTHER: Angelessa?

LESSA: Yeah?

MOTHER: If you're in tennis, you're a professional athlete...

LESSA: Yeah?

MOTHER: ...if you're in track and field, you're a professional athlete, even if you catch on with the Harlem Globetrotters, you're a professional athlete, but if you're in Fantasy wrestling in the main feature attraction they pay for, you are nothing in this world...

DOLLY: But a nigger.

(*Lessa steps toward her but Bigman gives her a two-handed push that sends her crashing into the lockers.*)

NETTY: Lessa! Go easy now, go easy!

LESSA: (*Steadies herself against the lockers and leans there.*) I'm cool.

MOTHER: (*To Bigman.*) Take the girls out there.

NETTY: I don't know, Bigman.

BIGMAN: Dani, Frenchy, let's move it.

(*Crowd roars. He exits. Dottie and Dolly remove their cover-ups, revealing red, white and blue sequin peekaboo outfits with five-inch heels.*)

DANI: (*Hesitates a moment, then:*) O.K. We pull hair, kick each other, stuff like that. Work the crowd. You pull off my top. I pull off yours. I mess you up with the Argentine. I full press, it's over. We grab the clothes, we're out of there. Six, eight minutes max.

NOLA: Just lead me.

DANI: You got it.

NOLA: (*To Tiger.*) Thanks.

TIGER: Don't mention it.

(*Nola and Dani exit.*)

NETTY: I don't know…

MOTHER: She's got tits, how bad can it be? (*Handing Bigman a Xeroxed sheet.*) When they come off, hand 'em this. Breaks down how they wrestle my girls.

(*Bigman takes it, starts to leave.*)

MOTHER: Dottie doesn't work off her feet. I got those legs insured for thirty thousand.

DOTTIE: You said fifty.

MOTHER: Fifty. Nothin' in the face. They don't go through the ropes. Crowd gets messy, they split.

(*Bigman starts out again. She stops him.*)

MOTHER: Do right.

(*Bigman exits.*)

(*Simultaneously.*)

    RING ANNOUNCER: Gentlemen, we got a little change of program here…

    DOTTIE: How do we look, Mama?

MOTHER: Turn around.

DOTTIE: Do we look like queens, Mama? Are we sweet as pie?

MOTHER: I could eat you for breakfast.

DOLLY: Tryin' Passion Flower on my nails.

MOTHER: You look good.

DOTTIE: You look good too, Mama. You are part of the circle.

MOTHER: Stay away from the young one, she doesn't know shit.

DOLLY: No problem.

MOTHER: Stay off the ropes. I don't want you marked.

DOTTIE: Yes, Mama.

MOTHER: Smile to the crowd, they fans.

DOLLY: Yes, Mama.

MOTHER: (*Handing them miniature American flags.*) Wave the little flags.

DOTTIE: We will.

MOTHER: You are stars in the Fantasy Entertainment field.

DOLLY AND DOTTIE: Yes Mama.

MOTHER: We are just workin' out a little political setback...

DOLLY: Yes, Mama.

MOTHER: Usin' drugs was a bad thing, a bad, bad thing.

DOTTIE: Yes, Mama.

MOTHER: But fuckin' the Mayor of Los Angeles was a good thing.

DOTTIE: Yes, Mama.

MOTHER: That's part of a career. That's networking.

DOLLY: Yes, Mama.

MOTHER: All right, go on up there and get ready. Get inside yourselves.

DOTTIE: You didn't say we were goddesses, Mama.

MOTHER: You are motherfuckin' goddesses.

DOTTIE: (*Hugging her.*) You sweet ol' thing. (*Turns to the room.*) Bye, y'all. You keep evolving now, y'hear?
(*She blows them a kiss and they are gone. We hear music and crowd cheering.*)

MOTHER: (*To those still in the room.*) Let me give you a little personal advice. Get yourself a husband and a shit job. You don't have it. You never will have it. You got no future on T.V. (*She leaves.*)

NETTY: How you feelin', Tiger?

TIGER: I'm feeling bad.

NETTY: You look bad. You want some morphine?

TIGER: You got?

NETTY: I got.
(*A crowd reaction. She reaches into her bag and pulls out a small commercial vial.*)

TIGER: Where you get it?

NETTY: Well, darlin', we have our little ways.
(*Crowd roars.*)

TIGER: You always a surprise, ain't ya?

NETTY: Girl's got to live, honey.

TIGER: Hard as that may be. You got a syringe?

NETTY: (*Handing her one in a packet.*) Fresh as a daisy.

TIGER: (*Feeling her ribs.*) Makes my day.

NETTY: Cementville, Tennessee. I'm too fat for Fantasy Entertainment.

TIGER: An I'm too far out there. (*Tiger starts changing from Pocahontas back into street clothes.*)

NETTY: What about you, Lessa?

LESSA: Just fine.

NETTY: What you doin'?

LESSA: Gettin' dressed. (*Lessa puts on her Olympic warm-up suit.*)

NETTY: Never saw you pull that out.

LESSA: Just seemed like what I wanted to wear.

TIGER: (*To dog.*) You sweet sweet thing.

NETTY: You want to catch a beer tonight?

LESSA: I'm catchin' a bus.

TIGER: Shit, Lessa, cool off.

LESSA: I'm cooled off. I'm way, way cooled off.

NETTY: Where you catchin' a bus to?

LESSA: Wherever seventeen dollars and change gets me.

NETTY: Probably Memphis. Shoot we're all goin' to Memphis. Get the bus with us in the mornin'.

LESSA: I don't think so.

(*An old man, in his late sixties, early seventies, cane in hand appears in the doorway. He is African American.*)

KID: Good evening.

NETTY: (*Caught off guard, She startles.*) Good Lord!

KID: Didn't mean to make you jump. (*Takes off his hat.*) Pay my respects.

LESSA: What do you need?

KID: Well, ladies, I don't have much and I don't need much.

TIGER: This here is a dressin' room. We got a show on, Granpa.

KID: (*Points to a poster.*) Willie "The Kid" Cayman, that's my picture. (*They look. He laughs.*)

NETTY: This is you, honey?

KID: Light on my feet. Lookin' real sweet. TNT in both hands.

NETTY: Honey, you got million dollar charm.

KID: Much obliged.

NETTY: Don't mention it.

(*Roaring and whistling from the crowd.*)

KID: Could I bother you ladies to step in? On my way from Key West, Florida to Catafalque Bay, Alaska in a '79 Cadmium Red Pontiac Firebird. Stoppin' here, stoppin' there.

NETTY: Come on in, darlin'.

KID: Just call me Kid. (*Turns to Tiger.*) Kid Cayman.

TIGER: Tiger.

KID: Tiger who?

TIGER: Just one name.

> (*Simultaneously.*)

>> RING ANNOUNCER: …winner of our lingerie interlude, lusty, busty Dani Malowsky!
>> (*Crowd reaction.*)
>> KID: (*Smiling.*) Uh-huh, I can understand that. (*Sees cat case.*) I got me a small yellow dog. (*Turns to Lessa*) Seems to me I know you, sister.

LESSA: I don't think so.

KID: Sure I do. I got a memory they come miles for.

LESSA: Angelessa.

KID: Oh, it'll come to me. I'm workin' on it.

> (*The crowd breaks into applause.*)

KID: You're all in the wrestlin bouts, huh?

NETTY: That's right, honey.

KID: Now I had one hundred seventy fights, featherweight to middle-weight, but I still got my brains 'cause they couldn't hit me. I was kinda here, kinda gone at the same time. What you'd call a will-of-the-wisp. (*To Lessa.*) Your daddy wasn't the cut man for Sugar Ray Robinson, was he?

> (*She shakes her head.*)

KID: Fought here two times. Once with Jose Higucia, an old veteran with a good left hand. Carried him eight rounds so he could set up another payday. Once with Sandy Sadler. Oh, he was the dirtiest fighter alive, thumbed me so bad. Took forty-six stitches 'round my left eye. Knocked me down seven times. It's in the book. Fought Sandy three times. (*To Lessa.*) You ever won a beauty contest?

LESSA: Kid, I never won a beauty contest.

KID: Well, the fix musta been in. You ever married to a high hurdler?

> (*Crowd roars, applauds and whistles.*)

LESSA: (*Smiling.*) You ought to move on pretty soon, Kid.

KID: Oh, I plan to. Yes, you got to keep movin'. (*Looks around room.*) Oh my, ladies…memory lane.

> (*At this moment Dani and Nola enter like whirlwinds. They have*

covered themselves with the kimonos. They change into ninja costumes for the main event. They have masks.)

NOLA: Whoa! Hot patootie, was that somethin'?

DANI: Into it, honey! I'll say that for them.

NOLA: ...Throwin' money...

DANI: Bills...

NOLA: Change, bills, I didn't have a...

DANI: Five dollar bills...

NOLA: ...Have a place to tuck it...

DANI: (*Passing Kid.*) Who's he?

KID: Bon jour, how you doin'?

TIGER: Used to fight here.

DANI: Pop, you got my sympathies. (*Handing money to Netty.*) Eighty bucks off the floor. Split it up.
   (*Tiger starts humming "Me and My Shadow," occasionally singing a few words of the lyric.*)

NOLA: Am I gettin' this on straight?

NETTY: Come over here, honey.

DANI: How you doin', Tiger?

TIGER: Feelin' no pain.

DANI: (*Holding up Xeroxed sheets Mother gave Bigman.*) You see this shit? The Dolly & Dottie Show.

NETTY: How it goes?

DANI: Yeah, how it goes. They parade around, we fall down. They writhe around on the floor, we're amazed. Va-Va-Voom, we collapse unconscious.

LESSA: Damn.

DANI: Fuckin' stupid. Tiger, Dammit!
   (*Tiger stops singing.*)

DANI: Well, you got to play it like it lays.

LESSA: Get goin'.

DANI: I'm gone.

NOLA: (*Tying the laces.*) One minute.

DANI: (*Exiting.*) Catch you up there.
   (*Simultaneously.*)
      NOLA: (*Finishing.*) I am sweatin' buckets.
      LESSA: Lemme look you over.
      RING ANNOUNCER: And now our featured bout of the

evening…the fine, fabulous femmes fatales of American wrestling…direct from national television…

NOLA: (*Moves over to her.*) I hope I can do this.

LESSA: Turn around.

(*Nola does. Lessa pushes her into the broom closet and slams the door, turns the twist lock. Tiger chuckles.*)

NOLA: Hey!

NETTY: Now, Lessa…

NOLA: (*From inside.*) Come on, Lessa. I got to get up there. Stop playin' around.

LESSA: The bitch as called me a nigger is mine.

NOLA: Let me outta here! I got to be wrasslin', I can't be in here.

NETTY: Lessa, what the hell…

LESSA: Payback.

NETTY: Don't be crazy now.

LESSA: I'm gone.

(*She moves rapidly to the outside door. Just as she gets there, two hands fasten on her throat and drive her back into the room. It is Eddie. He wears a hospital robe over hospital pajamas. There is some blood staining through his bandages and onto the robe. Eddie is big. His face is gray. His voice a gurgle in his throat. He's a little like the Frankenstein monster only he moves faster.*)

EDDIE: You bit my dick off. (*He drives her up against the wall.*) You…bit…my…dick off.

NETTY: Eddie…come on, Eddie

(*Lessa fights, but he maintains the grip.*)

EDDIE: Bit…bit my…dick.

TIGER: (*Trying to move.*) Get him off her.

(*Eddie makes only a gurgling roar now. He bends Lessa backward over the bench.*)

NETTY: Come on, Eddie. Come on, Eddie.

(*A very loud voice cuts across the ruckus. It is Kid.*)

KID: Stosha!! Stosha "The Wild Man" Oronovsky!

(*Eddie throws Lessa down and turns. The Kid opens his arms with a radiant smile.*)

KID: You the cream in my coffee, man.

(*Kid slaps his own hand and holds it out. Eddie, trancelike, slaps it and they are into a six or eight beat streetshake at the end of which*) *the Kid drives his knee upward into Eddie's groin. Eddie lets out pain that lasts an eternity. When he stops the Kid says:*)

KID: You slicker than a snake on ice, baby.

(*Eddie crashes to the floor insensate. Unfortunately he falls on Tiger's cat box. Tiger doesn't see it. Netty does.*)

NETTY: Oh God!

TIGER: You O.K., Lessa?

LESSA: Yeah. I'm fine. Stay off me.

(*The Kid turns to Lessa who has stumbled to her feet.*)

KID: Did you ever put the shot in Seoul, Korea?

LESSA: (*Nods.*) Down in Seoul, Korea.

KID: Ooooooo, you were fine! Now you go on up there and have a good time. I like to see people enjoy themselves.

(*Lessa nods and moves out of the room.*)

TIGER: How'd you know his ring name?

KID: Read the poster on the way in. I got me a memory I could point out the same fly five days apart.

TIGER: You think he's hurt bad?

KID: (*A big smile.*) He might be if she bit his dick off.

TIGER: (*Sings lightly.*) "Walkin' down the avenue..."

NETTY: Tiger honey, I got bad, bad news.

TIGER: What?

NETTY: Well, he fell on your dog.

TIGER: Where?

NETTY: Kind of flush, direct *on* her. (*She kneels by Eddie and lifts his upstage side a little.*) Oh my. Tiger darlin', I'm afraid she passed.

TIGER: Yeah?

(*Netty nods.*)

TIGER: O.K.

NETTY: Honey, I'm sorry.

TIGER: (*Tears rolling down her cheek.*) O.K.

NOLA: (*Pounding on the door.*) Let me outta here!!

NETTY: Oh my God, I forgot. (*Heads for the closet.*)

KID: Let her cool down.

TIGER: (*Trying to get up.*) Whoa, got the nods.

KID: No last name, huh?

TIGER: No name.

KID: You know what I see when I look in your eyes, Tiger?

TIGER: Yeah, what?

KID: Morphine. Morphine, am I right?

TIGER: Yeah.

KID: Oh, that's a sweet low, isn't it? I had me several months of that down in Calcutta. Oh I'd cry and I'd cry and I'd sleep like a baby.

(*There is an ugly roar from the crowd upstairs.*)

TIGER: We're all fucked.

NETTY: We are.

KID: Not me, I got Florida real estate.

NETTY: I hope Bigman don't hurt her.

TIGER: Yeah.

NETTY: (*To Tiger who is throwing stuff in a bag.*) What are you doin'?

TIGER: Movin' out. (*Starts tossing stuff in the flight bag.*)

NETTY: You got no place to go.

TIGER: I can go where that crowd ain't.

(*Another roar.*)

TIGER: Fuck this place.

NETTY: (*Looking down at Eddie.*) One thing, Lessa, she'll be gone.

TIGER: Eddie don't look like he's wrestlin' in Memphis.

NOLA: Tiger? Somebody?

(*There is a tremendous ROAR from upstairs.*)

KID: (*Looking at the ceiling.*) Uh-huh, they like it.

TIGER: (*Looking around the room.*) Ain't much works out.

KID: I had an uncle lost his greeting card business, on the next day, the next day he won an *all expenses paid vacation* for two in Hawaii.

NETTY: That ain't us, old-timer.

KID: Outside his hotel he put fifty cents in a machine to get a papaya juice an the can got stuck. He shook that machine and it tipped over on him, broke both his legs.

TIGER: Sure, it works that way.

KID: In that hospital he met a beautiful nurse who a year after became his wife...

NETTY: You're kiddin'?

KID: That's right, two years after that she poisoned him for his insurance. Oh, you never know what's coming off next.

(*There is shrieking in the hall and moments later Dottie appears holding one hand over her face. Her head and face seem covered with blood.*)

DOTTIE: My face! Oh God, my face. My eye. Where's my eye?

NETTY: Jee-sus.

DOTTIE: (*Trying to see the damage in the makeup table mirror.*) I'm ruint. Ruint in the race wars. My God, I can't see out of my eye.

NETTY: Let me look.

DOTTIE: (*Raging.*) I got to be in the movies!

NETTY: Sit still! Where's your sister?

DOTTIE: Went under. Some thyroid giant drug her into the crowd by one leg. I seen somebody rip off her G-string an eat it. They've gone crazy.

NETTY: Looks like it's mainly the nose.

DOTTIE: (*Shrieking.*) Oh Jesus, I'm disfigured!

(*Lessa enters, she has Mother, her dress ripped and completely disheveled, in a headlock.*)

MOTHER: Three hundred dollars.

(*Lessa bangs Mother's head into a locker.*)

MOTHER: Six hundred dollars.

TIGER: Hi there, Lessa.

(*Lessa bangs Mother into the lockers again.*)

LESSA: (*To Tiger.*) How you doin'?

MOTHER: You bitch, you tore my artificial breast off. (*Mother pulls free.*)

LESSA: So long, Mama.

(*She hits her cleanly with a punch. Mother goes down.*)

NETTY: Godammit, stop roughhousin'!

TIGER: Bye, Netty.

NETTY: Hold on.

TIGER: Adios, Bigman.

(*Bigman enters, his shirt is torn, his suit jacket a collage of spilled coke, crackerjacks and beer. He's obviously been on the floor in the arena.*)

BIGMAN: (*Acknowledges her without thinking.*) Yeah.

DOTTIE: Is that a broken nose?

TIGER: Lef' three cans of gourmet dog food.

DOTTIE: My God, that's a broken nose.

(*Tiger exits. Bigman focuses on Lessa.*)

BIGMAN: You have screwed with my hustle. You miserable slimeball, five-way cunt.

(*Simultaneously.*)

(*Lessa charges him knocking him down. For the first moment of the fight she seems to dominate him. She gets him in a hammerlock. He breaks it. Slowly the fight begins to change. Soon Bigman dominates. Then he begins to administer a real beating. He brutalizes Lessa. It must look like He might actually kill her. During the fight other dialogue takes place.)*

NETTY: Lessa! Lessa, for Christ's sake, blow it off! Lessa!

DOTTIE: (*Over to the fallen Mother.*) Mama, she broke my nose, Mama.

NETTY: Bigman!

BIGMAN: (*To Netty.*) Off me.

DOTTIE: There'll be media, Mama. We got to go. We can't be on the T.V. all ruint. Come on, Mama. (*She pulls at her.*) My God, it's the apocalypse. (*Pulling her to the door.*) They ate Dolly, Mama. They like cannibals, Mama.

BIGMAN: (*Beating Lessa.*) Yes. Oh yes. Oh yes.

DOTTIE: Come on, Mama. I got you. I got you, Mama. (*Pulls her out the doorway and exits.*)

(*Bigman slams Lessa against the lockers. She falls down. Without warning, and from where he sits, the Kid shoots him with Dolly's gun. Bigman sits suddenly down, awkwardly, as if surprised. The room freezes. Sound from the arena where a full-scale RIOT is in progress rocks around them.*)

BIGMAN: Who shot me? (*He focuses on the Kid.*) You shot me. (*He sees Eddie.*) What's Eddie doin' here? Christ, he shot Eddie. You're a serial killer.

(*Lessa lurches to her feet; feels if she's in working order; crosses to bucket of water. Throws some on face.*)

NETTY: (*Looking at the carnage.*) You O.K., Lessa?

DANI: (*Enters.*) The rubes they...unbelievable...on the floor, in the ring, like a bee swarm...broke pipes, water gushin' in...I'm tellin' ya...the rubes gone apeshit...(*Sees Bigman, Eddie.*) What the hell?

BIGMAN: I'm shot. I'm shot down.

NETTY: Let me see.

BIGMAN: Get off me!

(*Lessa still in a rage trashes the sisters' makeup tables. Sweeps tubes and bottles onto the floor. Rips tables away from the wall and upends them.*)

LESSA: Yes!!!

DANI: Goddammit, Lessa.

    (*Lessa opens the Knockout Sisters' trunk, goes through the clothes, flings them around the room.*)

DANI: (*To Bigman.*) Who shot you?

BIGMAN: (*Vastly irritated.*) Who gives a shit? I'm shot.

DANI: (*Indicating the Kid.*) Are you still here?

KID: Just passin' through.

DANI: Is that Eddie? Eddie, is that you?

NETTY: Jesus.

LESSA: Sequins, man. I hate sequins.

DANI: (*She checks Eddie.*) Jesus. This ain't my style. We got to blow, Netty, we got to blow now.

    (*Glass breaks somewhere outside the door.*)

DANI: You hear that? The rubes are comin'. (*Turns to Kid.*) Don't shoot. Don't shoot me.

KID: (*Chuckling.*) O.K.

LESSA: (*Surveying the damage she has wrought.*) Lookin' good.

    (*Nola pounds on the door. Dani startles.*)

NETTY: Oh, God.

DANI: Who is it? What is that?

NETTY: I completely…(*She unlocks the door.*)

DANI: We got Dwayne again?

NOLA: (*Emerging.*) I been…no air…banging. I been yelling…(*She sees.*) Jeeminy, holy cow, boy-Friday.

    (*Lessa packs her stuff.*)

DANI: Now. Out now.

    (*More crashes outside. Dani throws her stuff in her bag. She scoops up the money from her fight with Nola. Netty kneels by Bigman.*)

DANI: There's gonna be cops and bad shit.

NOLA: We're gonna die, we're all gonna die.

NETTY: You want me to stay, Bigman?

    (*She touches him, he yells.*)

NETTY: Sorry.

BIGMAN: That hurt, O.K.?

DANI: (*To Netty.*) Let's roll. Come on, Netty.

NETTY: (*Back to Bigman.*) Poor darlin'.

BIGMAN: Will you get your fingers out of the bullet hole?

NETTY: Bigman.

BIGMAN: You could kill a fuckin' tree.

DANI: (*Pulling Netty away.*) Cops, Netty, freaked out rubes...
(*Gestures at the fallen bodies.*) They gonna pin this shit on us.

KID: Say...

DANI: (*Whirling.*) Don't even look at me.

KID: Kid Cayman...How you doin'?

DANI: Screw off.
(*Angry crowd burst.*)

DANI: (*A sudden thought.*) You got a car, Pop?

KID: A car, huh?

DANI: A driveable car.

KID: Got me a '79 Cadmium Red Pontiac Firebird parked right out
front in a handicapped zone.

LESSA: You lookin' for company?

KID: Always lookin' for company. Got a workin' radio, a part-time
clock, and she seats six comfortable. (*Tosses her the keys.*) Pull it in
the back; I'll be along.

LESSA: (*Looking at him.*) O.K.

KID: Don't mention it. Ooooooo, you was poetry in motion!
(*People are standing around.*)

DANI: Are you all like *deranged?* Let's split.

NETTY: Where?

DANI: When the hell did we ever know where?
(*Lessa moves out without speaking.*)

DANI: Move it. Hump it. Move it.

NETTY: (*Taking the terrified Nola's hand.*) Come on, honey. Mama
take care of you.

DANI: (*Pulls and pushes Nola and Netty out.*) Move it. Move it. Beat it.
Go! Go! Beat it. Beat it!
(*Nola and Netty exit.*)

LESSA: Eddie. Hey Eddie.
(*He suddenly shoots out a hand and grabs her ankle.*)

LESSA: Let go.
(*He doesn't. He tries to pull her over. She stamps on his wrist. He lets
go with a grunt. She goes down on one knee just outside his grasp.*)

LESSA: I hope you don't die, but I hope you come goddamn close.
Amen. (*She rises.*)

DANI: (*Speaks to Kid.*) Hell, that oughta make him feel better.
(*Lessa exits.*)

DANI: So long, Bigman.

BIGMAN: Get me some help.

DANI: (*Ambivalently.*) Sure. (*To Kid.*) Move it out, Pops. (*She exits.*)
(*Kid rises and closes the hall door. He twist-locks it. We hear the sound of the approaching crowd.*)

BIGMAN: You snuffed me.

KID: You won't die. I didn't hit you in the right spot. (*Looks at Eddie.*)
I hit him in the right spot.

EDDIE: ...My dick.

KID: Uh-huh. (*To Bigman.*) You Jack Vag's boy, used to be a coffee
kid down to Joe Louis Gym.
(*Bigman looks at him amazed.*)

KID: Now you doin' this trash.

BIGMAN: What the hell are *you* doin'?

KID: Keepin' you company.
(*Crash from outside.*)

BIGMAN: Don't ditch me.

KID: You want a smoke?

BIGMAN: Yeah.

KID: Hurtin' people, now that's a serious gig, see. I don't play with it.
I don't fool nobody. (*Big smile.*) When I hurt 'em, I hurts 'em.
(*Puts the cigarette in Bigman's mouth.*) I ever tell you I fought
Sandy Sadler three times? Second fight a woman come to the
dressing room, bare shoulders, ball gown, took off a diamond
bracelet, give it to me, said, "You, sir, gave a fine account of
yourself." (*He tips over a bank of lockers, stage right. Points at a
door behind the locker which has been revealed.*) Come right
through there in that China silk dress. Took me to her home on
a bluff overlooked a wide turn in the Mississippi and there we
danced the Samba to a sixteen-piece all-girl orchestra from
Venezuela. Sandy Sadler, he was there. Two-Ton Tony Galento,
he was in town. Ooooo, he was light on his feet. The referee, he
danced with the Governor's wife and a Secret Service man. Ol'
Jake Lamotta, he slow danced with a nine-year-old girl standin'
on his shoes. Oh, that was a sight. The waiters in their white
coats, they joined in. All of us laughin', hummin' along, all doing
the rumba, while the moon went down. (*He heads out.*) There
was a girl playin' clarinet in that band later left a camellia on my
pillow. (*His voice recedes down the hall.*) 'Course those were
different times. Different times. Different times.

(A moment. Someone begins pounding on the hall door. We hear, "Y'all in there...you're road kill, you hear me." Bigman startles awake.)

BIGMAN: Eddie?

EDDIE: Yeah?

BIGMAN: You there?

EDDIE: Yeah?

BIGMAN: How much you got left?

(No answer. The lights start to fade. A fire axe breaks through the panel of the door. Once, twice, a third time. The lights are out.)

END OF PLAY

Criminal Hearts

A Comedy in Two Acts

ORIGINAL PRODUCTION

Criminal Hearts received its premiere at the Theatre Company, Detroit, Michigan, on April 24, 1992. It was directed by David L. Regal and had the following cast:

Ata	Miriam Yezbick
Bo	Jennifer Jones
Robbie	Tim Pickering
Wib	Joe Hislop
Voice of Mrs. Carnahan	Cathy Allen

Scenic and Costume Design: Melinda Pacha
Lighting Design: Mark Choinski

CHARACTERS

ATA, a romantic agoraphobic in her mid-30s. She is in a lot of trouble.

BO, a grifter in good times, a burglar in bad. Truth is the least of her worries. 32-40.

ROBBIE, Bo's getaway man. He has low-down sex appeal and loves malt balls. 28-33.

WIB, a man in the worst sense of the word. He is 38-45.

MRS. CARNAHAN, an offstage voice. 50-60.

CRIMINAL HEARTS

ACT ONE
Scene One

The bedroom of an expensive condo in Chicago. It's 3 AM and pitch dark in the room. What we can't see is how empty it is. There is nothing but a mattress with silken sheets on the floor, and a wilderness of empty pizza boxes, Dr. Pepper cans and hundreds of sharpened pencils on the floor. New supplies of pencils and soft drinks are stacked in a corner, plus the best battery-operated pencil sharpener money can buy. There's a window leading to a fire escape, a door to a walk-in closet, an outside door, and a door to the rest of the apartment. There is nothing on the walls, and a phone with a long cord sitting somewhere. A woman, Ata, in her early thirties in an expensive nightgown sleeps on the silken sheets. But we can't see that yet. Silence. City Sounds. Light Snoring. Suddenly, cans being kicked.

ATA: (*Out of sleep.*) What? Hello? (*Silence.*) Oh, my God. Who's in here? Somebody's in here. Oh, my God. Don't hurt me. Don't kill me. I have eighty dollars, but I don't know where my purse is. I could write you a check. Tell me your name, and I'll write you a check. (*Silence.*) I have jewelry, but it's dumb stuff. I was robbed last year, they got the jewelry. You can have my jewelry, though. I'll give you my jewelry and the eighty dollars. (*Silence.*)

Listen, I'm frightened, I'm very frightened, I'm suppressing a scream here.

BO: Shut up.

ATA: Oh, my God. Oh, my God. You *are* in here.

BO: Yeah, I'm in here. I want you to shut up.

ATA: I've got a gun.

BO: Bullshit.

ATA: I do. I have a gun. A big gun.

BO: You don't have a gun. *I* have a gun.

ATA: My husband gave it to me. It's a thirty-seven. A police thirty-seven.

BO: Turn on the light.

ATA: Don't hurt me, I have herpes.

BO: On these lights I'm counting to three here.

ATA: I can't.

BO: You can't what?

ATA: I have a problem.

BO: So?

ATA: I freeze. I freeze with fear.

BO: Get outta here.

ATA: All my life. My nervous system shuts down. Its called kinetic hysteria. I'm in therapy.

BO: I don't give a goddamn if you're in therapy, turn on the lights!

ATA: Don't shoot. Don't shoot. I'll tell you where it is.

BO: What is?

ATA: The switch.

BO: I can't believe this.

ATA: To the left of the door.

BO: What door?

ATA: The front door.

BO: Lady, I don't fuckin' live here, I'm sneakin' around in the dark.

ATA: If you're facing the bed...wait...where exactly are you?

BO: Will you turn on the light!!

(*Ata begins to make sounds preliminary to screaming.*)

BO: Okay, okay, I'm below the bed.

ATA: If you could see how I'm shaking, and I'm clammy, I'm very clammy.

BO: And I'm below the bed.

ATA: On a clock, if you're facing the twelve, the door to the living room would be at 8:30.

BO: I'm facing which number?

ATA: The twelve.

BO: To my left. Okay, I'm going. (*Cans are kicked over.*) What the fuck is this. Are you screwing with me?

ATA: It's nothing. Keep going.

BO: How far?

ATA: Ummm. Eight feet. Well, maybe ten feet.

BO: I'm going to fall over like some little table and kill myself?

ATA: No.

(*More Cans.*)

BO: Damn it. Okay, doorway. Listen, I turn on this light I want no noise. (*She feels around.*) Okay. There is no switch here at any height.

ATA: Left of the door?

BO: Nowhere. None.

ATA: As you come in.

BO: I'm not coming in, I'm going toward! Jesus, okay now. I don't want noise. No noise. You hear me?

ATA: Yes, yes I do.

(*Bo turns on the light. The apartment is barren. All furniture gone except the mattress. The walls have been stripped of decoration. Ata is like a squatter in a luxury apartment.*)

ATA: Don't hurt me, don't hurt me, don't hurt me, don't hurt me.

BO: (*Looking around.*) Gimme a goddamn break! What the hell is this? What the hell is going on here?

(*Ata opens her eyes. She sees Bo, a burglar in her late 30s dressed in jeans and a black T-shirt. She has a pistol, now pointed at Ata. She has a cast on her wrist.*)

BO: Hey, you...

ATA: You're a woman.

BO: Yeah, right. Where the hell's the stuff, the goods?

ATA: I'm a woman. We're women.

BO: V.C.R., silver, lap-top, television, videocam, I'm talking negotiables here.

ATA: Women shouldn't shoot each other. Men shoot each other. Women relate.

BO: Stuff, where's the stuff, the goods, the items?

ATA: That's a question, I can tell you that.

BO: Right.

ATA: But, I'm…actually I can't…I'll, I'll tell you where's the stuff, I'd like to, but the gun is making me itch.

BO: You have negotiable stuff, I know that.

ATA: I have stress allergies, I pass out…I just…you know, out, flat gone. I have a suspect nervous system…wait! Wait, I know you, I do, yes…oh, God…why do I know you?

BO: Because I've seen your goddamn stuff, lady. I'm not some geek I go in cold, like on the off-chance it could be worth my while, right?

ATA: At the deli? No. No.

BO: Sit there. Don't even blink. (*She moves toward the door leading to the rest of the apartment.*)

ATA: Smoke alarms!

BO: (*After a quick look out the door.*) Un-fuckin'-real.

ATA: You were here about smoke alarms, that's right, isn't it?

BO: Yeah. Where's your life, lady? Where's your furniture, for instance?

ATA: We have a relationship. I told you about my marriage. I confided in you. You admired my decor. We exchanged.

BO: I cased you out. Right. Now I'm back for the stuff, okay?

ATA: I'm more than an object to you. I'm a dimensional person who feels pain and fear. I'm a woman, I have breasts. Don't shoot me.

BO: Hey! Downstairs I have a guy with a truck, get it? He's a professional, okay? I'm supposed to hop on down the fire escape, tell him, "Guess what? The bitch has Dr. Pepper and pizza, come on up help me load it out?"

ATA: He did that. He did that. That is exactly…I can't believe you said that. He…he…I was…I went to work…oh, I'm Ata, Ata Windust. Hi.

BO: Get away from me!

ATA: Sorry, sorry…but, he…I don't know…rented a truck, I'm at work, bam, cleans me out…the apartment, furniture…the stuff.

BO: Who?

ATA: Wib.

BO: Wib?

ATA: My…my, uh…whatsit, whatsit…words. Husband, husband. My husband had the truck.

BO: Your husband is Wib?

ATA: Wib, yes, he's Wib. Was. Well, still is but probably will be was. Husband, I mean. He'll still be Wib.

BO: He took everything but the mattress?

ATA: Mainly, almost. Yes. All of it. Paintings, rugs, corkscrew. (*A sudden rage.*) Stop pointing that gun at me! I'm sorry. I'm sorry.

BO: You got jewelry?

ATA: This, this, my wedding ring.

BO: I don't want your fucking wedding ring. I want your jewelry.

ATA: Took it, took it, gone.

BO: Cash?

ATA: Eighty dollars. My purse. There.

BO: Credit cards.

ATA: He canceled them. Well, I have my mother's VISA, but it might be expired.

BO: (*Seeing an object on the floor.*) What's this thing?

ATA: It's a battery-operated pencil sharpener.

BO: I oughta fuckin' shoot you for wasting my time.

ATA: (*A blood-curdling scream.*) Brent, no!!
(*Bo, completely taken aback, whirls around looking behind her. Ata throws herself at Bo, who caught off-guard, is knocked to the floor. They wrestle clumsily.*)

BO: Ow! Shit. Okay, ow.

ATA: Yes, yes, yes, yes, yes…oh, my God.

BO: Hey!

ATA: Yes…

BO: Gimme that…

ATA: Yes!! (*Ata, through luck and adrenaline, comes up with the gun.*)

BO: Son-of-a-bitch.

ATA: Yes!! I have a gun, I have a gun, I have a gun!

BO: Right, okay, watch it, watch it!

ATA: You watch it, you watch it. Back. Go on. I could kill you, I could kill you a million times. I could pull this trigger, I could stab you, I could gouge out your eyes, I could eat your flesh!

BO: The trigger…watch the trigger.

ATA: Do you have any idea how angry I am? Deeply, deeply emotionally angry? Coming in here, violating my space? Turning me into an animal? Yes, yes, an animal. That is what you have done to me. I'm a human being not an animal do you understand that?

BO: The trigger, the trigger.

ATA: I have problems do you hear me? I have more problems than I should demographically have. And you have pushed me, kicking and screaming, over the edge, and I could cheerfully and without a second thought see you bleeding on the floor…is that clear to you?

BO: I get it, okay, I got it. Look in my eyes here, right? You're pissed off. Good. You should be pissed off, take your finger off the trigger.

ATA: I'm flipped out, do you see that? This is a suprarational state, a fragmentation, a reality-declining-perceptual-veer and you can only pull me out of this by proving to me that you are a human being and you have about three seconds.

BO: The trigger!

ATA: One, two…

BO: Kids. I have kids.

ATA: Their names.

BO: Yolanda, Gitch, Sarah?

ATA: Sarah?

BO: Sarah Claire.

ATA: You have a girl named Sarah?

BO: Yeah.

ATA: I don't want you to have a Sarah. Don't tell me you have a Sarah. I have a Sarah. I had to leave her at my mother's. Oh my God, you have a Sarah. (*She starts to cry.*) I have problems. I have an empathy problem. I hate this. You are making me cry. I'm in control here because I have the gun, is that right?

BO: Yeah.

ATA: All right. I'm in control. This isn't something just happening to me. This is *my* movie.

BO: Absolutely.

ATA: Tie yourself up.

BO: Tie myself up?

ATA: Fast.

BO: You are fuckin' nuts, lady.

ATA: What do you think I've been trying to tell you? What do you think I'm dealing with? Why do you think I'm drinking all this

Dr. Pepper? Why do you think I'm sharpening pencils hour after hour? (*Ata puts a second hand on the gun in the pose she's seen in cop movies.*)

BO: Easy now, okay? We're playing with an eighth of an inch here, okay? Just give me a hint how I should tie myself up?

ATA: Soon. You should do it soon.

BO: Right. With what?

ATA: How do I know? I didn't break in here. I don't live a life of violence and crime. Just do it.

BO: You got cord?

ATA: No.

BO: Electrician's tape?

ATA: No.

BO: String, you got string?

ATA: Hurry this up!

BO: You hurry up, I can't tie myself up with pizza boxes.

ATA: You think anybody cares if I shoot you?

BO: You got an extension cord?

ATA: No.

BO: What then?

ATA: The phone! The phone cord. Move it!

BO: I'm going.

ATA: Faster.

BO: I'm doing it. (*She ties herself up with the phone cord.*)

ATA: He took the string. I had a lot of string. Can you believe that? He took the time to empty a drawer full of string and take it. Is that sick? Tell me, is that sick or what?

BO: I'm tying here, okay.

ATA: I liked that string. I liked it.

BO: Listen, okay, I got a...look, I tie this tight, hands together, I can't knot it...I get it out here where I can knot it, it's long, it's loose.

ATA: Just tie it!

BO: I'm tellin' ya, I can't tie it. You try tying yourself up, it's not so goddamn easy.

ATA: Step through it.

BO: What?

ATA: Step over it so it's tied behind you.

BO: I'm not a fuckin' contortionist, I'm a criminal.

ATA: Try it.

BO: Look, let me propose something to you here...okay?...easy on the trigger. I'm out here scrounging for my kids, right? I'm in the goddamn projects scarfin' powdered eggs and government cheese in a goddamn jungle where my ten-year-old deals, okay? You, what can I say, you got problems of your own, you don't need me. What say I untie this shit, I go out the window, you get some sleep, everything looks better in the morning. Pretty good, huh? Whattayasay?

ATA: (*Furious.*) That's not the big picture!

BO: Right.

ATA: (*Intense.*) Society, do you hear me? What about society? Not to mention right and wrong. What about walking down the street, for instance? You're a woman, and you walk down the street? Look at me, I'm a prisoner in my own city.

BO: (*Angry herself.*) Hey, lady, you're a wacko, living off Dr. Pepper and Italian sausage with a short circuit brain, and I'm the biggest fuckin' screw-off in fuckin' history fallin' for that "look out behind you shit," so don't give me this crap about some big picture!

ATA: Step through the cord.

BO: Wait a minute...whoa...let's get real here, okay? What I can do is this. I can put one leg through, see, I can do that. Good, okay, now I'm sitting on this mattress, all right? I'm your prisoner, no kidding, like this, no problem. Like what could I do now, see my point? Now get your fuckin' finger off the trigger.

ATA: You're my prisoner?

BO: Yeah.

ATA: You are.

BO: Right.

ATA: (*Begins to cry.*) I hate this, I hate this.

BO: Right, right.

ATA: You're a vulture.

BO: Right.

ATA: You feed off me. Everyone feeds off me. I have to call the police.

BO: Right.

ATA: You tied yourself up with the phone. (*Realizing Bo is tied up with the phone.*)

BO: Right.

ATA: Who told you to do that?

BO: You did.

ATA: Not with the phone. How can I call on the phone? My God, I'm completely isolated.

BO: We got a problem.

ATA: Yes.

BO: Two problems.

ATA: Yes.

BO: To phone, you gotta get close to me an' you don't want to get close to me. On the other hand, you put me in jail the city of Chicago takes my fuckin' children.

ATA: Stop it!

BO: What?

ATA: I hate that. I hate it! You're debasing the language.

BO: I'm doing what?

ATA: Swearing. Profanity. Don't you realize that's the last resort of people with a limited vocabulary?

BO: I got a limited vocabulary.

ATA: All we have is language and trust between two human beings, and look at us. This is what it's come to? Violence, weapons. I'm pointing a gun at you, can you believe that? Everything has been taken from me, and I'm lost in a homicidal rage. What kind of a life is that?

BO: Sad shit.

   (*Ata levels the gun.*)

BO: Sorry. I got these habits, take it easy.

ATA: I can only stand up or lie down here, do you realize that? I am thirty-three years old, and I don't have chair. Man has had chairs for thousands of years. Egyptians had chairs. Do you have chairs?

BO: Yeah, I got chairs.

ATA: Because you stole them!

BO: Hey, wacko, I picked 'em up in the street. From people for whom chairs are no problem in million dollar condos they are dumping 'em in the street every goddamn day, an' I am out there livin' off their fuckin' garbage. You want chairs, leggo the pistol, unfuckin' tie me an' we'll go down an' get chairs. Jesus.

ATA: I'm sorry.

BO: Forget it, it's okay.

ATA: Wait. Oh, my God. Did I say I'm sorry? I'm not sorry. How dare I say I'm sorry to you? I must be out of my mind. I should apologize for having chairs? I worked for those chairs. And should I want to put *my* chairs in the street…which I don't do, I have never done, but should I want to put them in the street which is built with *my* taxes, I have the right to do that. Is that clear?

BO: But you got no chairs, the guy took 'em, is that right?

ATA: Wib.

BO: Wib took the chairs.

ATA: My husband.

BO: Your fuckin' husband Wib took the chairs.

ATA: Yes!

BO: You wanna know something? Me too.

ATA: You too?

BO: Yeah.

ATA: You too what?

BO: I also got cleaned out.

ATA: (*Indicates the room.*) Like this?

BO: Yeah.

ATA: Someone took all your things and left you like this?

BO: Worse, no mattress.

ATA: What kind of a world is this?! I can't take this in. Who did this?

BO: My old man.

ATA: Your father?!

BO: No, not my father. Try to follow the conversation here. My old man. The guy I was fuckin'. My live-in.

ATA: With a truck? He just pulled a truck up and then this?

BO: You got it. That's right. Him an' his wigged-out half brother Frankie, right, they like swipe this Ryder ton and a half, see, an' while I'm out takin' my kid a neck brace over to Ethel's, they do it. Plus, plus they go down to the river, right, run a truck sale offa the tailgate, fade my stuff, come back here, dump the truck, now I got Ryder all over my ass, pay the day's rental or I'm slammed up for auto theft.

ATA: For the truck they used to rob you?

BO: Yeah, so I'm sleepin' on the floor in my coat cause it's fuckin' February, and I got Sarah, eighteen months, in some cardboard box, right, covered up with like paint rags 'cause they offed my crib with the blankets still in it.

ATA: This is sub-human behavior. What, what did we do to these men? We existed, that's what we did. We nurtured, we existed. We gave them our bodies and our minds and they pull up a truck!

BO: Wait. Wait. Dis, that's my live-in, Dis, he runs a crack joint.

ATA: This is appalling…

BO: Wait. Wait…crack joint in this fucked up apartment he won offa this guy playin' knuckles, but he's gotta pay protection to these Haitian street lords, bein' on their turf, right, so this guy dealin' to him gets pushed out a window by some bitch in his stable, Dis' business is fucked, he's got street lords in his face "where's the money" see, fades my stuff to pay them but it's like not enough, get it, he splits, I got the street lords on my ass for the rest in like five minutes. They break my wrist to remind me. Bingo, I gotta make some money, here I am.

ATA: You had the baby in a cardboard box?

BO: Yeah. The other two kids I got one with Ethel, one the city took but Sarah stays with me, you understand? She needs her mother, that's that.

ATA: Mine is sixteen months.

BO: Yeah, mine too!

ATA: You said eighteen.

BO: Nah, sixteen. I got an eighteen year old an' a twenty-eight year old.

ATA: A twenty-eight year old child?

BO: Yeah. She poured boiling Gatorade on a guy. She gets out a few months.

ATA: You can't…How old are you?

BO: Forty-two.

ATA: My God, you had a child when you were twelve?

BO: Yeah. Cesarean.

ATA: And two more?

BO: Live ones, yeah.

ATA: And you have nothing in your house?

BO: Nah. You neither. That how come your kid's at your mother's?

ATA: She wasn't safe here.

BO: That bad?

ATA: He says she's his. He says he'll take her.

BO: (*Emotion showing.*) That sonofabitch.

ATA: (*Beginning to break.*) I couldn't stand that.

BO: How come he took your stuff?

ATA: Because he hates me! He hates me because I found out he was a creep. He couldn't stand my knowing. He's a lawyer.

BO: So why's he a creep?

ATA: Because he calls me babe, plus he was sleeping with his secretary. He was sleeping with one of my friends. He was sleeping with *two* paralegals. He was sleeping with the woman at the dry-cleaners. That's the one place you're supposed to feel safe.

BO: I never been to a dry-cleaners.

ATA: He had another apartment where he took these women. Twelve years. Twelve years I lived in ignorance. On his birthday I would write songs for him. I would buy sexy underwear and go to his office wearing a raincoat and carrying my guitar. I would take off my raincoat and sing to him, and we would make love on his desk.

BO: (*Admiringly.*) Pretty fuckin' kinky.

ATA: I noticed he started coming home without his clothes. You know, he would have one sock, or one cufflink, maybe no tie. I thought it was endearing. He was working so hard for us, his mind was so busy, he was going to work with one sock. I loved it. *I* loved that he was absentminded, it made me feel close to him. Idiot! Idiot! Then I noticed he left with two socks and came home with one. I laughed. I asked my friend Cathy how a lawyer could come home with one sock and she said, "Nooners." Do you know what "nooners" means?

BO: Yeah.

ATA: It was like a sliver in my brain. Nooners. Nooners. Nooners. I tried to give him the benefit of the doubt. I made harmless scenarios for one sock. Then I found panties in his raincoat pocket. They weren't even cotton! I waited all day in the apartment. I would pace to one end and hit the wall, then I would pace to the other end and hit the wall. He came home and I confronted him. "Panties," I said, "panties, you have panties in your raincoat pocket!" "Gosh," he says, slapping his forehead like this, "Gosh, thanks for reminding me. They're evidence in a case, I wanted you to take a look and tell me what store might carry them!"

BO: Lawyers.

ATA: I go to Cathy, she says hire a private detective. I said that's demeaning and surreptitious, and suspect and tasteless…

BO: So you hired one…

ATA: Yes! And it all came out, six simultaneous affairs. Sometimes he would make love to three women in one lunch hour. His secretary would schedule them and *she* was having an affair with him. I started having trouble going out of the house, my heart would pound, I would fight for breath. If I got to the elevator I would start sweating, get dizzy, get a terrible headache. I would have to lean against the wall when the door opened, I couldn't get out. I saw doctors. One gave me a prescription for Valium, another one said I was nervous and needed to lose weight, the third one asked wouldn't I be happier pregnant! I was so miserable I called Wib's partner Gil, we were friends, he and Wib had been together since law school, maybe he could help me understand. We went to dinner. He was quiet and soothing and empathetic and non-judgmental…

BO: So you fucked him…

ATA: We made love. We made love and the next morning I told Wib and the next afternoon Wib rented the truck. He rented the truck and now I live on pizza and pencils, and if I touch the doorknobs I get an electric shock.

BO: (*Looking around her at the cans of cola.*) Pizza and this stuff, huh?

ATA: Dr. Pepper. It's my only hope. It's made from the bark of the tamarind tree. If I drink enough, sometimes I can get to the drugstore.

BO: This stuff gets you out the door?

ATA: On a good day.

BO: So like in a strange way I can dig it, you know? You want to go out and you can't and I want to go out and *I* can't.

ATA: You're afraid to go out?

BO: Yeah, I'm afraid to go out. It's the fuckin' DMZ, man. You know elevator bingo? You get in the elevator, bingo they got your money, your shoes, an' you're down on the floor gettin' porked, right? Outside we got numbers runners, skag merchants, crazies, kids this high passing angel dust and sensimilla weed, everybody scramblin', carryin' a piece, a blade, a razor in their cheek, it's a fuckin' circus, you see what I mean? Hey, I look up, my neighbor's holding her two year old out the window by one arm

off the eighth floor. She already dropped the baby, right? She's
sending them back to God so they'll have a nicer time. Get the
picture? Do I want out? Yeah, I want out an' I want *your* fuckin'
V.C.R. to *get* out. You got a kid, right?

ATA: What are they doing to us? What are they doing to us? That's
what I want to know. Why are they doing this to us!
(*She slams her hand against the wall in frustration, and the Gun
goes off. There is a pause.*)

BO: Shit.

ATA: I shot the gun. I shot the gun.

BO: Yeah.

ATA: I could have killed you.

BO: Yeah.

ATA: What should I do?

BO: Maybe put the gun down.

ATA: (*Conflicted.*) Put the gun down?

BO: So what am I gonna do, jump on you?
(*A knock on the door.*)

ATA: Oh, my God, oh, my God.

MRS. CARNAHAN: (*Offstage.*) Mrs. Windust? Mrs. Windust, are you all
right?

ATA: My neighbor, Mrs. Carnahan. My God, it's three in the
morning.

MRS. CARNAHAN: Mrs. Windust, open the door.

BO: She'll go away.

ATA: She won't go away, she never goes away.

MRS. CARNAHAN: I heard the gunshot, and I've called the police.

BO: Talk to her.

ATA: What?

BO: Say something. Through your mouth.

ATA: Mrs. Carnahan?

MRS. CARNAHAN: Mrs. Windust?

ATA: Yes, it's me, Mrs. Carnahan, I'm perfectly all right.

MRS. CARNAHAN: You're not shot? There was a gunshot.

ATA: Ah...well...not exactly.

MRS. CARNAHAN: Open the door, Mrs. Windust.

ATA: I can't do that, Mrs. Carnahan.

MRS. CARNAHAN: I'm afraid I'll need to satisfy myself you're all right if
you don't mind.

(*Robbie, Bo's accomplice, a man of 40, appears in the window. He wears a Walkman with earphones and a Chicago Cubs cap. He has a pistol.*)

ROBBIE: (*To Ata.*) Drop the piece, lady.

BO: Robbie…

ATA: Oh my God, oh my God.

BO: It's O.K., it's O.K. All right?

MRS. CARNAHAN: Do you hear me, Mrs. Windust?

ROBBIE: It's not O.K., I want her to drop the piece.

BO: She can't drop the piece, O.K.?

ROBBIE: Why?

BO: Because she freezes to things, O.K.?

ATA: Oh my God, oh my God.

MRS. CARNAHAN: (*Pounding.*) Mrs. Windust!

BO: (*To Robbie.*) Beat it.

ROBBIE: No way.

BO: Trust me.

ROBBIE: Yeah?

BO: Yeah.

ROBBIE: Where's the fuckin' furniture?

BO: It's a long story. Go.

ROBBIE: Yeah?

BO: Yeah.

ROBBIE: Cubs are up 3-0 on Cincinnati.

BO: Robbie.

ROBBIE: You're not makin' a mistake here?

BO: Yeah.

ROBBIE: To err is human.

BO: I'm okay.

ROBBIE: Whatever you say. (*To Ata.*) Hey, lady. Sorry I almost blew your brains out.

ATA: Oh, well.

ROBBIE: Maybe next time.

ATA: Oh my God.

(*He goes.*)

MRS. CARNAHAN: (*Pounding.*) Open this door or I will begin to scream for help.

BO: (*To Ata.*) Well?

ATA: I don't know. I don't know. You have kids?

BO: Yeah.

ATA: Sweet, beautiful, vulnerable, trusting kids.

BO: Yeah.

ATA: Go on. Go. Go!

BO: (*Bo is immediately on her feet and untied, obviously she could have done it all along.*) Catch you later. Y'oughta start eatin' from the four food groups.

ATA: I'm coming, Mrs. Carnahan.

BO: (*At the window.*) Hey.

ATA: (*Startled.*) What?

BO: Thanks. (*Bo exits.*)

ATA: You're welcome. Mrs. Carnahan?

MRS. CARNAHAN: I'm here, Mrs. Windust.

ATA: I'm all right, Mrs. Carnahan. Really, I'm all right. I'm not in any danger, no danger of any kind. I'm not harmed or threatened or in trouble. But, the thing is, Mrs. Carnahan, I'm not going to open the door because there's no need and the other reason is…I'm with a lover, Mrs. Carnahan, a lover, a beautiful man who makes my life worth living, who gives meaning to my existence and the thing is, you see, that we are without clothes, that's the thing, we are scented and oiled and pomaded and fresh from the act of love, and so to open the door would be a betrayal for us and an embarrassment for you and then we would feel judged, you see, and the spell, the spell would be broken, because having lived the life you have, you know how fragile these things are. And after our pleasantries, after you were satisfied with my condition and had gone back to your rooms, my lover, the spell broken, would dress and kiss me somewhat impersonally and close the door behind him with the faintest click, Mrs. Carnahan, and I would be alone, at a time when being alone feels…well, feels very worrisome because other things that give meaning…well, they get harder and harder to come by, don't they, Mrs. Carnahan? (*The lights beginning to fade.*) Harder and harder to go out and meet these things which seem more and more without meaning and feeling more and more alone and feeling more and more as if that is perfectly all right, that it's very compelling to be alone without meaning when that's probably the worst idea really. So I won't be opening the door, Mrs. Carnahan, because I don't want to end up alone

in here and liking it. (*It is down to a single spotlight.*) I really
don't. I really don't. I really don't. (*The light is out.*)

Scene Two

*It is two weeks later. 3 AM. The room is in darkness as before. There
are more cans and a new stack of pizzas. Ata is asleep; we hear her
snore. Bo appears in the window in silhouette. She raps on the
windows; it does not penetrate Ata's state. She raps again. Nothing.
She jimmies the window and enters the room.*

BO: (*In black.*) Hey, Ata. (*She kicks Dr. Pepper cans.*) Goddammit.
Ata. Ata, it's me, Bo. (*She finds the mattress and shakes her.*) Ata,
for hell's sake.
ATA: (*Startling awake.*) Oh my God. Oh my God. I've got a gun, I'll
use it. I'll eviscerate you. I'll dance on your coffin.
BO: It's me, Bo.
ATA: Bo?
BO: Bo. Bo the burglar. You remember, a couple weeks ago.
ATA: Bo!
BO: Yeah.
ATA: You're back.
BO: Yeah. Don't shoot.
ATA: Bo the burglar.
BO: Yeah. You want some company?
ATA: Company?
BO: Sure, you know, shoot the shit for a minute.
ATA: Shoot the shit.
BO: Yeah. (*A pause.*) You want me to go?
ATA: No! No, stay. This is wonderful, turn on the light.
BO: To my left as I'm facing the bed, right?
ATA: I need to see you. I'm going crazy. Well, I am crazy. I'm
hallucinating.
BO: Wait a minute. No. O.K.
(*The lights go on. Bo is dressed precisely the same. Ata is wearing a
startlingly red, high-fashion formal. She's sleeping in it.*)

BO: How ya doin'?

ATA: I'm quite mad.

BO: Nah.

ATA: Look at me.

BO: Nice dress.

ATA: It's a Calandrini. His prices are astronomical.

BO: I can see that.

ATA: I sleep in them. I use them to dust. It's the only thing he didn't take, my clothes. I'm so glad to see you.

BO: You got the gun.

ATA: Oh. I forget.

BO: You got it in your hand.

ATA: I can't let go of it. I don't think about it anymore.

BO: Still?

ATA: I suppose.

BO: For two weeks? That sucker is still loaded.

ATA: Sometimes I see I've put it down but other times without realizing I must pick it up. When I think about it I can't let go of it. Your wrist?

BO: Not bad.

ATA: How's Sarah?

BO: (*Still focused on the gun.*) Sarah?

ATA: Your baby.

BO: Ear infections. She don't like me to leave her for a minute.

ATA: Mine's still at Mother's.

BO: You don't see her?

ATA: No. No, I don't. I love her. Her little body. She's all I love. Mother says I'm not competent, she says I can't care for her. She says I need professional help, I live like a pig.

BO: Hey, tell her go screw herself, a pig don't drink Dr. Pepper.
(*Ata smiles. Bo focuses on the two or three hundred pencils by the bed.*)

BO: Nice pencils.

ATA: I sharpen them. It's very soothing. Then I can sleep.

BO: Right.

ATA: (*Sharpening a pencil.*) Listen.

BO: Very soothing.

ATA: Try one.

BO: Maybe later. I was doin' a job upstairs, so I dropped by.

ATA: In this building?

BO: A doctor. We made out good.

ATA: We?

BO: Robbie, my sideman. Used to be a driver for a made guy. He's ace.

ATA: The one in the window?

BO: Yeah. He don't like sittin' around, you know the type? Always doin' somethin', guy always tappin' his foot, right?

ATA: Robbing people. Robbing people. I don't know.

BO: I rob insurance companies.

ATA: Yes! That's it! Robbing the rich to give to the poor.

BO: I am the poor.

ATA: Yes! (*A pause.*) Did you go to your prom?

BO: I didn't even go to my fuckin' school.

ATA: I'm hallucinating. I just saw green balloons. Prom balloons while you were talking. (*Bo looks around her.*) I think about things and they're so real, I think I'm actually there. My prom, my birthday parties, the Miss Carolina Junior Pageant.

BO: You shittin' me?

ATA: No.

BO: Like a beauty thing?

ATA: I played the xylophone.

BO: Man, they all play the xylophone. Dis, he used to watch that shit every year. What's weird is who ever saw a xylophone in real life?

ATA: I played "Lady of Spain."

BO: You win?

ATA: I have a misshapen breast. It's oblong.

BO: So whattaya do now?

ATA: Do?

BO: Do. Work. Job. Whattaya do?

ATA: Oh…

BO: Yeah?

ATA: Things.

BO: Yeah?

ATA: (*Suddenly angry and defensive.*) I do things!

BO: (*Matching her.*) What?

ATA: Dances. I plan dances. Steeplechases. Masked balls. Auctions. Charitable events. I organize. I volunteer.

BO: (*Frustrated.*) But, what's your job?

ATA: *That's* my job.

BO: You mean for money?

ATA: No, not for money!

BO: Then it's not a job!

ATA: You say that? You a burglar?

BO: (*Pointing a finger.*) I'm no burglar?

ATA: You just jimmied my window.

BO: I'm a shag. (*No comprehension from Ata.*) A shag, a hustler, a grifter, a boost.

ATA: You tried to burgle my apartment.

BO: I'm outta work.

ATA: You're an avocational burglar?

BO: Ata?

ATA: What?

BO: Shut up! Okay, someone comes up to you onna street. They got a lottery ticket. A winner. They can't cash it, they're an illegal immigrant. Wants you to cash it; you split the money. That's the shimmy. Woman comes up, overhears, says it's a good idea. Everybody should put up a hundred dollars faith money. She's the switch. Money goes in an envelope. You hold it. The switch goes to cash the ticket. The shimmy disappears. You look in the envelope. Cut up newspaper. You start screamin'. You're out a hundred dollars. That's the shag, the grift, the hustle. That's my fuckin' job.

ATA: Who would give you a hundred dollars?

BO: You would. The immigrant is the shimmy, the come-on. I'm the switch doin' the envelopes. My cousin Alicia was the shimmy, hey, great accents, sweet lookin', somebody you'd take pity on, she gets offed in a drive-by. Listen, the switch ain't the hard part, a good shimmy's the heart of the shag. I do accents, they fall down laughin'. So I go back to breakin' an' enterin' an sellin' phoney smoke alarms door to door.

ATA: I bought smoke alarms from you.

BO: Well, don't smoke in bed.

ATA: Why? Why am I the victim? Why am I singled out? I was always admired, pampered, successful, always getting the plums, but inside it's as if I was fertilized, pregnant with this...oh, God...this seed of self-doubt, and it...oh, I hate this...grew until I, yes, smell of it, radiate it…my aura says take me, use me, siphon me, it's what I'm for!

BO: You gotta wise up.

ATA: Yes.

BO: You gotta retaliate.

ATA: Yes!

BO: You gotta say "fuck you."

ATA: I will not use profanity!

BO: Because you're fucked up.

ATA: Civilization…we have to free ourselves, we have to rise, we have to fulfill, we have to heal. My God, the old woman next door says it's kill or be killed, she's trying to sell me an AK-47!

BO: How much?

ATA: No, I say no. We have to stop the cycle, we have to trust.

BO: Forget it.

ATA: We have to!

BO: Don't trust nobody. It's for suckers, I'm tellin' you. Your own mother, I'm tellin' you, will sell you for a price. Trust like incites other people to fuck with you. You know that. You don't trust 'em, you keep 'em honest. It's like doin' them a favor. Don't trust 'em, don't tell 'em nothin'. What they know, they use on you. You fucked that guy, he ratted on you. You came clean to Wib, he stole your stuff. You trusted your mother, she took your kid. You got the whole thing backwards. Don't trust 'em, don't tell 'em nothin'. Trust me.

ATA: But how can you live like that!!?

BO: Ata.

ATA: What?

BO: I need the pistol.

ATA: (*Holding it up. It's still in her hand.*) This?

BO: Yeah.

ATA: Why?

BO: Why?

ATA: What would you do with it?

BO: Ata, what are we talking about here? I left it, I need it.

ATA: You mean it's yours?

BO: Yeah.

ATA: So you should have it?

BO: Yeah.

ATA: (*Exploding.*) Then what were you doing coming in here to take all *my* things?

BO: You got no things.

ATA: That's not the point.

BO: I borrowed that piece from a guy wants it back.

ATA: What does he do with it?

BO: (*Exploding.*) He's a fuckin' hit man an' I don't wanta get hit.

ATA: He would kill you?

BO: Why not?

ATA: Why not?

BO: Ata, the way you *keep* stuff, you fuck over people who *take* stuff. This guy, he can't afford it to be known you can rip him off.

ATA: So I should see a professional murderer gets his gun back?

BO: In this case he could kill people or he could kill me. Take your pick.

ATA: You see why I'm crazy?

BO: Actually, yeah.

ATA: Why I can't go out of my room?

BO: Why you are crazy is because you let people piss on you, you don't do nothin'.

ATA: That is not why I'm crazy.

BO: It is, trust me. Lemme ask you somethin'?

ATA: What?

BO: What happened to your eye?

(*Ata goes over, lies down in bed and pulls the covers over her head.*)

BO: This is an answer? (*She goes over and tries to dislodge Ata.*) Hey, wacko, I'm talkin' to you? You got belted, right? An' the payback was what? Hey. You got belted, what did you do? You did nothin', right? You got under the covers.

ROBBIE: (*Appears in the window. He has the Walkman.*) What're you doin'?

BO: What're you doin'?

ROBBIE: I'm checkin'.

BO: I'll see you down to the truck.

ROBBIE: Takin' a little break, huh?

BO: Yeah.

ROBBIE: In the middle of a robbery?

BO: Yeah.

ROBBIE: It's interestin'.

BO: I don't speak English? I said I'll be down.

ROBBIE: This year?

BO: Fuck you.

ROBBIE: I'm down there with a truck fulla hot stuff with cops tellin' me I'm double-parked an' you're up here havin' a tea party. Plus the Cubs is losin' 10-2 to fuckin' Montreal, which is Canadians for Christ sake, an' I got to listen to that. On top of which you walked off with my malt balls.

BO: Shut up. (*Back to Ata.*) I'm gonna tell you one thing, everything, all of it, everything in life is based on respect. You hear me? With respect, you got peace and quiet, you got business as usual, you know, everything goin' along hunky-dory. No respect, you got your black eye and no chairs, right? (*To Robbie.*) Whattaya say?

ROBBIE: Absa-fuckin'-lutely.

BO: (*To Ata.*) So, who belted ya? Your old man, right? I'm right an' I know I'm right. (*To Robbie.*) Whattaya do someone belts you?

ROBBIE: Chainsaw his legs.

BO: This would be one approach. Come outta there. (*She pulls the bedclothes off Ata.*)

ROBBIE: (*To Ata.*) How ya doin'?

ATA: Hi. (*To Bo.*) We had a little disagreement, you know, money. It was my fault, I yelled at him. It was all my fault…(*She begins to cry.*)…and then he hit me.

BO: Ata. Let's go get the stuff.

ATA: What stuff?

BO: The V.C.R., the mini-cam, the silver, the jewelry, some chairs, the Nikon, a couple paintings and his fuckin' wallet.

ATA: The things he took?

BO: Yeah.

ATA: We would go and rob him?

BO: I could go for that.

ATA: No.

BO: Yeah.

ATA: No.

BO: Yeah.

ATA: Violence is a circle, don't you see that? It goes on, it feeds on itself, he'll just take it again.

BO: No, he won't.

ATA: Why not?

ROBBIE: Because we'll sell it.

BO: It'll be money then. Money for you, money for me. Because you didn't turn me in. Robbie and me, we only take sixty percent.

ROBBIE: You're kiddin?

BO: Sometimes you gotta do right.

ATA: But we won't get what it's worth.

BO: But will he be pissed.

ATA: It's wrong to steal.

BO: But, will he be pissed.

ATA: He would be.

BO: Yeah.

ATA: He would be irate.

BO: Yeah.

ATA: He has to win. He has to dominate.

BO: Yeah.

ATA: He'd get hysterical and irrational. He would be out of control. He hates being out of control. And he never forgets. It would be like a sliver in his brain.

BO: Tough fuckin' nuggies.

ATA: And I would like it.

BO: Damn straight.

ATA: I would really like it. I would enjoy it. He would deserve it, and I would revel in it. I would be ecstatic and mad with joy! But we can't.

ROBBIE: Why is that?

ATA: Because he has it in the country.

BO: We can go there.

ROBBIE: We got a truck.

ATA: It's a very exclusive enclave.

BO: What's an enclave?

ATA: Several homes set into a hill. One road. And where you turn in there's a 24-hour checkpoint with a security guard. They either need confirmation from the person you're visiting or they need to know you.

(*A pause.*)

BO: Like they know you, right?

(*A pause.*)

ATA: Me?

BO: You.

ATA: I can't go out.

BO: You sure?

ATA: I can't. I can't go out. I can't go out!
   (*The phone rings. Ata looks at Bo.*)

BO: Why not?

ATA: (*Answers the phone.*) Hello. Yes. It's very late. What? I don't
   know. Yes, I will. (*She puts down the receiver and goes to the closet
   door. Looks inside. Closes the door and returns to the phone.*)

ROBBIE: (*To Bo.*) You wanta serve five for a traffic ticket?

BO: (*Tossing him a pack.*) Eat your malt balls.

ROBBIE: (*Disgusted, pointing to his earphones.*) Hey, back off, I'm losin'
   to Canadians here.

ATA: (*Back on phone.*) Yes, it is. You are asking me? Yes. Yes. Yes. I
   can't go out. Yes. Yes. All right. Yes. You're welcome. (*She hangs
   up.*) When he took everything he forgot his golf clubs in the
   closet.

BO: Yeah?

ATA: He's playing with an important client tomorrow and he wants
   me to bring them over to his office in the morning.

BO: You can't go out.

ATA: Yes. He said failing that would I call a cab and have them sent
   over.

BO: He wants *you* to *bring* them?

ATA: Yes.

BO: Fuck him.

ATA: I said I'd do it!

BO: Yeah?

ATA: I said I'd do it!!

BO: Yeah.

ATA: It walked out of my mouth. I got a headache when I heard
   myself saying it. (*She gets gradually wilder.*) I said I would subvert
   every instinct, every impulse, every sense I might possibly have of
   myself and make sure his golf clubs are delivered. I said I would
   do that. But before I do that, there is one other thing I have to
   do. (*She goes to the closet and drags out the bag of clubs. While she
   pillages, she talks to the clubs. One she bends by stamping on it.
   Another she smashes over a radiator. A third she warps over a
   window sill.*) Nooners...nooners...sand traps...you...you I
   will...mangle...dry-cleaners...right at the dry-cleaners... golf...

hate, hate golf…yes…hate…there, yes…putt with that! (*She takes the rest of them and, with Robbie stepping aside, throws them out the window.*) Bring them to his office…put them in a cab to his office…(*Over the edge they go.*) Vaya con Dios! (*Turns to them.*) Now, how will we rob him?

BO: You would have to go out.

ATA: Out? Out there? Me go out? (*A roar.*) I'll go out!!!

BO: (*Calmly.*) You're on. Here is what I would suggest. (*To Robbie.*) How is your truck?

ROBBIE: It's a shitmobile.

ATA: I thought so. We would have to rent a late model van. Next week is Wib's birthday, he goes drinking and he can't walk. It's disgusting. We would dress formally. We would carry champagne and flowers. We would drive up to the checkpoint and I would tell the guard we are going to surprise Wib when he comes home with a party. We would say we're going now to decorate. The guards like Wib. They would like us to surprise him on his birthday. Then we would rob him and put it in the van and drive back out saying we forgot scotch tape, and we would give them a bottle of champagne so they could celebrate too, and we'd wave and smile and leave and sell everything. (*A pause, roaring.*) And then I'd be happy!!

ROBBIE: Not bad.

BO: I could go for that.

ATA: (*A faraway look.*) Yes.

BO: Dress formally?

ATA: Beyond reproach. (*She goes to the closet.*) In my world they don't believe what you say, but they believe how you look. In there I have forty thousand dollars worth of clothes they will believe. I have Wib's tux. I have accessories. I am revenge on a horse, I will flay him alive.

(*Ata exits to adjacent room.*)

BO: Could I say something here?

ATA: Yes.

BO: Don't laugh.

ATA: No.

BO: I never wore a dress.

ATA: In your whole life?

BO: Yeah.

ATA: Never?!

BO: Yeah.

ATA: (*Returns with an armload of dresses and a tux.*) Nobody's perfect. I will shred him. I will drain him like a Dr. Pepper. I will sharpen him to a stub. I will gnaw him like a vegetarian double cheese. (*She laughs grimly but wildly.*) Here we have a Christian Dior. (*She separates gowns.*) Here we have a Jean-Paul Gaultier. Here we have a Gianni Versace. You will wear a dress!

(*Lights out.*)

END OF ACT ONE

ACT TWO
Scene One

It is 1 A.M., a bell rings in the hour somewhere in the city. The room is much the same. In the darkness, we hear people singing "Roll Me Over In The Clover." [Footnote: Please note: Mention is made of songs which may or may not in the public domain. Producers of this play are hereby cautioned that permission to produce this play does not include rights to use these songs in production. Producers should contact the copyright owners directly for rights. End Footnote.] *As the lights come up, there is a key in the lock and Ata, Bo, and Robbie enter. They are dressed to the nines, the women in formal dresses, Robbie in Wib's tux. They are carrying two champagne bottles. Ata carries an old teddy bear. They sing another verse standing inside, backlit by the light from the door.*

ALL: "...and do, do, do it again." (*A chorus of "Yes," "All right," "Fuckin' killer, man." As a matter of fact, they sound good.*)

BO: Can we sing or what?

ATA: We can sing!

BO: (*To Robbie.*) Were we slick, or were we slick?

ROBBIE: Real good.

ATA: Real good!

BO: (*About Ata, to Robbie.*) Was she a pro, I'm askin' ya? Did she do a job?

ROBBIE: She did good.

BO: You gotta say it.

ROBBIE: She did good, you did good, the Cubs win two.

BO: Unbelievable, man. Am I in a dress here?

ROBBIE: You are *in* a *dress!*

BO: And did they buy it? Did they buy me in fuckin' drag?

ROBBIE: (*An affirmation.*) Did they buy it!

BO: That guard in the glass booth, he tipped his hat, man. He fuckin' winked at me.

ATA: You look wonderful.

BO: Yeah, but you went out. Out the door, down the elevator, into the van, man, you were so far out you weren't even out, you were gone. You were flyin'.

ATA: I was. I didn't get sick, I didn't get dizzy, no panic, no shakes. We could've just driven on to California. Caught a plane to Hawaii. Moved right on to New Zealand. Out, out, out past the edge of the planet.

ROBBIE: Yeah.

BO: Yeah.

ATA: (*Astounded.*) I did a burglary. (*Intrigued.*) Would you call yourself hardened criminals?

BO: (*To Robbie.*) Whattaya think?

ROBBIE: Pretty much, yeah.

ATA: Professionals?

BO: Definitely.

ATA: (*Adopting the lingo.*) Been in the joint?

BO: Yeah.

ATA: (*Holding up the gun she can't let go of.*) Armed. Armed and *dangerous.*

ROBBIE: You betcher ass.

ATA: I'm pretty proud.

BO: You should be proud. You laid out the job. You did the job. You're a criminal.

ROBBIE: Technically, she stole her own stuff.

BO: Yeah, but she broke 'an entered. She carried a piece. She showed class.

ROBBIE: I'm not sayin'…

BO: Right. Look. What *I'm* sayin', *we* pulled a job. It went good. She's a fuckin' criminal.

ATA: Really?

BO: Yeah.

ATA: Oh, Bo.

(*She hugs her. Bo, surprised, is stiff as a board. Ata has a thought.*)

ATA: Oh, no.

BO: What?

ATA: You wouldn't call me a volunteer?

BO: A volunteer fuckin' criminal? No.

ROBBIE: Nah.

BO: You're a criminal, you're a criminal, that's it.

ROBBIE: Hey, two years old I would steal change from my old man. Six I would do lookout. Ten I'm hot-wiring cars. Like, it's *in* me.

ATA: Yes! Yes!! *In* you. Yes. Because I've never been, I mean *been,* embodied anything I *was* because those things, a student, a daughter, a beauty contestant, a wife, a volunteer, well, they are very unclear, very nebulous to the point that I felt, well, ashamed. I did. More and more and more ashamed until I turned in on myself like a pretzel and couldn't go out, because there was *no one* to go out. My God, could that possibly be it? Do you think that's it?

BO: You're getting whacked out again, Ata.

ATA: But if you don't *exist*, can you go out? *That's* the problem!

BO: (*Holds up bottle.*) The problem is we got a dead soldier here.

ROBBIE: In this monkey suit, I get thirsty.

ATA: But what if I don't exist?

BO: You don't exist, you're gonna save a lot on toilet paper. You got no *problem*, you wanna see a problem? (*She whirls on Robbie.*)

ROBBIE: You lookin' at me?

BO: Empty your goddamn pockets, man!

ROBBIE: Hey!

BO: Your pockets, man, you got bulges in your pockets.

ROBBIE: Pardon my registering an exception here.

BO: Haul 'em out.

ROBBIE: Car keys.

BO: Bullshit, you're skimmin'.

ROBBIE: Would I skim you?

BO: You wanta wake up tomorrow. Pull it out your pocket.
  (*He does. It's gold chains.*)

BO: Nice lookin' car keys.

ATA: Wib's chains. My earrings.

ROBBIE: I didn't want to leave 'em in the truck, we could get ripped off.

BO: (*Walks over and slaps him.*) You're too dumb to skim me, man. (*To Ata.*) A little for himself, right? Somethin' we don't split. (*To Robbie.*) Don't ever skim me! (*To Ata.*) See, he got to try an' I got to catch him. (*To Robbie.*) Am I right here?

ROBBIE: Yeah.

BO: (*Giving Robbie a friendly whack.*) My man.

ATA: (*Upset.*) But, how do you *trust* each other?

BO: You don't trust nobody, you keep your eyes open. I'm gonna pretend he ain't a thief? He's gonna pretend I ain't a thief? How could we do a job together? (*Noticing.*) Shit, I got somethin' on your dress. What is this crap?

ATA: Dab it with club soda.

BO: What's club soda?

ATA: We are from different planets.

BO: This dress is fuckin' with me, I'm tellin' you. (*She smiles.*)

ROBBIE: (*To Bo.*) You look good though.

BO: Yeah.

ROBBIE: Absolutely.

BO: It's weird, man. You wear this stuff you feel weird. Like I don't wanna get dirty. I mean what could you *do* in something like this? (*To Robbie.*) You're lookin' at me funny.

ROBBIE: You got legs.

BO: Yeah. Creepy. You're talkin' to a guy, you both got pants on, it's one thing. You got this stuff on, I dunno. I can't, like, you know, talk. (*To Ata.*) That guard, you know, usually on a job I would hustle him, jive him, you know, get him goin'. What did I say? Nuthin'. You hadda do the talkin'.

ATA: I did. I liked it.

BO: Yeah. So how do you talk to a guy in a dress? (*Robbie laughs.*) Shut up, I'm not talkin' to you.

ATA: You smile, you agree, you ask questions, you praise him, you debase yourself, you go down on him, and then they marry you.

BO: You got a fuckin' mean streak, I like it.

ATA: I would like a beer. I would like several beers. I don't like champagne. I never liked champagne. I would hate it when men brought me champagne. And I would smile.

BO: You need a beer.

ATA: To get plastered.

BO: Right.

ATA: Extremely plastered.

ROBBIE: I tell you one thing.

ATA: What?

ROBBIE: Criminals like beer. Let's get beer.

BO: You go. I gotta get out of this tube. You know what this teaches me? I like a protected crotch. (*She starts out to change.*)

ROBBIE: (*To Ata.*) So where do I get beer?

ATA: On Congdon.

ROBBIE: Where's Congdon at?

ATA: Never mind. I'll go with you.

ROBBIE: (*Simply.*) Or we could stay here where I would remove your items of apparel, roll Milk Duds over your luscious body and then clean you up with my tongue.

ATA: I see.

(*A stunned moment; Bo reappears.*)

BO: Okay, there's one thing I always wanted to do in a dress.

ATA: What?

BO: It's fuckin' stupid.

ATA: What?

BO: Dance. I'm not kiddin'. Like in the fuckin' movies. Every time there was a dance, I was in jail. Plus, I wouldn't wear a dress. I used to practice with my mother, though. To the radio. Like, next door they had a radio. We would go out in the hall, we could hear it playin', we would twirl. My old lady, she was light on her feet from bein' a taxi dancer, she would show me. I don't mean this fuckin' sex they call dancin' now. I mean dancin'. Like in the movies.

ATA: I'll dance.

BO: Nah.

ATA: We could.

BO: Nah.

ROBBIE: (*Hits his transistor radio.*) So who's watchin'? (*Finds a station.*) Oldies.

BO: Nah. I was talkin'. Get the beer.

ATA: (*Walks over and puts her arm around her.*) I'll lead.

BO: Get offa me.

ATA: No.

ROBBIE: You said dance. So dance.

BO: I was jokin' around.

ROBBIE: Hey, give a guy a thrill.

BO: This is stupid.

ATA: Shut up.

(*They dance.*)

BO: This is a weird fuckin' night, man.

(*Ata sings along.*)

BO: I'm in a dress dancin' with my victim. What are you, queer? Don't press in on me.

ATA: This is dancing, Bo.

BO: Forget it.

ATA: I dare you.

(*A pause.*)

ROBBIE: She dares you.

BO: Fuck you. Dance.

(*They do. And not badly either.*)

BO: What're you doin'?

ATA: I'm leading.

BO: No, you're not.

(*They dance.*)

BO: The world is fucked, y'know. I don't like touchin' people. I don't like their hands on me. I like the music, y'know. Movin' around. I would like dancin' you could do by yourself.

ATA: Shhhhh.

BO: I liked dancin' with my mama. She had a hand she could hold two grapefruit. She was light on her feet, y'know. There was a lot of heat come off her body in the wintertime.

ATA: Be quiet, Bo.

(*They dance.*)

ROBBIE: Bee-yoo-tiful, no crap. Very beautiful dancing.

(*A few moments and the song ends. An awkward moment as they disengage.*)

BO: Thanks.

ATA: You're welcome.

ROBBIE: Beer. An' malt balls. I got a habit for those babies.

ATA: O.K.

ROBBIE: Take my arm. Hey, I seen movies.

ATA: (*A moment. She does.*) My pleasure.

ROBBIE: Fuckin' A.

(*They move to the door. He opens the door. Ata pulls back.*)

ROBBIE: I did what?

ATA: I'm dizzy.

ROBBIE: We been drinkin'.

ATA: I can't.

BO: (*Suspicious.*) You can't what?

ATA: I need a Dr. Pepper.

ROBBIE: You need a beer, come on.

ATA: I really don't feel well.

BO: Bullshit, get the beer.

ATA: I can't.

BO: Because you can't go out the door?

ATA: I don't know why I can't.

BO: You not only went out the door, you took me out the door.

ATA: It was different.

BO: How?

ATA: I was on fire, it was revenge. I could go out for revenge and for beer I can't.

BO: We're talkin' a lousy beer here, we're thirsty!

ATA: What kind?

BO: What the fuck do I care, whatever you get.

ATA: Budweiser, Miller, Heineken, Moosehead, Schlitz, Sharp, Guiness, Coors, Guadalajara Light.

BO: Whatever you want!

ATA: I can't pick!!

ROBBIE: (*To Bo.*) Is she goin' out for a beer?

BO: She's goin' out for a beer.

> (*They take her from each side and start with her to the door.*)

ATA: (*As she is taken.*) This is abuse, I'm being victimized, if I was a person I wouldn't stand for this...

> (*As they get her to the door, there is a knock. The room freezes.*)

ROBBIE: Cops.

ATA: Cops?

ROBBIE: They knock like that.

> (*Ata instinctively points the gun at the door.*)

BO: No! (*She grabs Ata's hand.*) Gimme that.

ATA: I can't.

BO: Hand it over.

ATA: I can't let go.

BO: This is ridiculous.

WIB: (*Outside the door.*) Ata?

ATA: It's Wib.

WIB: I know you're in there, Ata.

ATA: It is, it's him.

WIB: Don't force me to lose my temper, Ata.

ROBBIE: How about I rearrange him?

WIB: We are adults, and I want us to behave like adults.

ATA: We could hide, we could go out the window.

> (*Bo moves toward the door.*)

ATA: What are you doing? Where are you going?
  (*Bo opens the door. As she does, Robbie leaps into the closet.*)
WIB: (*He is expensively but casually dressed. He is smoking. To Bo.*)
  Hello.
BO: Hey.
WIB: Is Ata here?
BO: Right (*To Ata.*) It's whatshisname.
ATA: (*Moves where Wib can see her.*) Hello, Wib.
WIB: Hey, babe. May I come in?
BO: Can he come in?
ATA: Of course. Please do.
WIB: You have a gun, Ata.
ATA: Yes.
WIB: Why is that?
ATA: It's stuck.
WIB: The gun is stuck?
ATA: I can't put it down.
WIB: Whose is it?
ATA: A hit man's.
WIB: This is not a turn for the better, Ata. (*To Bo.*) I don't believe
  we've met?
BO: Nah.
WIB: I'm Wib Windust, the soon to be ex-husband.
BO: Yeah.
WIB: And you?
ATA: This is Bo. My friend Bo. Wib, Bo, Bo, Wib. Bo Smith.
WIB: My pleasure.
  (*They shake.*)
BO: Right.
ATA: Bo is…Bo is…a criminal anthropologist, very famous, like Jane
  Goodall only with criminals. Yes. Amazing. She lives with them
  for months at a time. In their habitat. Assessing their rituals and
  recording their tribal life, becoming part of the urban village,
  wouldn't you say? I would say so, and her new book, *Clinical
  Memoir* didn't you call it, Alfred Knopf, already on the lists "The
  Anti-Social Tribe," well, it's really remarkable, really, just
  remarkable, and so…so thick…really…so, Bo, Wib.
WIB: (*To Bo.*) That's amazing.
BO: Well, you know…

WIB: I don't think I ever met an anthropologist with such great legs.

BO: No shit. (*Wib laughs.*) Too bad I can't see your legs. (*He laughs again.*)

WIB: (*To Ata.*) She's terrific.

ATA: It's very late.

WIB: I know. I'm sorry I was out when you came by.

ATA: I'm sorry?

WIB: (*To Bo.*) Ms. Smith, excuse me for bursting in, especially at this hour, and I hope I don't embarrass you, but is there any possibility that I might have a word alone with my wife?

BO: No.

WIB: Just for a minute?

BO: No.

WIB: With my wife?

BO: No.

WIB: I see. You are very direct. In that case. (*To Ata.*) I was out this evening with friends...

ATA: With bimbos and sluts and diseased creatures of the night.

WIB: (*Unfazed.*) ...and I returned home to find myself robbed. Very professionally robbed, I might add, no upset, no drawers overturned... (*To Bo.*) Is that common?

BO: No.

WIB: And, strangely, they took mainly items which are bones of contention between us, Ata...

ATA: When I was robbed...

WIB: You were never robbed...

ATA: With a truck...

WIB: Yes, truck, when I picked up...

ATA: Robbed.

WIB: Things of mine...

ATA: Mine...

WIB: Subsequent to discovering your very upsetting affair with my dearest friend and business associate, which could be described at the very least...excuse me, Ms. Smith...as tasteless and abusive.

ATA: You were having...

WIB: (*Cuts her off.*) So. (*To Bo.*) As an anthropologist, this is probably interesting to you. (*To Ata.*) I came home hurt, very fragile, over your disregard for our bond, my feelings, my professional embarrassment, feeling very betrayed and most things, objects, mementos, at the heart, the center of my existence, had been carted off, but oddly enough...I can say this really astounded me, I found your earring in the hall...this malachite earring which, if I remember clearly, was an anniversary gift, Ata. So I thought I'd take the opportunity to drop by and ask you personally what the hell is going on here?

ATA: Wib, I'm sorry...

BO: (*Indicating the room.*) She doesn't have your stuff, right?

WIB: No, but she has a terrific supply of Dr. Pepper and pizza.

BO: So you could be wrong, right?

WIB: I could be, I could be wrong, Bo, but I believe Ata just told me she was sorry...didn't you say you were sorry, sweetheart?

ATA: It's not right...

WIB: No, it isn't, babe, it's not right to sleep with my partner, who is an easy mark, by the way, because most women find him physically unattractive, and it's not right by anybody's standards, and I'm sure Bo will bear this out, to steal. It is corrupt, degenerate, and desperate.

ATA: They were my things.

WIB: They were things I gave you, Ata. You know it, I know it, if we detailed it for Ms. Smith, she would know it.

ATA: My things!

WIB: My money. Money I was glad to share with you. Money I was glad to see on your back and on our table. Support I could give you so you could do whatever it is you do. Volunteer or social or whatever, and I respect that because the society needs more than a good lawyer, and a woman doesn't have to work to be a meaningful human being. A woman doesn't have to *be* a meaningful human being because what we define as meaning is often just materialism when what is real meaning might be intuition. But none of this, none of it, Ata, deflects the fact that on that material level I bought the stuff, and it's mine. I don't have intuition, that's yours, I lack in empathy, that's yours, but the stuff, Ata, the stuff, goddammit, is mine.

BO: Or whoever has it.

WIB: Yes. For the moment. But this earring...this earring...you were in my house...and what I am going to do, I'm going to light a cigarette, babe. (*To Bo.*) One for you?

BO: Yeah.

WIB: I'm going to light a cigarette...(*He lights Bo's and his.*)...then I am going to count to three, and Ata is going to tell us what's going on...one, two...three.

(*Ata is silent. Wib looks around the room.*)

WIB: It is very depressing how you live now, Ata. This is a disordered mind made manifest. This will attract roaches. (*He sees something.*) What is this? This is a clubhead. This is the head of a one thousand dollar Coursefleet wedge. Oh, wait a minute, this is something else, Ata, something else we don't even want to think about. The reason you didn't send over the clubs...you destroyed my clubs, didn't you...this has been like severed...a severed head...I don't think I'm calm now. No, I don't think so...because everybody has something, something they care about for no good reason, something that is like an arm to them, a heart, and when you...you sever that...goddammit, where are my clubs!

ATA: I'm sorry.

WIB: You're sorry? What the hell is that, you're sorry? You are sorry on every level, but that is as nothing at all now. That is nothing! (*He picks something up.*) Do you know what this is? This is a battery operated pencil sharpener. This is something she cares about because whenever things are too much for her, which is most of the goddamn time, she sits on the floor and sharpens pencils, hundreds of pencils that I buy for her, as if she were a committed lunatic, but it isn't a sharpener for long because I'm going to put the goddamn thing out of its misery. (*He puts it on the floor.*) For no other reason than because you inexplicably care about it, do you understand me? (*He stamps on it.*) There and there and there. Well, now, by God, it's a dead pencil sharpener, and I'm counting to three again, and don't say you're sorry.

ATA: Sorry?

WIB: Yes.

ATA: I never said I was sorry.

WIB: (*To Bo.*) You see what I deal with here?

ATA: Never.

WIB: Day after day. Time after time.

ATA: No.

WIB: You are apologizing half the time you're awake, Ata, and unfortunately for good reasons.

ATA: (*Wildly and passionately.*) Because I am not…I am not, not, not, not sorry, because to be sorry *would* be madness, and I am not sorry. I am, I'll tell you what I am, I am bemused at what has happened to me because *I* signified at one time, *I* was redolent with promise, fecund with promise, and now I am bleached like a cow skull in a Georgia O'Keefe painting. And what is the sun I curled up under? The radiance I melted away in? Why it's you, Wib. Under your influence I sharpen pencils and eat pepperoni pizza, confined to an empty space with my Dr. Pepper. I am the victim of evaporation of moral fluids, and you are the drought. You are smug and conventional with your place assured and your habits ingrained. You are a second-rate lawyer in a corrupt system doing unimportant paperwork for the scum of the corporate earth in a salmon and green office in an architecturally insignificant skyscraper in the midst of an urban sprawl six blocks from your pre-fab condo that you got a brain-dead interior designer to fill with mail-order furniture that thousands of other second-rate lawyers have dignified with their purchases and mistaken for something they liked. Your conversation is a rehash of magazines you subscribe to, newspapers you read and television you watch without a single self-generated idea or actual concern you didn't co-opt from whatever conservatively correct positions you have self-consciously adopted. You have no passions, or politics, or pain, or paradise; you have golf clubs. The books you don't read are the seminal works of the century, and the books you do read are the junk mail of publishing. You can't fix your car or your toilet, you can't make anything, build anything, or change anything. You've never eaten something you caught or killed or grew or cooked other than to throw it on a barbecue and make sure it's rare. You have no sense of the transcendental or the mystical, or the spiritual, you don't even have a cookie-cutter religion to give you something to do on Sunday, other than the Chicago Tribune. You never fought in a war or lost a child or lost anything except your car keys and your glasses and your temper and your credit cards. You don't have a coherent family or a community you love, or close friends, or even a pet, a dog, a cat, or a parakeet; you have a car phone. Your idea of love is getting it up, and getting it up is all you think about when you make love so that nobody gets anything back from you even when you're inside them because you are a new kind of super-hero, you are scarecrow man got up for a power lunch and completely devoid of a center or a soul or a commitment except to keep the birdshit off your shoulders with a smile painted on your face as you scare everything alive out of its wits with this phoney intimidation that wouldn't even kill or maim because it's just another function of any empty vessel which is all you are, Wib, you are the Flying Dutchman of the 90s, plowing right along, wind in the sails, pretty as a picture, and nobody, *nobody*, at the wheel! So I am going out, far out, way out, out beyond you, because I need to see what few real things I can get inside me before it's too late, and there is no way to get them from you, because the lights are on at your house but there's nobody home! (*She accidentally squeezes off a round with the gun pointed toward him.*) I'm sorry. Excuse me. (*She slams out the door, but unfortunately she has mistakenly gone into the closet with Robbie.*)

WIB: (*To Bo. Cool, taking a drag.*) She seems to have gone into the closet.

BO: Yeah.

WIB: If I'm not mistaken, there was a guy in there.

BO: Yeah.

WIB: Too bad, let's talk about you. There's something hot here, Ms. Smith, something I haven't seen before.

BO: Call me Bo.

WIB: You're in a dangerous profession, Bo. You're brave, you're smart, and you have extraordinary breasts.

BO: Beside the legs.

WIB: Beside the legs. What's the central motivating factor of the criminal mind? What makes them tick?

BO: You have it, they want it.

WIB: Really?

BO: Yeah.

WIB: Interesting insight. Let's talk about me.

BO: Why not?

WIB: I'm smart, I'm skilled, I'm avid, I last.

BO: No shit.

WIB: Exactly. Listen babe, what do you see?

BO: You mean now?

WIB: I mean me.

BO: Smooth. Real smooth. All the parts together. Like a good car.

WIB: I function.

BO: I'll bet.

WIB: That's right. No point in taking a great car apart to talk about the pieces. Listen…

BO: (*She suddenly moves in and kisses him.*) Shut up.

WIB: (*A smile.*) Surprising. Very surprising. Perhaps you'd like my card?

BO: Yeah.

WIB: (*Handing her one.*) Business phone. Country phone. Where could I reach you?

BO: You can't reach me.

WIB: Your work.

BO: Right.

WIB: Another book.

BO: Yeah.

WIB: Criminals. I'm a buff. Give me a call.

BO: Why not?

    (*He kisses her.*)

WIB: (*Another look at her.*) Very surprising. (*He goes to the closet and knocks.*) Hey babe, I'm sorry to interrupt you, but I've got a long drive. I'll send over a list of the things I'm talking about. If they mysteriously reappear, well, I know you're impulsive. Otherwise, twenty-four hours from now I call the police. We can still be friends, Ata. I'll send over a case of Dr. Pepper. Don't forget to tell your friend you're frigid. (*He turns back to Bo and puts out his hand.*) A pleasure, Ms. Smith.

BO: Fuckin' A.

    (*He laughs then shakes his head in amazement and goes out, closing the door. Bo stands for a moment and then goes over to the closet and opens the door. Robbie and Ata are discovered, partially disrobed in a feverish embrace which continues even after she has opened the door. Bo crosses away, picks up a Dr. Pepper and opens it. She drinks and turns to watch the closet.*)

BO: (*A moment.*) Yo, Robbie.

ROBBIE: (*Seeing her.*) Yeah.

BO: Come on out.

ROBBIE: Right.

BO: Now.

ROBBIE: I'm trying.

BO: Ata!

ATA: What!?

BO: He's gone.

ATA: Good. (*She reaches out and slams the closet door shut.*)

BO: (*Chuckling.*) Man.

   (*The closet flies open and Robbie escapes.*)

ROBBIE: Easy, easy, you've given me a stick shift here.

ATA: (*Roaring.*) I want it! I want life!

BO: (*To Robbie.*) So, is it hard to get out of a tux?

ROBBIE: You tell me.

   (*Ata starts toward him. Robbie moves to the door.*)

ROBBIE: I oughta get the truck out to the fence.

ATA: No.

ROBBIE: So he can't trace the stuff. So we can split the money.

ATA: But he knows.

BO: He don't know, he's got an opinion.

ATA: But the police.

BO: It ain't so easy to prove shit. They got a conviction every time they found an earring, they'd have to make the whole state a joint.

ROBBIE: I'm out of here.

ATA: But you'll come back?

ROBBIE: I gotta take care of business.

ATA: Later tonight?

ROBBIE: Hey, trust me.

BO: You heard the lady.

ROBBIE: (*Flicks an eye at Bo, then back.*) Sure. Yeah. I'll be back. (*To Ata.*) You're a fuckin' firecracker. (*To Bo.*) I'm gone. (*He goes.*)

BO: (*To Ata after the door closes.*) So, whattaya think?

   (*Ata suddenly embraces her.*)

BO: He was settin' you up.

ATA: (*Pulls back from the embrace.*) No.

BO: Yeah. He figures maybe there was something left to hustle.

ATA: From me. Hustle me?

BO: Yeah.

ATA: No.

BO: Yeah.

ATA: He is rat mucus.

BO: But he's a good kisser.

ATA: He's despicable; he's an animal; I want him.

BO: I noticed.

ATA: I hate that.

BO: Hustle him. It's possible.

ATA: But he's hustling me.

BO: But he's a good kisser.

ATA: Would you come here and live with me?

BO: You're fuckin' wacko.

ATA: You could bring Sarah. You could get out. You could get a job where I volunteer.

BO: Where is that?

ATA: Parker Community Center. Drug counseling. We drive dealers off our street.

BO: Yeah?

ATA: It's very successful.

BO: You know where they go? They go six blocks up.

ATA: They would love to hire you.

BO: Yeah, right.

ATA: You're the underclass, you have the real problems the underclass have, you're abused, you've been driven to crime, plus you're intelligent, you're a woman, and you're a mother. If you would say you're Republican, you'd be perfect for funding.

BO: How the fuck do you live in the world?

ATA: Please, Bo.

BO: It pays what?

ATA: Minimum wage…to start.

BO: Minimum wage is like fuckin' your sister. I don't cross the street for minimum wage.

ATA: But, to get out of the projects.

BO: Ata, whattaya want here?

ATA: I want a friend.

BO: Me?

ATA: Yes, you're my friend.

BO: What the fuck makes you think that?

ATA: You got me out.

BO: I got no friends.

ATA: Live here. You could bring Sarah.

BO: Sarah who?

ATA: Your Sarah, your daughter.

BO: I got no daughter.

ATA: She slept in a carton. Sarah. In the projects.

BO: I don't live in the projects.

ATA: After Dis cleaned you out.

BO: Nobody cleaned me out.

ATA: You said. You told me.

BO: No.

ATA: You told me your life.

BO: You had a gun, you were calling the police.

ATA: You broke into my house.

BO: It's my fuckin' job.

ATA: I let you go because of your life!

BO: Get real, goddamn it. This is the fuckin' world, O.K.? Hoppin'
from your condo, to your limo, to the mall, to your hairdresser,
to your fuckin' grave, what do you know? You think I'm goin'
back to the joint an' get punked in the shower by iron bitches an'
their rubber dicks? You're a fuckin' virgin from life. You got ideas
a four year old don't have. Off the welfare mothers, fry the bad
guys, send the winos to Iowa. You are so screwed you think these
are ideas! Get outta here an' truck over to Jamison Avenue for a
couple days on the street, an' then you come back, if you're still
alive, and call me a liar.

ATA: (*A pause.*) Who are you?

BO: Don't start with me.

ATA: I have to know! I have to know! !

BO: Shut up.

ATA: I thought *I* didn't exist, *you* don't exist. You're the only human I
have left to relate to and you don't exist. You have broken into
my space, put a gun in my hand and led me into a life of crime
and unbridled sexuality, and I want to know who you are!

BO: No.

ATA: No? What do you mean, no? I am careening off into the void,
do you understand me? Sarah is gone, Wib is gone, my mother
thinks I'm an animal, my friends want me committed, I'm
enjoying unnatural acts in a closet, you're the only person I
believe, and you never tell me the truth!

BO: So fuckin' what?

ATA: Because if you don't exist and I don't exist and none of that...
(*Gestures outwards.*) ...exists, I might as well put this in my
mouth! (*She puts the gun barrel between her lips.*)

BO: Hey, I'm a shag. I'm a grifter, okay? I work the circuit. Robbie, he
was a guard in the joint. I put him wise.

ATA: You said he drove for the mafia.

BO: Wintertime, we do a city a month. Me, Robbie, Alicia 'til she
married a mark...

ATA: You said she died!

BO: We do the con, the shifty, like I told you. No Alicia, we got no
shimmy. We're doin' burglary, which is for dumb shits. Now fuck
the truth, who cares about the truth, I never made a dime off it,
now get the goddamn barrel outa' your mouth!

ATA: (*She does.*) You don't have children, and my Sarah is a poodle.

BO: Get outta here.

ATA: Sarah Bernhardt. I was embarrassed in front of you I didn't have
children.

BO: Nice hustle.

ATA: AAAAARRRRRGGH! How do I know, how can I tell, how can
I be sure who you are?

BO: Fucked if I know. Who are you? Who cares?

ATA: Because, because...when you're here, I'm awake, I'm not
hallucinating...I can't explain it...because!

BO: Tell you what, *you* wanna job?

ATA: No.

BO: Yeah. (*Points to herself.*) The switch. (*Points to Ata.*) The shimmy.
We're missin' a shimmy.

ATA: No.

BO: Yeah.

ATA: The vulnerable one? The one who plays the victim?

BO: You are a victim.

ATA: That's criminal activity.

BO: You already pulled a job.

ATA: I would go with you?

BO: Onna Greyhound.

ATA: I've never been on a bus.

BO: What, not a city bus?

ATA: No.

BO: Nobody's perfect.

ATA: I can't leave here.

BO: Whatsamatter, you ain't finished your Dr. Pepper?

ATA: I can't get out the door.

BO: How about the window? (*She hands Ata something.*)

ATA: What's this?

BO: Wib's wallet.

ATA: How?

BO: Think about it. Between us, we got his social security number, his VISA number, his AMEX, his checking account, his saving account, you probably got a checkbook, a safe deposit number, his bonds, his securities. We got every number the bastard has.

ATA: We do.

BO: Yeah. Plus he wants to fuck me. Little does he know. You see to it his stuff goes back…

ATA: But Robbie…

BO: Fences got phone numbers. You do the shimmy for a month. Do his little victim. I get to know him. Trust me. I'll work his numbers. Shag his ass. We can cook him like a turkey. What's he worth?

ATA: (*A shrug.*) Several hundred thousand. More really. He owns property.

BO: We got his numbers. What I can do with those numbers you can't begin to imagine. Just keep him occupied, you know, be crazy.

ATA: I am crazy. I think I could do this.

BO: Fine. Then we hit Philly, the big Baltimore, Boston, down to Tucson, Albuquerque, man. Man, they got marks in the Sunbelt! A month in L.A. and then down to Florida to soak up some rays.

ATA: I'm the shimmy?

BO: Good shimmy's hard to find. Classy shimmy, that's big bucks. A shimmy with your wardrobe? Shit, I can probably retire off you.

ATA: Off me?

BO: Yeah. You got it all. You want a Dr. Pepper?

ATA: Bo, there is a fabric…a social…a social contract…the whole idea of, of private property…of the citizen…the, uh, the good, the idea of the good…the larger good…

BO: You just put down the gun.

ATA: I did?

BO: Yeah.

ATA: I put down the gun.

BO: Must be ready to go, huh?

ATA: I put down the gun.

BO: I'm not fuckin' with you. Robbie was fuckin' with you.

ATA: Robbie would travel with us?

BO: Yeah.

ATA: My God, I could do this.

BO: Yeah.

ATA: I could. You would teach me about the numbers, I would be a professional victim, I would soak up the rays.

BO: Why not?

ATA: I want a beer. I want a Coors. We could talk.

BO: Let's go.

ATA: I'll get it.

BO: Yeah?

ATA: Yeah. (*She heads for the window. She stops.*) So, I'm going out the window.

BO: Right.

ATA: Now. (*She doesn't move.*) Now. (*She doesn't move.*) I don't know who I'm getting it for.

BO: (*A pause.*) I did have a kid once.

ATA: Truly?

BO: Yeah. Truly.

ATA: Will you tell me?

BO: (*A pause.*) Yeah. (*A moment.*) Do I get a beer or what here?

ATA: (*Moves through the window.*) I'm out the window.

BO: Right.

ATA: I am out the window!

BO: Yeah. (*A moment.*) You're out. (*A moment.*) Beer.

ATA: (*Smiles.*) I'm gone.

(*And she is. Bo lights a cigarette. There is a knock on the door. Bo opens it. It's Robbie, with flowers.*)

ROBBIE: Jeez, I thought you was gonna jawbone all night. Me in the hall it's hard on your feet. Hey, I'm not complainin', you got the wacko out. O.K., let's load up the clothes. We can go out over the roof. You in the universe here?

BO: Yeah.

ROBBIE: So, what are we standin' here. Forty thousand bucks worth a rags, right? Must be worth five to somebody. Man, my lips are sore. She was like a piranha in there. C'mon, c'mon, she'll be back.

BO: No.

ROBBIE: What no? You sent her for a beer. We go, we don't split on the other stuff, we got the clothes.

BO: No.

ROBBIE: This is a steel wrap.

BO: No.

ROBBIE: We're talkin' big cash here.

BO: No.

ROBBIE: You're on to somethin', right? You got an angle, right? The little piece has a bank account. Am I gettin' warm? Her father runs a jewelry store? A bank! He runs a bank. Give me a little hint here?

BO: (*Picks up the gun but does not point it.*) See ya later.

ROBBIE: That's right, I'm goin'. Terrific. I'm workin' my fingers to the bone, I'm workin' on spec, I'm lettin' you use the truck, an' this is what I get.

(*She opens the door for him. He moves into the hall.*)

ROBBIE: Hey, no hard feelin's. I'll see you later.

(*She slams the door on him. He yells from outside.*)

ROBBIE: Fuck you and Montreal!

(*Bo lights a cigarette. He knocks. Bo gives him the finger. It's quiet. Bo whistles Blue Moon. Ata appears in the window.*)

ATA: Hey.

BO: Yo.

ATA: I got Tuborg.

BO: No problems?

ATA: No problems.

BO: What I owe you?

ATA: Nah.

BO: Hey.

ATA: Forget it.

BO: Three bucks.

ATA: I stole it.

BO: Get outta here.

ATA: Knocked over a bottle of vodka. While he cleans up, I took the beer. (*Hands six-pack to Bo. She takes two out and opens them.*)

BO: How come?

ATA: He called me babe.

BO: So how did it feel?

ATA: It felt like *I* did it.

BO: Yeah?

ATA: Yeah. We'll cook him like a turkey.

BO: Gimme the beers. (*Ata hands her two out of the six-pack.*) O.K., sucker, watch this shit. (*She uncaps both simultaneously with her teeth.*)

ATA: Fantastic.

BO: Yeah. (*Bo hands her a beer and clicks it with her own.*) Here's lookin' at ya.

ATA: Fuckin' A.

(*They drink and the lights go out.*)

END OF PLAY

Keely And Du

ORIGINAL PRODUCTION

Keely and Du was given its professional world premiere at Actors Theatre of Louisville during the 17th annual Humana Festival of New American Plays, March 1993.

In the cast were:

Du ....Anne Pitoniak
Walter ....Bob Burrus
Keely..Julie Boyd
Cole..J. Ed Araiza
Prison Guard ....Janice O'Rourke
Orderlies..............Jeremy Brisiel, Jennifer Carta, Jeff Sexton

Directed by ....Jon Jory
Scenery designed by ....Paul Owen
Costumes designed by ....Laura Patterson
Lighting designed by ....Marcus Dilliard
Stage Manager..Paul Mills Holmes
Assistant Stage Manager...Emily Fox

CHARACTERS
Du
Walter
Keely
Cole
Prison Guard
Orderlies

TIME AND PLACE
Working-class neighborhood, Providence, R.I.
Present.

PRODUCTION NOTE

Keely and Du is written to be played without an intermission. In production, it runs ninety-five minutes. If an act break is required, it should fall at the end of Scene 13.

No scene change, except the last, took more than fifteen seconds with two people assisting. The bed can be held in place by drop bolts and, when removed, along with the water heater, knee-high fridge, stool and chair in the last change, it took thirty-five seconds.

The author recommends that *no* pre-show or between-scene music be used. The only sound cue should be that of an ambulance siren to cover the change from basement to prison.

MUSIC NOTE

Caution: Professionals and amateurs are hereby warned that live stage performance rights for the song *K-K-K-Katy* by Geoffrey O'Hara are controlled exclusively by EMI Fcist Catalog, Inc., 810 7th Ave., 36th fl., New York, NY 10019 Attn: David Wolfson. Royalty arrangements and licenses must be secured well in advance of presentation by anyone choosing to perform this song in the play.

KEELY AND DU

Scene 1

An unfinished basement in a working-class home in Providence, R.I. Architectural details are meager; a few pipes, a water heater, a cement floor with a drain. There is an old cast-iron bed bolted to the floor, a small box refrigerator, a rocking chair and a stool. The only door has been framed with sheet metal with a viewing slot added. Beside the door is a speaker monitor. On the other side is an electronic keypad used to control access and egress from the inside by inserting a five-number code. In the room a sixty-five-year-old woman is finishing making the bed. She wears a housedress. The time is now.

DU: (*Singing the song K-K-K-Katy absently, her mind elsewhere. She finishes the bed and puts two pillows on it from the rocker. She starts the song again. The buzzer rings through the speaker monitor. Du moves to it and presses the button.*) Yes?

WALTER: (*On the speaker.*) She's here.

(*Du stands lost in thought for a moment.*)

WALTER: Hello. She's here.

DU: Yes.

(*She pulls back the bedclothes neatly. Walter enters. He is a man of fifty, neatly dressed in inexpensive slacks, sport shirt and jacket. He wears a mask. He carries a suitcase which he places by the rocker. Du laughs.*)

WALTER: I know. (*He looks over the room.*) You need to put yours on.

DU: (*Crosses to get her mask.*) I hope she's not allergic. I scrubbed, but... (*She gestures helplessly.*) Old basements...uh...you see.

WALTER: It's fine.

(*She puts on her mask. He moves to the door and speaks out it.*)

WALTER: Now, please.

(*He re-enters. Moments later two men bring in a hospital gurney. On it is a young woman, early thirties, strapped in. She wears a hospital gown. She is unconscious. Over the foot of the gurney is a dress and, on it, shoes.*)

DU: (*Involuntarily.*) Oh, my.

(*The two men wear jeans and T-shirts or short sleeves. One is young; one isn't. They pull the gurney parallel to the bed and unstrap it. They move the young woman onto the bed. One places the dress and shoes in the suitcase by the rocker.*)

WALTER: Thank you.

(*One nods, neither speak.*)

WALTER: Please be at dispersal in twenty-three minutes, we are running seven minutes late.

(*The two men look at their watches.*)

WALTER: Seven twenty-two.

(*One adjusts his watch. They take the gurney out and close the door.*)

WALTER: (*Speaks to Du.*) Is there anything needed?

DU: (*Stands over the young woman, looking down.*) I don't think so.

WALTER: The anesthesiologist says she might sleep through or she might not.

(*Du stands looking at her.*)

WALTER: I'll be back in four days. Someone will be upstairs. It went very smoothly and cleanly; we have no reason to be apprehensive. (*He puts down the small suitcase he carries.*) Everything is here. Your husband wishes you well. Please memorize this. (*He hands her a slip of paper.*) Only in an emergency. (*He takes it back. He takes both her hands in his.*) God be with you.

DU: (*She smiles.*) Yes.

(*He suddenly leans forward and kisses her cheek. Du is surprised.*)

WALTER: We will prevail.

DU: I know.
(*He goes out the door and closes it. Du inserts locking code into the keypad. A pause.*)
DU: We're fine. (*The viewing slot closes. Du turns, moves to the bed and takes the young woman's pulse. She moves to the suitcase and opens it, taking out a fairly thick file folder. She thumbs through it. She finds what she is looking for.*) Right handed. (*She puts the folder in the bag and takes out a pair of chromed handcuffs. She goes to the bed, handcuffs Keely's left hand and clicks the other cuff on the headboard. She makes sure this arrangement is comfortable for Keely. Now Du folds the clothes she has removed from Keely and places them back in the bag and re-zips it. Du goes to the bed and takes Keely's pulse. Finished, she goes and checks the door and then moves to the rocker, where she sits watching the bed and its occupant. She sings "K-K-K-Katy, K-K-K-Katy..." The Lights go down.*)

Scene 2

Lights almost immediately up. Keely is moving.

DU: (*Experimentally.*) Keely?
(*Keely moves.*)
DU: Keely?
KEELY: Ummmm.
DU: It's all right, honey. Keely? You're all right, you're just waking up. (*Nothing from the bed. Du sits a moment. She takes off her mask, thinks, puts it back on.*) Keely? (*Takes the mask off, moves to the suitcase and puts the mask in it. Crosses to the bed.*) Keely, I'm a friend, I am. You're just waking up. You're not hurt in any way. You're in bed, and I'm here to help you.
KEELY: (*Struggling toward consciousness.*) What?
DU: Nothing's wrong with you, you're just waking up.
KEELY: Who were they?
DU: Who, Keely?
KEELY: On the street?
DU: Good people who wanted to help.

KEELY: I feel nauseous.

DU: That's perfectly normal. Try not to move quickly.

KEELY: Thirsty.

DU: I'll get you some water. (*She goes to the large thermos with spigot.*)

KEELY: Hospital.

DU: (*Returning.*) What, honey?

KEELY: Those people…I'm so foggy…where is this?

DU: Is it a hospital, well, no, it's not.

KEELY: I don't know you.

DU: Well, I'm easy to know.
(*Keely drinks.*)

DU: Not too much now. (*She takes the cup.*)

KEELY: Thank you.

DU: You're welcome.

KEELY: Dried out. (*Now aware her left arm can't move.*) Wait…

DU: I'll just come sit down with you…

KEELY: What…

DU: Right here.

KEELY: Hey… (*Pulls arm against restraint.*) Hey… (*She twists to try to look at the arm.*) What, what is that?

DU: Don't worry, Keely.

KEELY: Hey! What is this? Who are you? Get me out of this, you, whoever you are…please…where am I?

DU: It's for your own safety…I'll tell you, but we should…

KEELY: Now! Take this off me!

DU: I can't…

KEELY: Take it off, it's hurting me…take it off me!

DU: I'm your friend, Keely.

KEELY: I feel sick, I don't feel right. This is…I'll start screaming…it's cutting my wrist…not right…take this off.

DU: You'll hurt yourself…

KEELY: Now! (*A bloodcurdling scream.*)

DU: Stop it.

KEELY: Help me! Help! Help me!! (*She glares at Du. She twists and fights until she falls off the bed.*) What the hell did I do to you? Hahh? Please. Let me go!

DU: You need to calm yourself, honey.

KEELY: Help! Laura! Help me! (*To Du.*) Who are you? This hurts, it's hurting me. Ow. Ow, ow. I can't stand this. (*She's on her feet, yanking the cuffs, grabbing with her free hand. She tries to drag the bed. She tries to tip it over. She starts to cry out of frustration. She tries to go after Du, yelling:*) Let me go! You better let me go!

DU: Please don't hurt yourself.

KEELY: Get these off. My dad's alone. He has to be fed. Do you understand that? He can't move, do you hear me? Come on, what are you doing? Tell me? What do you want me for? Who do you think I am? I'm not anybody; why would you do this? Let me go! Come on, I'm not kidding. Listen, I got seventy bucks in the bank, I can't get laid off.

(*Her diatribe becomes less and less controlled, builds to a peak and then declines into a beaten, exhausted silence that leaves her staring at Du, who sits in the rocker.*)

KEELY: Get this off me. I can't do this. Help! Let me out! Get me out of this. Do you hear me, are you deaf, or what are you, lady? Help! Help! Help me, help me, help me! (*She screams in rage and frustration.*) What are you? Tell me what you want. Tell me what you want. Please, talk to me, talk to me. Please. Please. (*She stands, sweat pouring down her face, her voice hoarse, panting. She yanks against the cuff. She stands staring at Du. The lights fade.*)

Scene 3

Lights up. Keely lies sleeping. An outside lock turns. Du enters with a bucket of water, a towel, washcloth and sponge. She puts the towel on the stool and the bucket on the floor. Keely sits bolt upright, startled. She stares at Du.

DU: Rise and shine, the British are coming. In the army my husband had a sergeant used to say that every six A.M.! Heavens. Well… would you like to wash up, Keely? I hoped we'd have a shower, but something about the pipes.

(*Keely doesn't respond.*)

DU: Are you a bath person or a shower person? I was bath, but I changed over when I got so that I didn't like looking at myself.

You're so aware of yourself in a bath, don't you think? Did you sleep at all? Heavens, I don't see how you could, I really don't.

(*Du reaches out to touch Keely's shoulder, but she turns away.*)

DU: Keely?

KEELY: Get away from me!

DU: I can do that, yes. Keely...

KEELY: Don't talk to me!

DU: I thought you might want to wash yourself.

KEELY: You heard me!

DU: (*Sits in rocker.*) You can tell me if you change your mind.

(*Keely doesn't move. The lights fade.*)

Scene 4

In the dark, a tray falls. Lights up. Keely has knocked a breakfast tray presented by Du to the floor.

DU: (*Looking down.*) Well, honey, what is that? What does that mean? I would like you to keep my arthritis in mind when I'm on my hands and knees cleaning that up.

KEELY: (*Eyes flaming.*) I'll keep it in mind.

DU: You need to eat.

KEELY: I'm not eating.

DU: Then they'll feed you intravenously. Well, I'm upset if that's satisfying, I'm not cleaning this up now.

(*She sits in the rocker. She waits. Keely will not respond.*)

DU: No ma'am. No ma'am. Well, not everyone likes 'em scrambled. My middle son, he was poached, and he's still poached if you ask me. That boy was, is and will be a trial. It was his born nature and his grown nature, I swear I had no effect, but that child can make you laugh! Lordy. From this high. Three boys, and lived to tell the tale. Every single one of them on the basketball team, and if that's not the dumbest human activity the mind could come up with, I don't know what is. Run one way, put it in a hole, run the other way, put it in a hole. Lord have mercy.

(*No response.*)

DU: You can talk or not talk. You'll be here almost five months, here in this room with me. How will we pass the time? You have a special burden, I believe that. I would lift it from you if I could. You are not what I would have chosen, but...wiser heads. What we think is not everything in this world. You'll be having a baby; perhaps we should start from there.
(*Lights down.*)

Scene 5

In the darkness we hear a buzzer. Walter, on the speaker: "I will be coming down." Lights up. Du moves to the door, pushes the speaker's button, and says:

DU: Yes?

WALTER: I will be coming down.

DU: Yes. Good. (*She turns to Keely.*) I hope you aren't so angry that you can't listen because it would be important to listen now. Keely? He is blunt spoken sometimes, and he is a man, don't let that close your heart. Keely?
(*Du goes to the suitcase and puts on her mask. There is a light knock on the door. She goes to it and unlocks it. She opens the door. A man wearing a mask, dressed in a suit and tie enters with a briefcase. He speaks to Du.*)

WALTER: Good morning, sister.

DU: Good morning.

WALTER: Good morning, Keely. (*No answer. He goes to the rocker and pulls it closer to Keely but still beyond her reach.*) Nana is taking fine care of you, I'm sure. (*He looks at the tray on the floor.*) I see you've had your breakfast. You seem alert and well. The anesthetic we used, 100 milligrams Ketamine, is very mild and will not harm the baby, we're very sure of that. I know you have other concerns. Funds have been arranged for your father's care. I wanted to reassure you. (*A pause.*) Will you talk to me at this point, Keely, or shall I just talk to you? I know this must be hard to take in.

KEELY: Who are you?

WALTER: I am a member, Keely, of Operation Retrieval. We are a group of like-minded Christians motivated by a belief in the sanctity of life and the rights of unborn children.

(*Keely puts her head in her hand.*)

WALTER: Now, Keely, western man has firmly held to life-supportive principles as promoted by Hippocrates from 450 B.C. until the turn of the century. Since then, certain groups and individuals have been promoting death as a solution to social problems. I do not condone that. You are almost three month's pregnant, Keely.

KEELY: I was raped.

WALTER: You were, Keely, and I find that horrifying. That a man you knew and cared for...

KEELY: Wait a minute; wait a minute.

WALTER: You are the injured party...

KEELY: Yeah, right...

WALTER: In God's eye, and in ours...

KEELY: And handcuffed, and kidnapped.

WALTER: ...but your unborn child is separate from that issue.

KEELY: No, it isn't.

WALTER: It is a separate life which may not be taken to solve your very real problems.

KEELY: Hey, it's cells, little cells.

WALTER: (*Very clearly.*) It is a separate life.

KEELY: And what about my life?

WALTER: I need to clarify the situation for you...

KEELY: (*Pulling on her restraint.*) Oh, it's clarified.

WALTER: Keely, there are 1,500,000 abortion deaths on this planet each year, and that is spiritually unbearable. Now, you are one of four young women, geographically distributed, all with child, all seeking abortion, who have been taken into protective custody. Each of you sought out a clinic for different reasons and in different situations. There is, of course, a political dimension here. We chose you as a rape victim, Keely. Rape has always been understood as the extreme edge of abortion policy, and we must make clear that infant rights extend even into this catastrophic area. The rape victim must be given support on every level, but the fact of the child is critical. If medically we must lose or severely harm mother or child, we must choose. If both can survive, both must survive. We intend to document and assist these children's lives, which would otherwise have been lost.

KEELY: What do you mean, document?

WALTER: Document, Keely. We'll discuss it later.

KEELY: Who the hell are you? Screw you people. I'm not a goddamn teenager. You're not God. I want an abortion!

WALTER: Keely...

KEELY: What do you want from me?!

WALTER: We want you to hold your baby. We will care for you here until the seventh month of your pregnancy and then return you home for the birth in the best medical circumstances.

KEELY: Oh, man.

WALTER: We assume the following responsibilities: all expenses relating to the birth of your child will be taken care of, adoptive parents eager to raise the child and capable of so doing will be in touch with you, should you decide to raise your child...

KEELY: How the hell do you think I'm going to do that, huh? You knew I was pregnant, you knew I was raped, do you know I take care of my dad? Do you know he's paralyzed? Do you know I hold his bedpan? Is that part of what you know? Do you know I work two jobs? Do you know what they are?

WALTER: A child-care subsidy will be provided for the first two years, and there will be an education fund...

KEELY: What is your name? What...what...who are you?

WALTER: You're going to be famous, Keely. You're going to be a famous American. There will be many opportunities open to you and your child. This is difficult for you to understand, but your life has already changed for the better...

(*Keely laughs.*)

WALTER: I know it's ironic. Are the handcuffs hurting you?

KEELY: Yes.

WALTER: I'm sure there is something we can do. Everything I know about you, Keely, and I know considerable, leads me to believe you will fall in love with your baby.

KEELY: My sister-in-law, she threw her baby on the floor. You think "in love with your baby..." is all that's out there?

WALTER: It's what should be out there. You are in your third month, Keely. Your baby is sensitive to the touch. If you stroke its palm, it will make a fist.

KEELY: You're going to prison, mister. I'll put you there.

WALTER: You may send me to prison…(*He gestures toward Du*)…we are both prepared for that spiritually and practically. We have committed our lives. What can I say to you? I am a father, and caring for, learning from my children…well, you wouldn't understand. They resurrected my life through our Lord Jesus Christ.

DU: She's exhausted.

WALTER: Keely, the abortion procedure you were seeking Wednesday morning is called Suction Curettage. A powerful suction tube is inserted through the cervix into the womb. The baby's body and the placenta are torn to pieces and sucked into a jar. The baby's head is crushed and then extracted.

KEELY: Screw off.

WALTER: It's sometimes hard to recognize a friend at first, Keely, we need direction sometimes, we need people to tell us what to do when we act out of panic or confusion. I have limited your options and taken control to give you the chance to step outside your runaway emotions. I will return your options to you when you are thinking clearly and ready for them.

KEELY: (*Indicating Du.*) She took off her mask, I'll remember her.

(*Walter looks at Du. A pause, and then he takes off his mask.*)

WALTER: There, now you've seen us both. Hello.

(*Keely doesn't reply. Du takes off her mask. Walter looks at her again briefly. He rises and moves to the door.*)

WALTER: I am a pastor if you wish counseling about your rape or your pregnancy. One of our doctors will visit you weekly. This lady is a registered nurse. (*A pause.*) You could be my daughter, Keely, and if you were I would do this for you. I'll see about the handcuffs. Goodbye, Keely. (*He exits, closing the door behind him.*)

DU: (*Goes to the door and locks it. Turning back, she cleans up the breakfast.*) I'm sorry they chose you.

(*Lights out.*)

Scene 6

A tray crashes in the dark. Lights up. Du stands over another fallen breakfast.

DU: (*Looking down.*) My husband can eat the same breakfast one hundred times in a row. Goes the same route in the car to the same places. Buys the same color socks by the gross. He is very set in his ways. (*She kneels down and cleans up.*) Please talk to me. (*A pause.*) Please talk to me. (*A pause.*) My husband isn't much of a talker. Well, are they ever? To us? I don't know. Oh, about some things. Not about others. I never could understand it. (*She pauses. Keely doesn't reply.*) Now, Keely, truly, are we going to sit here like this? You talked to him; am I so much worse? Well, he's a good man if he doesn't sound like one. The language you use? Honestly. You know what he says where another man would swear? Flub-a-dub-a-dub! Right out in public. Flub-a-dub-a-dub. (*She laughs.*)

KEELY: Why should I talk to you? (*Referring to the cuffs.*) Look at this. Why the hell should I talk to you?

DU: (*She has finished cleaning. She looks at Keely.*) Because you have a life to lead, young lady. That is why "the hell" we should talk. And don't play Miss Self-righteous with me, this is beyond that. None of this is going away, Keely. Deal with it.
(*Keely stares at her, furious.*)

DU: Foolishness.
(*Lights out.*)

Scene 7

The lights come up on Walter talking to Keely at the bed. She has her hands over her ears. Du stands somewhere above the bed.

WALTER: By twenty-five days, the developing heart starts beating; by forty-five days, it has eyes, ears, mouth, kidneys, liver; it has a brain and a heart pumping blood it has made itself. I know you can hear me, Keely.

KEELY: No.

WALTER: Three months, right now, there is sexual differentiation. The

baby sleeps and wakes and excretes and has vocal cords he even
tries to use.

KEELY: You have no idea...no idea...

WALTER: At four months...it has eyelashes and expressions you could
recognize from your grandmother.

KEELY: Please stop talking.

WALTER: Why wouldn't you let the baby live, Keely? You never have
to see it again if that's what you want.

KEELY: No.

WALTER: The baby isn't rape, Keely, the baby is a baby...

KEELY: Please... (*She starts to cry.*)

WALTER: Last year there were 700,000 people wanting babies who
couldn't get them...listen to me...

KEELY: Don't touch me.

WALTER: I know carrying this baby is difficult and emotional...but,
after abortion there are frightening side effects.

KEELY: Please...

WALTER: ...serious depression, terrible guilt, mental illness, self-
destructiveness.

DU: That's enough.

WALTER: Spare yourself, Keely, finish this in a life-giving way so you
can respect yourself.

KEELY: Screw you!

WALTER: (*Forcibly turning her face to his.*) Your mouth should be
washed out with soap.

DU: That's enough!

WALTER: (*To Du.*) What are you doing?

DU: I am suggesting that she isn't hearing you...

WALTER: Yes?

DU: They are important things, and we would want her to hear them.

WALTER: (*Coming back to himself. Understanding.*) Yes.

DU: That's all I'm saying.

WALTER: Thank you.

DU: That's all I'm saying.

WALTER: Sometimes I don't realize...sometimes I am over-emphatic.
(*To Keely.*) Please accept my apologies. (*He lightly touches Keely's
arm.*) That certainly won't happen again.
(*She stares at him.*)

WALTER: I, umm...I'll be back this evening.

DU: I didn't...

WALTER: Is there anything I can bring you?

(*No answer.*)

WALTER: Well, then...(*He goes and collects his things. To Du.*) Thank you for pointing out that I had overstepped myself.

DU: I just...

WALTER: I'm sorry, Keely.

(*No answer. He leaves and closes the door.*)

DU: (*She goes to the door and locks it. She comes back and sits on the edge of the bed.*) I'll just be here. I won't touch you. I won't say anything. I'd just like to sit here.

(*Lights down.*)

Scene 8

Lights up. Du is mopping the floor.

DU: ...so, the stock market crashed, three days later, there I was. The doctor asked my father what they planned on calling me... "Calamity Jane," he said. There were ten kids, I was the fourth. Would you like me to stop talking?

(*Keely shakes her head "no."*)

DU: My mother, Jesus watch over her, died of leukemia at thirty-seven, leaving ten children, God help us, you can imagine. Well, God provides. I took care of the little ones, and my sister, 'til college took care of me. So much to learn, such a stupid little girl. Thousands of meals I put together. Sometimes I would step into a closet for the peace and quiet. Oh, mercy! Oh, my father was quiet, Lord he was silence in shoes, I mean it...so tall...he wore one suit, and he would move through the mess and noise and contention and tears, and he would pick up the fallen, dry the ones who were wet, find the lost and admonish the fallen away with an old wooden spoon. And then he'd go and sit in the midst of the madhouse and read his Bible. When his eyes tired he'd have me read it, on the floor beside him, one hand on my shoulder. You know, I remember a hundred things he did and nothing of what he said. He died of throat cancer, and he died so hard I don't even like to think about it. (*A pause.*) What about your father? (*A pause.*) What about your father? (*Irritation.*) I think you're spoiled rotten, what do you think? You care for your father, and you think that's hard? It's a privilege to do that, young lady. You work two jobs and think you're put upon? There are millions suffering because they can't provide. Your husband forced himself on you? You should have gone to the police. You want to end the life of the baby you are carrying? It's contrary to God's will, it's murder, it's not necessary, it's as selfish an act as you could conceive, and we will not allow you to harm that child or yourself. You are better than that, you know you are, and how you feel or what trouble you might have is not so important as a life. Now grow up and talk to me. (*A pause.*) What about your father?

KEELY: My father? He can move his right arm and the right side of his face.

DU: I'm sorry.

KEELY: He's a cop who got shot during a drug bust. You mess with a cop's daughter, they will skin you alive.

DU: I am truly sorry.

KEELY: You know what you get for kidnapping?

DU: Well, not to the year I don't.

KEELY: All you've got left. All of your life.

DU: I'm a Bible Christian, Keely, and you can have my life to stop the slaughter is my perspective, I suppose. Not that I could take the prison, Lord, I don't even like low ceilings. I don't know what I'd do. But…Isaiah 44:24, "This is what the Lord says – your Redeemer who formed you in the womb: See, I set before you today life and prosperity, death and destruction, now choose life, so that you and your children may live." (*A pause.*) I don't know if you care anything about the Bible.

KEELY: (*Flaring.*) Hey, I didn't choose to have this baby.

DU: And the baby didn't choose, honey, but the baby's there.

KEELY: And I'm here. I don't have, you know, Bible reading to hold up. I'm not some lawyer, all right, with this argument, that argument, put in this clause, fix the world. I can't do this, take care of my dad, get myself straight, take on a baby, I got, you know, nightmares, stuff like that, I see, whatsername, Princess

Di, on some supermarket magazine, I'm there crying, they have to call the manager, because what we've got here, I could get messed up, who knows, killed by who impregnated me, not to mention I might, I don't know, hate this baby, hurt this baby, throw the baby or something like that, I'm not kidding, what's inside me. Now, do you have some Bible quotes for that, or am I just beside the point, handcuffed to this bed, carrying the results of being fucked by my ex-husband while he banged my head off a hardwood floor to shut me up.

DU: I'm sorry.

KEELY: You're sorry?

DU: That was the act of an animal at that time.

KEELY: At that time? You don't know who he was, who he is. You don't know who I am, and God knows you don't care, with your scrambled eggs and your grandma act, either let me out of here or leave me alone, do you understand me? I wouldn't eat I don't know what if it came from your hands, I wouldn't touch it, I wouldn't let it inside me. You're filth. I don't care what church you come from or who your God is. You're criminal filth, and I will see to it you get yours. Now, leave me alone. (*She turns away. There is silence.*)

DU: I can't leave you alone, honey. Nobody wants to be left alone. Not really.
(*The lights fade.*)

Scene 9

The light comes up on Walter sitting by Keely's bed taking things out of a grocery bag beside him on the floor.

WALTER: Feeling the baby move. I've always thought it must be the most extraordinary sensation. Mouth wash. I believe peppermint was required. Oranges, I hope they're ripe. It wasn't apples, was it?
(*Du nods that it was.*)

WALTER: I'm not an expert shopper, if you hadn't noticed. Emery boards. Kleenex. Catsup. And the, uh… (*Small hangers with panties.*)

DU: …underthings.

WALTER: Size 7 if I'm not mistaken. (*Nods.*) Now… (*Takes books out.*) "The First Year of Life," very informative… (*Another.*) Doctor Spock, of course. Proof you can't spoil good advice with bad politics, and this, on pregnancy, my wife suggested.
(*Keely doesn't look up.*)

WALTER: Do you know that I love you, Keely? I love and understand your resistance. I am very proud of you, oddly enough. You believe you are right, and you stick to it. If you were swayed by reason or found new understanding, I believe you would have the guts to admit it. (*No response.*) Listen to me. You have life inside you. It perceives. It now recognizes your voice. Your voice among all others. It cannot be dismissed by calling it a fetus. (*He waits.*) The child is separate from how it was conceived and must also be considered separately from you. I have no wish to choose between you, but if I must I choose the child who has no earthly advocate. I can love you, but I must protect the child. This is my responsibility. Keely. Keely? You *will* have the child, Keely, so the book on pregnancy, at least, will be of practical value to you.
(*He puts that book on the bed. Keely doesn't look up.*)

WALTER: This is a pamphlet on abortion. (*He opens it.*) Please look at the picture, Keely. (*Again.*) Please look at the picture, Keely.
(*She doesn't.*)

WALTER: If you cannot look at these photographs, Keely, you have no right to your opinions. You know that's true.
(*She looks up.*)

WALTER: This. (*He turns the page.*) This. And this. This. This. This.
(*The lights go down.*)

Scene 10

Lights up immediately. Du is in the chair by the bed. She takes a pair of baby shoes out of her purse. She puts one in the palm of her hand and holds it out to Keely. Keely looks. She takes it. She smells it. Lights out.

Scene 11

Lights up on Keely and Du. They sit silently. The time stretches out to almost a full minute.

KEELY: (*Finally.*) I'm hungry.
DU: (*Rising.*) I'll get you some breakfast.
  (*Lights out.*)

Scene 12

Keely sleeps. Du dozes in the rocker. Walter enters. Du wakes as the door clicks behind him.

DU: (*Startled.*) What is it?
WALTER: Shhhh.
DU: What? What time?
  (*They converse quietly, aware of Keely.*)
WALTER: A little after midnight.
DU: Something's wrong.
WALTER: Not at all. I brought you a milkshake. I just got here from Baton Rouge.
DU: Baton Rouge!
WALTER: A note from your husband. (*He hands her a folded sheet of lined paper.*) Your husband's been injured. It's not serious.
DU: What?
WALTER: Du, nothing, read it. He broke a finger in a fall.
DU: A fall?
WALTER: They rushed a clinic. He was right in the front where they told him not to be. I'm a little tired.
DU: He's too old for the clinics. It could have been his hip.
WALTER: He wants to be with the children who protest. He doesn't want them to be afraid.
DU: He's seventy years old. How many times do I have to tell you?
WALTER: You try and stop him.

DU: (*Reading.*) He's arrested.

WALTER: Trespassing. Out tomorrow. Write a letter, we'll get it to him. How is she?

DU: Well, she gets her sleep.

WALTER: And?

DU: She's thinking about it now.

WALTER: (*Nods.*) Split the milkshake with me, I haven't eaten.

DU: Did we close the clinic in Baton Rouge?

WALTER: (*Shakes his head "no."*) They put up a chain link fence. They're still killing twenty-five a day.

DU: (*Brushes hair out of Keely's face.*) Thank God we took her.

WALTER: (*Shakes himself.*) I'm asleep on my feet.

(*The lights fade.*)

Scene 13

Lights up on Keely sitting up in bed eating breakfast.

DU: (*She watches as Keely eats around the eggs.*) You ever try catsup?

KEELY: What, on eggs?

DU: Oh, we'd buy this spicy kind by the case, Lone Star Catsup. My brothers would heat up the bottles in boiling water so they could get it out faster.

(*A moment. Keely pokes at her eggs.*)

KEELY: (*Finally.*) For what?

DU: Eggs, rice, they put it on cantaloupe which like to drove my mother from the house.

(*An involuntary smile from Keely, and then, sensing her complicity, silence.*)

DU: So, he left high school, Cole?

KEELY: Listen… (*Having started to say something about the situation, she thinks better of it, then her need to talk gets the better of her.*) He took a factory job. He was into cars, he wanted this car. His uncle worked a canning line got him on.

(*A pause.*)

DU: And?

KEELY: We still went out…off and on. We got in an accident, we were both drunk, I got pretty cut up. My dad's cop pals leaned on him. After that…don't know, lost touch.
(*A pause.*)

DU: Lost touch.

KEELY: I don't want to get comfortable talking to you.

DU: Keely…

KEELY: Forget it.

DU: Please…

KEELY: I said forget it. (*A long pause.*) I'm going crazy in here. I could chew off my wrist here. That paint smear on the pipe up there, I hate that, you know? This floor. That long crack. Everywhere I look. Wherever I look, it makes me sick. (*She tears up.*) Come on, give me a break, will you. I gotta get out of here, I can't do this. (*Mad at herself.*) Damn it.

DU: (*Gently.*) Help us pass the time, Keely. You're not giving up. I know that.
(*Keely looks down.*)

DU: You lost touch.

KEELY: Yeah. (*A pause.*) There were guys at school, you know, different crowds…thirty-seven days, right?
(*Du nods.*)

KEELY: I was…man…I was, umm, waitressing, actually before he left, down at the Gaslight…he didn't like me working. I just blew him off. (*A moment.*) If I talk, it's just talk…only talk, that's all…because this is shit, what you do to me, worse than that.

DU: Only talk.

KEELY: Because I don't buy this, you tell him I don't buy it.
(*Du nods. They sit. Then:*)

KEELY: So I was at a Tammy Wynette concert, you know, somebody else's choice, and there he was, definitely his choice as I found out, and my date is…well, forget him, so we got together and it got hot really fast and we ended up getting married, which nobody I knew thought was a good idea, which made me really contrary which is a problem I have…like up to here…so, you know, what I said, we got married, plus… (*Finishing the eggs.*) The catsup's all right.

DU: Oh, it's good.

KEELY: I mean I knew who he was, and I did it anyway. I knew about the drinking, I knew about the temper, I don't know where my head was, in my pants, I guess.

DU: Well, I married a man deemed suitable and that can be another problem. There is only one way a man is revealed, and that is day in and day out. You can know a woman through what she says, but don't try it with a man.

KEELY: Yeah, he had a line. I even knew it was a line.

DU: I'll just take the tray.

KEELY: And I knew he drank. Oh, hey, he down-pedaled it before we got married…way, way down-pedaled. He would drink, say two, two drinks, say that was his limit, take me home, go out pour it down 'til ten in the morning, I found that out.

DU: They talk about drugs, but it's still drinking the majority of it, now I have never been drunk in my life, is that something? I'm often tempted so I'll know what I'm missing, yes ma'am, I've tried the marijuana…

KEELY: Bull.

DU: Oh, I have, and it didn't do a thing for me and that's a fact, and I've been in a men's room which I doubt you have, and I've kissed three men in one day, so don't you think you can lord it over me.

KEELY: You smoked?

DU: Oh, yes. Found the marijuana in my son's sock, sat on his bed, waiting 'til I heard him come in the front door, lit up and let him come on up and find me there doing it. Shocked him down to his drawers I might say…straightened him up in a hurry. That's the one who's an accountant now. All boys. I would have given my heart for a girl baby. (*An awkward pause.*) It's noisy, too many boys in a house.

KEELY: (*A pause.*) Suitable?

DU: What? Oh, suitable. I was keeping company with a slaughter-house man who could pop your eyes out with his shirt off, but he was an atheist and a socialist and who knows what else, and that was one too many for my father so he ran him off and put me together with a nice German milkman whose father owned the dairy, if you see my point. August. His name, not the month. I married him at nineteen, in 1947, and two months later the dairy went under, so I got no money and he looked just terrible undressed. The fact is he was an uninteresting man, but he got into the storage business and turned out a good provider. Now, listen close here, we went along 'til he bored me perfectly silent, if you can imagine, and God found us pretty late when the kids were gone or near gone, and when God found that man he turned him into a firebrand and an orator and a beacon to others, and I fell in love with him and that bed turned into a lake of flame and I was, so help me, bored no more, and that's a testimony. There is change possible where you never hope to find it, and that is the moral of my story, you can stop listening.

KEELY: Right.

DU: It is. Still nothing to look at but I just close my eyes. The children kept me in that marriage until it became a marriage and the love I bore them kept me alive until the marriage could catch up.

KEELY: So what am I supposed to be? Glad?

DU: Things do change.

KEELY: Yeah, they get worse. He drank more, he got meaner, he screwed around. My dad got shot, Cole wanted to move to Arizona because he knew I'd have to take care of him. I'm waitressing, minimum wage, cashier at a car wash, seventy hours minimum, he drinks himself out of his job, real thoughtful, right? The recession came on, we just fought minute to minute anytime we laid eyes on each other, I said I wanted a divorce, he hit me, and I left. I was out of there fifteen minutes after he hit me…I was a crazy, out-of-my-mind lunatic I lived with him all that time. Jesus! What the hell was I thinking of?

DU: It was a marriage, Keely.

KEELY: Yeah. After that, he was all over me. I'd look out the window, he'd be in the back yard. The grocery, the library, when I was hanging up laundry, walk into the same bar when I was on a date. He'd come down to the restaurant, say it was about borrowing money, but he knew I wasn't giving him money, forget that, he just liked me to be scared which is what I figured out. Then it stopped for six months, who knows why, then he came back, sent flowers, left messages, begged me to talk to him for one hour, so I invited him over, you know, I thought we could sit down and let go of it. I thought I could take his hand and say we're clear, we're two different people. You know, some dumb ass idea like that. So I fixed him something to eat, and he brought me this stuffed animal, and we were doing, well, not perfect but all right, and I just touched his arm so he would know it was all right, and he locked onto my hand, and I said "let go now," and he started in…said he needed…pulled me in, you know, hard, and I got a hand in his face, and he…he bit down…bit down hard, and I…I don't know, went nuts…bunch of stuff…got me down on the floor…got me down on the floor and raped me. That's how he caught up with our marriage, that's how he changed.

(*They sit in silence.*)

DU: It's in the past, Keely.

KEELY: Well, this isn't. (*A pause.*) You believe God sees you?

DU: I do.

KEELY: He sees you now?

DU: I believe he does. (*A pause.*) Keely? …Keely? (*No answer.*) Almost time for your birthday.

(*A pause.*)

KEELY: How do you know that?

DU: Now, Keely, that's the least of what I know, and you know it.

KEELY: From my driver's license.

DU: The man says you can have a cake.

KEELY: The man?

DU: The man in charge.

(*A moment.*)

KEELY: If I do what, I can have a cake?

DU: Oh, a few pamphlets.

KEELY: I'm not reading that crap. I mean it. Don't you bring it anywhere near me.

DU: You're not afraid of information, are you, honey?

KEELY: You call that information?

DU: Well, there's facts to it.

KEELY: I'm not having a baby. I'm not having it and have somebody adopt it. I'm not having it and keeping it. It won't be. It won't.

(*A pause.*)

DU: What would you like for your birthday, honey?

(*Keely looks at her.*)

DU: Besides that. That's not in my power.

(*A pause. Will Keely speak?*)

KEELY: I would like to get dressed. I never liked being in a nightgown.

I don't like my own smell, I know that's crazy. You know how you can smell yourself off your night stuff.

DU: Oh, I can share that. That's something doesn't get a bit better with age, let me tell you.

KEELY: I want a chocolate cake. I want to stand up. I want my hands free, I don't care if it's for ten minutes, one minute. I want to walk into a bathroom. I want to stand up, not bent over on my birthday.

DU: Oh, honey. We only do this because we don't know what else to do. We can't think what else…I don't know, I don't…birthdays when they're little, the looks on those faces…those little hands…

KEELY: Little hands, little faces, you make me sick…Jesus, can you listen to yourself? All this crap about babies. You don't care about this baby, you just want it to be your little…I don't know…your little political something, right, God's little visual aid you can hold up at abortion clinics instead of those pickled miscarriages you usually tote around…hold up, Baby Tia, wasn't that the one you had downtown trying to pass it off like it was aborted? I can't believe you don't make yourself sick…throw up…you make me sick, how do you talk this garbage?

DU: (A moment.) I have that dress you had on…something the worse for wear…I might get it cleaned…cleaned for your birthday. (A moment.)

KEELY: I don't hate babies, if that's what you think.

DU: I know that.

KEELY: What the hell is your name? You can…you can…you can give me that for my birthday. I would like to know what the hell to call you when I talk to you!

DU: Du.

KEELY: What?

DU: I get called Du.

KEELY: Du.

DU: Uh-huh.

KEELY: Du what? Du why? Never mind, forget it…I would like to be free for ten minutes on my birthday.

DU: You might have to read some pamphlets.

KEELY: What the hell happened to you, Du? Do you see where we are? Look at this where you got to. Look at me. You used to be a person sometime, right? You look like one. You sound like one.

You see the movie "Alien" where they end up with snakes in their chests? What happened to you?

DU: They tear apart the babies, they poison them with chemicals, and burn them to death with salt solution, they take them out by Cesarean alive and let them die of neglect or strangulation. Over and over. Over and over. Little hands. Little feet. I've held babies. I've lost babies. I took my own baby through three heart operations and lost that baby. I need to sleep. That's what happened to me.

KEELY: (*Almost gently.*) I can't raise this baby, Du. I'm so angry and fucked up, I just can't do it. I dream how it happened over and over all the time. I'd be angry at the baby, I think so. I'd hurt the baby sometime and might not even know it, that could happen. If I had a baby, my first one, and I gave it away, I'd just cry all the time, I would. I'm doing this on empty and, if I did that, I would be past empty and I don't know. I have such black moods, it frightens me. The baby would come out of being chained to a bed, you know what I mean. It's not my baby, it's the people's who made me have it, and I couldn't treat it as my baby, not even if I loved it, I couldn't. He'd come around, see. He wouldn't stay off if I had his baby. He would never, ever in this world leave off me, and I think sometime he'll kill me, that's all I can think. Or hurt the baby, whatever, however in his head he could get me, he would do...would do it. Really. And I can't have his baby... uh...it's just not something I can do...because I'm about this far, you know...right up to the edge of it...right there...right there. (*A pause.*) So I guess it's me or the baby, so I guess that's crazy, but you don't...I don't show you...just how...how angry I really am. I don't. I don't.

(*A pause. The lights go down.*)

Scene 14

Du, wearing a stethoscope, sits on the bed, examining Keely.

DU: Probably just a urinary tract infection, as far as we can tell, oh, very common, practically nothing. The bladder is right there in front of the uterus, and it compresses when the uterus enlarges, so, it may not empty completely and the urine stagnates, and those bacteria just get after it. You see? So we need to wash more down there, lots of liquids, vitamin C... (*She moves the stethoscope.*) Now, there's the fetal heartbeat, would you like to hear...

(*Keely does not signify. Du puts the stethoscope on her, she doesn't resist. Du moves it on her chest.*)

DU: Anything? Anything? Now?

(*Keely nods. Du lets her listen. She does. Suddenly, Keely reaches up and takes off the stethoscope. Du takes it.*)

DU: We should get a Doppler probe, you could hear it better. (*No response.*) Oh, panty liners, I forgot, the vaginal discharge will be increasing.

(*She goes to make a note. Lights down.*)

Scene 15

The lights come up with Walter and Keely in heated argument. Du stands upstage.

KEELY: ...cannot do this!

WALTER: Living in a nation based on...

KEELY: ...do this to people...

WALTER: Christian values...

KEELY: Saving these babies...

WALTER: Because...

KEELY: While you rip up the rest of us...

WALTER: It is a central issue in a Christian society...

KEELY: My dad locked in a bed, man, who takes care of him...?

WALTER: We address those responsibilities, Keely...

KEELY: ...like I was some baby farm, baby sow, like they make veal by nailing those calves' feet to the floor...

WALTER: Because you will not confront...

KEELY: ...'til I'm fattened up for Jesus, right?

WALTER: That's enough, Keely.

KEELY: Enough, my ass!

WALTER: *Do not shout at me!* Christ says in the...

KEELY: Christ this, Christ that...

WALTER: Because you will not take responsibility...

KEELY: So you and a bunch of old guys...

WALTER: When you have alternatives that clearly...

KEELY: ...can do whatever you want and ram your Christ right up my...

WALTER: Enough! You listen to me, young lady, you are carrying a child and you will carry it to term. As to my Christ, he will speak to you, saying "Be fruitful and increase in number and fill the earth...

KEELY: Yeah, that's really worked out...

WALTER: "For your lifeblood I will surely demand an accounting. I will demand an accounting from every animal. And from each man, too...

KEELY: Animals and men, right?

WALTER: I will demand an accounting for the life of his fellow man.

KEELY: So I must be one of the animals...

WALTER: "...For in the image of God has God made man."

(*Keely spits full in his face. Walter steps back, takes out a handkerchief and wipes his face.*)

WALTER: Thank you. I have no right to speak to you in that tone. You are a young woman under enormous and unfortunate stress in a situation beyond your understanding where decisions must be made for you in a gentle and reasonable way. I apologize, it will not happen again.

KEELY: Fuck you.

WALTER: Thank you for accepting my apology.

(*Suddenly, both Keely and Du explode in laughter, it continues, they are overwhelmed by it. Slowly, they control themselves. It breaks out again. At last, as Walter watches them, unsmiling, it stops.*)

WALTER: You find obscenity amusing?

(*A beat. The women are again overwhelmed by laughter.*)

WALTER: We are one nation, under God. And the moral law of our God...

(*He waits for another outburst of laughter.*)

WALTER: ...is all that makes us a nation and within the boundaries of those laws we may speak and decide as a people...

(*One last fit of the giggles.*)

WALTER: …but when we transgress or ignore Christ's commandments we no longer have democracy, we have anarchy, we no longer have free speech, we have provocation, and this anarchy begins in the family which is a nation within the nation, which sustains and teaches and holds dear these precepts which makes us one. And when that family sunders, and turns on itself, and its children make their own laws and speak only anger, then will the nation founder and become an obscenity that eats its young. (*He waits a moment and then turns on his heel and leaves, closing the door hard behind him.*)

DU: Oh, my.

KEELY: Oh, my.

WALTER: (*Re-enters, picks up the briefcase he has left.*) We have further business in the morning. (*He exits again.*)

DU: I shouldn't have laughed, I don't know what I was laughing at.

KEELY: You were laughing because it was funny, Christ doesn't want this.

DU: I don't know.

KEELY: Well, He doesn't. (*She throws the pamphlets that have been on the bed on the floor.*) And this stuff is sewage. And I don't want any more hamburgers or catsup or microwaved peas. And I want a woman doctor instead of that dork with a "Turbo-Christian" T-shirt and his icy hands. And how about some trashy magazines, books with sex scenes, plus my back hurts, my legs ache, and I would like to see Batman VII, or whatever the hell they've got out there, hell, I don't care, take me to traffic school, I'll think I've gone to goddamn heaven!

DU: (*Holds up a key on a key ring.*) Happy birthday.

KEELY: Oh, my God.

DU: (*Tossing it to her.*) Yes, He is, whether you know it or not. (*She goes to the half refrigerator.*)

KEELY: (*Trying the cuffs.*) My God, does this open this?

DU: And from the fridge…

KEELY: What?

DU: (*Taking out the dress Keely was delivered in. It is freshly dry-cleaned, on a hanger, in see-through plastic. She holds it up.*) Nice and chilly.

KEELY: Yes!

DU: And one more thing...

KEELY: (*The handcuff opens.*) Oh, man. Forget the sex. This is...so cool. I can't believe this.

DU: (*Taking it from behind the heater, a six-pack.*) Warm beer. (*She brings it to Keely.*)

KEELY: I can stand up. Whoa, a little...

(*Du moves toward her.*)

KEELY: No, I'm all right. Beer, that's incredible. You don't have any idea. Nobody could have any idea. Standing up straight is this unbelievable pure high.

DU: I couldn't do the cake, I tried, I'm sorry. I could only get out once and I thought the dress was better...would you have rather had the cake?

KEELY: No, Du, the dress is fine.

DU: I could have gotten the cake.

KEELY: I'll put it on. Just give me a minute.

DU: Okay.

KEELY: Whoa. Walking. Let me give this a try. Oh, man. It feels like weird, you know? Don't let anybody tell you you don't forget how to do it.

DU: Please, please be careful.

KEELY: This is good, Du, this is really, really good.

DU: The beer is hot because I thought if he looked in the ice box I'd rather he found the dress, well, I don't know what I thought, I was so nervous.

KEELY: Hot beer, okay.

DU: Okay.

KEELY: Maybe I'll give that dress a try, what do you think?

DU: Can I help you?

KEELY: No, actually, Du, I would like to do it by myself, call me crazy, it seems like a real treat. Maybe you could crack the beer or something.

DU: I haven't had a beer in twenty years. On my birthday I would split a Fehrs beer with August.

KEELY: Hard to lift the old arm...

DU: His father would bring it over in his Studebaker. They don't make either one anymore. Those Studebakers. You couldn't tell if they were coming or going.

KEELY: Does the mystery man actually talk or does he just make speeches?

DU: Walter?

KEELY: That guy's name is Walter?

(*Du nods.*)

KEELY: Like he was really human? Okay, this is sort of on. Boy. I'm pregnant. I know I'm pregnant now. (*A pause.*) This life is strange, huh? (*A pause.*) I don't care, I'm in a dress. (*A look at Du.*) Thank you.

DU: Happy birthday.

KEELY: I never realized it had that word in it. Am I supposed to drink beer?

DU: (*Taken aback.*) I don't think one is dangerous.

KEELY: (*A moment.*) Could I have the opener?

DU: They twist off.

KEELY: Right. I spit in his face. I can't believe that.

DU: He provoked you.

KEELY: (*A moment.*) Whose side are you on?

DU: He is with God, but he is insufferable about it.

KEELY: Yeah.

DU: (*Nods.*) But he is with God.

KEELY: My idea is that after two beers he doesn't exist.

DU: Oh, I think one would be my limit.

(*Keely hands her one.*)

DU: Thank you.

KEELY: How do you know I just won't hit you over the head?

DU: Would you? (*No answer.*) Would you do that, Keely? (*No answer.*) Because there are people upstairs. Because you can't bar the door and, after hurting me, you would still be here.

KEELY: (*A moment.*) There are guys upstairs?

DU: Yes.

KEELY: Do they like beer?

DU: They call it the "blood of the beast."

KEELY: Right. (*Looks at her beer.*) To what?

DU: Honey, I think you're the birthday girl.

KEELY: (*Toasting.*) To the next half hour.

(*Du sips. Keely literally chugs the bottle.*)

DU: My stars! Oh, I wouldn't do that. Keely, have you lost your senses?

KEELY: I'm trying. (*She opens another one.*)

DU: We have all night.

KEELY: And I would like to spend it fucked up, begging your pardon, blasted, Du, I would really enjoy that. (*She drinks.*) Discount beer, don't knock it.

DU: You might want to sit down for a minute.

KEELY: No way. I forgot I had legs. (*Touching Du's shoulder.*) I don't want to sit down, okay? Boy, I never met anybody who would really take it to the limit like you and that guy. Have an idea or a feeling and just nail that sucker to the wall. Cole, my ex...you know...if you push, he'll pull, he'll just keep on, but he's crazy...I don't think you're crazy, are you? (*She drinks.*) Have this idea about how things should be and take it all the way to here? All the way to the handcuffs? Never met anybody like that.

DU: You look nice.

KEELY: Yeah, right.

(*Du hands Keely a pocket mirror.*)

KEELY: Whoa. I don't know about looking in this.

DU: You look nice.

KEELY: Was the kid that died a girl?

(*Du nods. Keely looks in the mirror.*)

KEELY: Well, that was a mistake. (*She looks again.*) Oh, God. I'm so wormy. No color. Look at this hair.

DU: I could put it up for you.

KEELY: Yeah?

DU: Curl you up the old way like I did for my sisters.

KEELY: How's that?

DU: Rags. Rag it. Yes, rag curls, they always come out nice.

KEELY: God, someone putting up my hair, that's been a long time.

DU: Make you feel better. Toward the end, my mother, nobody at home, but when I ragged her, she'd smile.

KEELY: Okay, if you drink your beer.

DU: Well, I can do that. (*Pats bed.*) You sit down here.

KEELY: Wow, I am already...plastered.

DU: Now I can't do it standing up. (*She goes to her purse.*) I brought a good piece of flannel just in case.

KEELY: I would really like someone to touch me.

DU: (*Holding it up.*) My favorite color. (*Keely sits.*) I do feel badly about that cake.

KEELY: Forget it. A little dizzy here. Cole wouldn't let me put her out for adoption, not even if I could stand it he wouldn't. (*A pause.*) You actually think you're my friend, don't you? I'm serious. It's a serious question.

DU: Yes.

KEELY: You always chain your friends to a bed?

DU: On her behalf, I would.

KEELY: Funny how there's always been somebody around who knew just what I needed and made me.

DU: Good or bad, depending.

KEELY: Yeah, and they were always men.

DU: Yes, they make a habit of it.

KEELY: I mean all the time. *All* the time.

DU: Sit still.

KEELY: My dad, oh yeah, it was *real* clear to him, my brother, he picked it right up, boyfriends, my husband, my boss where I work, they got right in there on *my behalf*...on my behalf. Hell, I even liked it, I even asked for it. I even missed it when I got over it and right then, right then you bastards were back on my behalf once again.

DU: Now, I don't do hair and listen to swear words.

KEELY: No problem, I'd rather have my hair done. Behalf. No kidding. Maybe less than half. Be less than half. I got the message. You finished that beer yet? (*She looks.*) Two more coming up.

(*She gets them, opens them. Du knocks one over.*)

DU: Oh, my.

KEELY: Where's your husband?

DU: Out doing the Lord's work.

KEELY: Like you?

DU: Like me.

KEELY: Nice marriage.

DU: (*Nods.*) Hm hmm.

KEELY: Somewhere out there?

(*Du nods.*)

KEELY: Know who else is out there? The FBI, fed cops, state cops, town cops, dry-cleaners, every living eye in Cincinnati.

DU: We're not in Cincinnati, honey.

(*A pause.*)

KEELY: Where am I?

DU: Well, you're a long way from Cincinnati.

    (*Pause.*)

KEELY: I know your face, bunch of stuff about you. I know your name.

DU: You might. We've been in our Lord's underground for three years, honey. That other person...well...

KEELY: For what?

DU: For lives. Our Lord. For an end to this holocaust.

KEELY: But you don't care what happens to me.

DU: I would give my life for you to be well with a healthy baby.

KEELY: (*Takes a long pull on her third beer.*) Forget this. (*She exhales, she drinks.*) Know what I like to do? I like to climb. Straight up. Straight, straight up. Colder than hell. The colder the better. I like the frost on the eyebrows, you know?

    (*Du has been working on her hair for some time.*)

KEELY: That feels good. I used to pull my own hair, it was like a habit. Fear of heights. I don't have it. I always thought I would have it, but I don't have it.

DU: Sit still.

KEELY: Cole screwed around with climbing...when he was sober. He like kept at me, you know, so I tried it. The pisser was, I was great...what can I say, I was, and did it frost him and did I love it? I could do stuff in rock shoes without an ice ax he couldn't even get near. It was so cool. Whip up a crack line, leave him on the wall. This one guy said I could be a pro, no kidding. Went solo, what a feeling, man. Cole yelled at me, Dad yelled at me, I really didn't give a damn, I didn't. Met some people, took a week off, caught a ride with these two women out to Fremont Peak in Wyoming. Man, I never saw anything like that. Make your hair stand up on your neck. They got these weird sleeping bags you can hang vertically from a sheer wall and get into? So I'm way, way up, right? And some weather blows through, so I roped myself in and got this hanging bag out and spent the night. I was hanging in this bag, see, 3,000 feet straight down, colder than hell, and I thought, well, you may pee from fear or freeze on the wall, but there is nobody up here to do any goddamn thing on your behalf. I got down from there and got a divorce. Boy, it was a good night's sleep up there, I'll tell you.

DU: Well, you shouldn't do a thing like that by yourself.

KEELY: It was...I don't know what it was.

DU: Turn this way.

KEELY: You ever done anything, like that?

DU: I'm not sure I know what you mean?

KEELY: Done...done anything.

DU: Raised sisters and brothers. Raised three good boys. (*A pause.*) I guess I'm doing something now.

KEELY: Yeah. You're way out there now.

DU: Yes, I suppose I am.

KEELY: Yeah you are. Get me out of here.

DU: I've thought about it.

KEELY: But you would?

DU: I would do for you, Keely, anything I didn't have to do against myself.

KEELY: You do this against me.

DU: No ma'am.

KEELY: You choose the baby's life over my life.

DU: No ma'am. Your life is in your hands. You liked that mountain because you were perfectly alone, Keely, but what I hope and pray for is perfect union and powerful life-giving connection...I long for it, need it, and I'm thinking that if you get your wish and I mine, my spirits will soar, and yours...well, I can't imagine "perfectly alone," I really can't. A mother can be together with a child in a perfect way, in a union that surpasses any wish you ever wished for yourself. If you haven't felt it, you can't imagine it, and it's within your power to feel it. There is union, they say, with a higher power. The baby though, that's a sure thing, oh, I can guarantee it.

KEELY: I would give all the babies and Gods just to be alone with myself now, I'm sorry but I would. I don't want to be in another box where something else is more important than I am.

DU: There is always something more...

KEELY: Maybe when I get healthy, but not now. They say an animal will go off by herself to heal. That's what I want.

DU: It's the wrong time, Keely.

KEELY: I haven't ever been alone! Sharing with my brother, moving in with roommates, moving in with Cole, moving back to Dad's, always other people in the room, always hearing other people talk, other people cough, other people sleep. Jesus! I dream about Antarctica, you know, no people, just ice. Nobody on your side of the bed, no do this, don't do that, no guys and what they want; what they have to have, just this flat white, right, as far, you know, as far as you could see, like right out to the edge, no items, no chairs, no cars, no people, and you can listen as hard as you want and you couldn't hear one goddamn thing. Where you can listen as hard as you want and you can't hear…whatever…so, if you wanted to hear something, you would have to hear yourself breathe, like you were in a white sack and there wasn't anything out there. (*A still moment.*) He said, "You want it? You want it? You want it?" Perfect rhythm, you know, banging my head off the floor. And I thought, this is like a beat, you know, had a beat, and I was inside this sound and I looked up and his eyes were completely blank, man, like moons. I almost got his eye. I came real close. I wanted that eye. I wanted it. Well, you don't get everything you want.

DU: Oh, baby.

KEELY: I kind of drifted off while he pumped. Yeah, I was out of there for sure…

DU: No more now.

KEELY: The sleeping bag…

DU: Shhhh.

KEELY: Up there in the sleeping bag…

DU: I know.

KEELY: It was real cold.

DU: I know.

KEELY: Then he went home. Hold me.

DU: Yes. I know. I know…

KEELY: More. Tighter.

DU: I got you. I got you.

KEELY: (*Letting herself be rocked.*) Forget this.

DU: Shhhh.

KEELY: (*Rage, not at Du but at the other.*) Noooooo!!

DU: (*Still rocks her.*) That's right. That's right. It's all right. It's all right. (*She sings the song K-K-Katy softly. The lights fade out.*)

Scene 16

The next morning. Keely is asleep in Du's arms. Du sleeps as well. The squawk box springs to life.

WALTER'S VOICE: Coming down.
> (*They stir.*)

WALTER'S VOICE: Coming down.

DU: (*Waking.*) Oh, my.
> (*She tries to disengage herself. Keely wakes.*)

WALTER'S VOICE: Coming down.

KEELY: What is it?

DU: The room.

WALTER'S VOICE: Please reply.

KEELY: Quick.
> (*They start to clean the room almost in a panic. Du grabs empty beer bottles and stashes them behind the heater. Keely shoves the hanger and plastic bag under her mattress.*)

WALTER'S VOICE: What is going on?
> (*Du moves to the microphone. Keely strips off her dress and puts it under her covers.*)

DU: (*Into microphone.*) Come ahead.
> (*Keely puts on the nightgown. Du unlocks the cuffs. We hear Walter's key in the lock. Keely gets into the cuffs and sits on bed. The door opens. Du begins to work on Keely's hair. Walter enters.*)

WALTER: Good morning.

DU: Good morning.

WALTER: What is going on, please?

DU: I'm sorry.
> (*Walter doesn't answer, he simply looks at her.*)

DU: Last night was her birthday, I brought her beer as a gift, I didn't answer you because we were hiding the bottles.

WALTER: May I see them, please?
> (*Du gets the six-pack and holds it up.*)

WALTER: Where are the bottle caps?
> (*She takes them out of her pocket. He looks at them.*)

WALTER: There's one more.
> (*She finds it and hands it to him.*)

WALTER: You used an opener?

(*She shakes her head "no." He looks at bed. She doesn't respond.*)

WALTER: I find this...unacceptable. (*An outburst.*) What the hell could you have been thinking of? (*He takes the time to regain control.*) That was stupid and destructive. You broke the discipline that protects us and the work. Alcohol is harmful to the child, which is our primary concern. Worst of all, you've made it impossible for me to trust you. What else were you doing?

DU: I put up her hair.

WALTER: And what else?

DU: I held her until she fell asleep.

(*A pause.*)

WALTER: Good morning, Keely.

KEELY: Hey.

(*A pause.*)

WALTER: You may finish her hair.

(*He moves around the room examining it. Du moves to Keely.*)

WALTER: Hell is a place, it is not an obscenity.

(*Keely and Du exchange a glance.*)

WALTER: It would be very difficult for two women in this circumstance not to develop complicity. I should know that.

(*Du goes on taking the rags out.*)

WALTER: The easy part of this for you, Keely, is that you have been coerced. We have had to coerce you because the laws which should have guided you are made by venal, self-serving politicians who invariably do the easy thing. You will shortly be returned to your home where you will be confronted by hard choices to be made without guidance. You will choose whether to love and raise your child or give the child up to young parents in a functioning and successful marriage who will become that child's family. You won't be coerced, you will choose. I don't need to tell you how difficult single parenting is. You've been kind enough to read the books I provided you.

(*Du finishes.*)

WALTER: People who make jokes at the expense of family and ridicule those of us who understand its central, unnegotiable worth are contemptible, callow, duplicitous fools. Believe me, they are the most dangerous people in this society. If I could teach you one thing, I would teach you that. (*A moment.*) Cole is here to see you, Keely.

KEELY: Noooo!

WALTER: Listen…

KEELY: Absolutely not! You keep him out of here, do you hear me? I don't want to see him. I won't see him.

WALTER: Cole is here to see you, you ought to listen to him.

KEELY: If you bring him in here, I'll kill him, or I'll kill myself, or I'll kill you if I get anywhere near you.

WALTER: He is changed from the inside out, actually transfigured, he wants your forgiveness.

KEELY: I'm warning you.

WALTER: You don't believe in forgiveness?

KEELY: Not for him, and you better not bring him in here.

WALTER: He has accepted Christ into his life. He has denied stimulants. He has cast out evil and accepted responsibility. He asked me, Keely, if he might mortify his flesh, begged me to witness, and in seclusion he lashed himself until he fainted.

KEELY: Yeah! Well, I wish I'd seen it.

WALTER: This man who has been cleansed is not the man who attacked you.

KEELY: Goddamn it! Are you crazy, you are all crazy, do you know that? You think I care about rapists who find Jesus? The two of you wailing away in some back room. Let him hold you down and do it and you might have some idea. Keep him out of here, man!

WALTER: He won't touch you, Keely. I have promised him ten minutes to talk to you.

KEELY: No!

DU: Don't make her.

WALTER: (*Looks at Du and then at Keely.*) I'll give you a moment to compose yourself. (*He exits.*)

KEELY: Du?

DU: I didn't know.

KEELY: Are you sure?

DU: (*A small pause.*) I knew he was saved.

KEELY: How?

DU: They found him and worked with him.

KEELY: They?

DU: We.

KEELY: So you knew?

DU: (*A pause.*) Yes.

KEELY: He was always going to come here?

DU: It was always possible. (*A pause.*) Let me brush your hair.

KEELY: No, thank you.

(*Du comes and sits on the bed.*)

KEELY: Don't.

DU: Keely...

KEELY: Don't sit on the bed.

DU: (*Gets up.*) If you forgave him, you'd be free of him, don't you think so?

KEELY: I should have put him in jail.

DU: Why didn't you?

(*Keely shakes her head, she doesn't know.*)

DU: You should have, honey. You gave us a harder time because you didn't. Sometimes you have to revenge before you forgive, but then the only way finally to rid yourself and clean yourself is the forgiveness our Lord makes sacred. It's the only armor.

KEELY: So it's my fault?

DU: I didn't say that, honey.

KEELY: I think you said it's my fault.

DU: I didn't say that. I believe that in extremity you must punish, which is God's wrath, or forgive, which is God's grace.

KEELY: This is from nowhere, this is just talk. You haven't been there, you don't have a clue. There are some things it's your job not to forget. That's God's grace if there is any.

DU: Honey...

KEELY: I forgive you, you brought me a beer.

(*Du moves toward Keely.*)

KEELY: No more.

(*It's quiet. Walter moves back into the room. Cole enters. He wears a neat blue suit, white shirt and conservative tie. He has short hair, recently barbered, and carefully shined shoes. He is serious and, if possible, handsome. He is, just below the surface, very nervous. The effect is oddly engaging.*)

COLE: Hello, Keely.

(*No answer. She regards him.*)

COLE: Your dad's well. I see him every day. I brought one flower because I didn't know what else to bring. I got it out of your yard. (*He puts it at the bottom of the bed and backs away again.*) Are you all right? You look all right. (*He turns to Walter.*) Does she have to be handcuffed?

(*Walter nods yes. He goes out into the hall and brings in a straight-backed chair which he places for Cole a few feet from the bed. Cole sits in it. Walter and Du stand.*)

COLE: What I did, it was something an animal would do. I should have been killed for it. I would wake up in the middle of the night and think that. Every night. I couldn't stand to look at myself. I didn't like to look down and see my hands or my feet. I wouldn't use a pen or a pencil because then you have to see your hand. I grew a beard because I couldn't shave. I wore the same clothes all the time, I was up to a quart a day.

KEELY: Save it for Jesus.

(*A long pause.*)

COLE: They found me. I was out. I wasn't human anymore. I won't describe it. Remember when we went down to Pensacola? That was some trip. Hey, I got your cat. I'm taking care of your cat. You got it after, right? I've been wondering what its name is? Your cat. What its name is? It's a great cat. I call it Stripes, you know, because I don't know. (*A long pause.*) I would cut off my hand, you know, like they used to do. I would do that if it would make a difference.

KEELY: Do it.

COLE: (*A moment.*) Okay, Keely.

KEELY: And don't ever use my name. I don't let you. I don't want your mouth on my name. (*A moment.*) You won't cut off your hand, you don't have the balls.

COLE: I could do anything.

WALTER: This isn't what we're here for.

COLE: Anything.

KEELY: To somebody else, you son-of-a-bitch.

WALTER: We are a family here. Like it or not like it. The father, the mother, two children.

KEELY: You're the father here?

WALTER: Effectively. Effectively, Keely. We are a family, because no family exists for either of you. We are a family because there is a child to be considered here. I ensure the child will live and hope to see it thrive. Because I have more experience of life than you, I know that later you will understand the wisdom of this position. Both of you have responsibilities to this child. The acceptance of these responsibilities is not optional in this family. I say that as the head of the family. We are here to discuss how to discharge those responsibilities. I will ensure that we do. (*To Cole.*) Say what you have to say.

COLE: Take me back. Forgive me. I loved you in a bad way, a terrible way, and I sinned against your flesh and spirit. God forgive me. I'm an alcoholic but I don't drink now. I don't know...I was...lived like...didn't know right from wrong, but I'm with Jesus now. I accept Him as my Lord and He leads me in His path. I will stay on the path. I will stay on the path. We were married, Keely, you are carrying my baby, let's start from there. I put you on a pedestal, Keely, I do, I wouldn't say it, and I am in the mud, I'm drowning and I ask you to lift me up and then we minister to this child. Jeez, Keely, our child. You know in my house, in my father's house, Jeez, what were those kids, they were nuthin', they were disposable. In your house, right, you know what a time you had. You know. But it can be different for him. I'm different, look in my eyes, you know that. Hey, my temper, you know, I don't do that, it's over... (*Indicating Walter.*) Ask him is it over. I think about you every minute, every day. I want to dedicate my life to you, because it's owed, it's owed to you. You got my baby. I hurt you so bad you would kill a baby! That's not you, who would describe you, you would do that? Jeez, Keely, don't kill the baby. I brought a book we could look up names, we could do that tonight. You pick the name, I would be proud. I'm going to wait on you. You're the boss. They got me a job. I'm employed. Five o'clock, I'm coming home. Boom. No arguments. I help with the house, we can be partners. I'm back from the dead. I don't say you should believe me but because the baby you should test me out. You gotta take my hand here, we could start from there, I'm asking you. (*His hand extended, he waits, a long time.*) Come on, Keely. I love you. I can't make love to another woman, you know what I mean. (*His hand is still out.*) You loved me and I destroyed that out of the bottle. But, Jeez, look at me, took off thirty pounds, I don't care what they tell me at A.A., I'm never taking another drink. I'm never. I wanted to suffer what you suffered so I had them whip me, I wanted to take off the flesh, I wanted more pain. I wanted more pain. I wanted more pain. I wanted your pain. I wanted to be even with you so I could put out my hand and we could be one to one. Come on, take my hand. Come on, Keely. Come on, Keely. (*A time.*) I dream of your body, baby. For all those years I knew the small of your back, it's burned into my hand. I worship your body, I adore you. Come on. Come on.. (*He moves off the chair.*) You don't have to ask me to be on my knees, I'm on my knees. What am I without you? I'm only what I did to you. I can't demand. What could I demand? Choose to lift me up. Who else can you save, Keely, but me? I'm the only one you can save. (*His hand is inches from hers.*) Take my hand, come on. It's five inches, you know what I mean? It's right here. It's right here for us to do. You don't have to make me promises, I'm not saying that. How could I expect that. I'm saying take the hand alone. (*A short wait.*) Let me touch your hand. Don't speak. Don't speak, I'm saying. Let me come this far and touch your hand, okay? Okay? Just the touch. Okay? (*He touches her hand. She doesn't withdraw it.*) Oh, my God. Oh, my God, there is stuff leaving me. Okay, Keely, I thought about a pledge, what I could make to you, if I could touch you. No harm. No harm is what I thought of. Look, I want to turn your hand over, make it palm up, okay? This is make or break, Keely. Right now. Right now. Close your hand, take my hand. You know what I mean? One gesture, you could save me. We could raise a child. With one gesture we could do that. Come on, Keely. Come on, Keely.

(*In an incredibly quick move, Keely brings his hand to her mouth and sinks her teeth into it.*)

COLE: Ahhhhhh…

(*He can't get the hand back, she goes deeper.*)

COLE: Ahhhhhhhhhhhhhhhhhhhhh… (*He screams. He puts his other hand on her head and tries to force her off.*) Ahhhhhhh…

(*Walter grabs him from behind, but he has pulled free and slaps her hard. Walter pulls him back. Du steps in front of him.*)

COLE: God love and forgive you!

WALTER: Idiot!

KEELY: Get out, go on, get out!

COLE: I can see the bone what she did.

WALTER: Come with me.

COLE: (*His fist doubled.*) What she did to me.

WALTER: Submit your will, come with me.

COLE: (*Angrily.*) I love you, Keely!

DU: There's first-aid upstairs.

WALTER: Come on, Cole.

COLE: Jesus, in thy name!

WALTER: Come on, Cole.

DU: I'll take care of him.

WALTER: (*Leading him out.*) This way now. Walk with Jesus, Cole. This way now.

COLE: Keely!

(*Walter and Du take him out. Without hesitation, Keely reaches under the mattress and pulls out the wire hanger her dress had hung on. She brings it up to her cuffed hand and untwists the hanger, straightening it out. She pulls the sheet over herself, puts the wire under the sheet with her free hand and works to abort herself. It goes on. The lights go down.*)

Scene 17

The lights come up. It is minutes later. The bed sheet covering Keely is soaked with fresh blood. Keely lies still; she has passed out. We hear Walter speak offstage.

WALTER'S VOICE: Did we leave it open?

(*We don't hear the answer. Moments later, He steps into the room.*)

WALTER: Oh, dear God. (*Over his shoulder, up the stairs.*) Help me! Come down here. (*He goes to the bed.*) Keely. Keely. (*He lifts the corner of the sheet. He drops it. Momentarily he puts his face in his hands.*) God help us.

(*Du enters through the door, sees, comes directly to the bed.*)

WALTER: She's aborted.

DU: (*Looks under the sheet; she removes the hanger.*) Call the paramedics.

WALTER: I'll try to reach Dr. Bloom.

DU: No. No time. You have to call 911.

WALTER: That's not possible. Where did she get it?

DU: It doesn't matter. I'll call.

WALTER: Think, this is kidnapping.

DU: She's losing blood.

WALTER: I know.

(*She starts past him; he stops her.*)

WALTER: You have to give me thirty seconds. (*He walks to the bed and touches Keely.*) We'll clear out. It will take five to seven minutes. We'll call the paramedics from a pay phone.

DU: I'm not leaving her. I'll call.

WALTER: Think.

DU: I don't care.

WALTER: Du.

DU: I won't implicate you. Go on.

WALTER: No.

DU: We're Christians. You're needed, I'm not.

WALTER: No.

DU: There is a larger world, a larger issue.

WALTER: Du, come with me.

DU: No. (*She goes to Keely.*) I'm getting help, honey, it's coming. I won't be gone two minutes. (*She kisses her forehead. She moves toward the door, touching Walter.*) God be with you.

(*She exits. He stands. He puts one hand over his eyes for a moment. He looks at Keely. He exits. The lights go down.*)

Scene 18

Lights up, the stage is empty except for a straight-backed chair off to one side. A female prison guard enters and presses a button on a speaker phone located on the wall.

GUARD: Code 417-26. Officer Carrington. Requesting pick-up 9923739 Visitors' Area. Time unit one-half hour. Over. Doing it now.

(*She exits and returns with Du in a wheelchair, dressed in a bright*

orange jumpsuit, prison issue. She positions her center. Buzzer
sounds. She goes to the speaker.)
GUARD: We're here. No prob.
   (She waits a moment. Keely enters. She wears a light summer dress.
   She carries a string bag filled with items and a McDonald's breakfast
   in a bag. The guard moves the other chair opposite Du. Keely sits.
   Du has had a minor stroke and lost the use of her left hand.)
GUARD: One-half hour.
KEELY: Hi. Breakfast. *(She opens the bag, takes out an egg and ham*
   biscuit, puts it in Du's good hand.) Catsup already on it. It's an
   unbelievable steam bath. Not bad in here. I had a migraine
   yesterday, but it's on the way out. So. You have more color. Any
   luck with the left hand?
   (In a tiny gesture, Du shakes her head "no.")
KEELY: Well, they said several months. They were saying you were
   ahead of schedule. Your hair looks nice. I just can't get mine
   done, I don't know. In this heat. *(She picks up the string bag.)* Let's
   see. Cranberry juice, pretzels, the hand lotion. Sorry about
   yesterday, I just…new Readers Digest, sequel to *The Clan of the*
   Cave Bear, peanut butter cremes. The Nyquil. *(To the guard.)* Is
   that all right?
   (Guard shakes her head "no.")
KEELY: Stationery. Something else, but I can't think what.
   (She holds up the bag and the guard moves forward to take it, and
   then back to her post.)
KEELY: Cole gave himself up. You probably heard that. Somewhere in
   Arizona. Dad had the flu. My God, he's ill-tempered when he's
   sick. The patient from hell, really. I could throttle him. I may
   throttle him. *(A pause.)* Every time I come here I come here to
   forgive you. Why can't I say it? I guess I come here to tell you I'm
   trying. "God's wrath and God's grace," wasn't that it? I don't
   seem to have either. *(A moment.)* Oh, there's a new waitress, she
   wears heels, green contacts, a Bible in her purse and her skirts up
   to here…you want to know the truth I think she's into my tips.
   She brings this dog to work, leaves it in the car, can you believe
   it, ninety degrees. Oh, I may go on a climb, I don't know, I don't
   know, the guy is married…yeah, I know…Boulder, Colorado the
   end of the month. Listen, he swears he's separated, plus he's
   paying. I just should get out, you know? I don't get out. Take my

mind off. Anyway. We could talk, you know? I would like that. What do you think? Boiling. So, what are you doing in crafts, that antimacassar stuff? Like you need more, right? (*A pause.*) Any more stealing?

(*Du shakes her head "no."*)

KEELY: The ring?

(*Du shakes her head "no."*)

KEELY: Boy, it never occurred to me like theft would be a problem in here. Hey, how's the Prozac? They still fooling with the level?

(*Du nods "yes."*)

KEELY: Maybe you could slip me some. Joking, you know? So, I went to a Judd concert. You know the one that sings without her mother now…(*She stops.*)…without her mother now. I don't know, I left. People, they're about half screwy, you know? People who go to those concerts? There was this guy next to me, he was smoking grass, right out there, had a little girl on his lap, maybe two. (*She tears up.*) Had this little girl on his lap. So. I don't know. I don't know. Anyway…

(*The conversation burns out. They sit. Du looks directly at her. They lock eyes. The pause lengthens.*)

DU: Why?

KEELY: (*Looks at her. A pause.*) Why?

(*They sit. The lights dim.*)

END OF PLAY

Middle-Aged White Guys

ORIGINAL PRODUCTION

Middle-Aged White Guys was first presented at the 19th Humana Festival of New American Plays at Actors Theatre of Louisville in March 1995. It was directed by Jon Jory with the following cast:

R.V. ....Karenjune Sánchez
Roy ....John Griesemer
Clem...Bob Burrus
Mona...Karen Grassle
Moon..Leo Burmester
King...Larry larson
Mrs. Mannering ....Anne Pitoniak

THE CAST
 Roy, The Mayor, 48
 Clem, The Businessman, 47
 Moon, The Mercenary, 46
 R.V., A Forerunner, 25
 Mona, A Woman in Transition, 40
 King, A Messenger
 Mrs. Mannering, Mother to the Brothers, 70

TIME
 The play is current

THE PLACE
 A dump

MIDDLE-AGED WHITE GUYS

A small-town dump and junk yard, its mounds and valleys of debris slightly steaming in the rose of the sunset. Piles of cans, boxes, barrels, the rusted hulk of an old car, broken bedsteads, refrigerators, garbage, old signs, mounds of the unimaginable. The effect created is a dark, eccentric, contemporary hell.

On top of the junked car, a young woman in a short, red dress, with a snake tattoo coiling up her left arm from wrist to shoulder, sits cross-legged. Heat lightning flashes in the distance. Far away, thunder rolls.

R.V.: Moon? Yo, Moon, can you hear me down there? Down, down, in that river of sleep? Down with one foot in the dark continent? You remember that day, Moon? You know the one I mean. Old guy leans over, touches my tattoo, says, "Hey, Snake, we got a no-hitter goin', woman; we're workin' a virgin top of the sixth." (*Thunder.*)
They say there's an hour in everybody's life where all the luck you shoulda' had comes together like drops on the windshield. You ever hear that? State championship high school game, and all the luck we'd never have again just riding your arm through the late afternoon. Roy, he was four for four; Clem caught that relay bare

handed for the double play. And there you were, right into the eighth, throwin' smoke and sinkers like Mr. Smooth in the bigs. And then, just then, some tanked-up dickwad on the third base side yells out, "Workin' a no-hitter, Moon!" And you froze stiff in your windup and looked over there like he woke you up from an afternoon nap, and then you shook your head and threw 14 straight, fat ones up there, and they put *five* runs on the board. I couldn't believe it, Moon. (*Thunder nearer; a dog howling.*) Omens and portents. (*She looks at the sky.*) Read 'em an' weep. (*She knocks on the car top.*) What the hell were you doin', Moon? How come you threw it away?

(*Roy Mannering, a man in his late 40s, appears over the ridge of the dump. He is dressed as Abraham Lincoln, including beard and stovepipe hat. Roy carries two six-packs of beer. He looks down and yells a name, apparently not noticing R. V.*)

ROY: Clem? You here, Clem? (*To himself.*) What damn color is *that* sky? (*He takes a step forward and falls ass-over-teakettle down the dump's incline.*) Well, that's just perfect. That's just sweet as hell. Clem?

(*The girl has disappeared. He wipes at his clothes with a handkerchief.*)

ROY: What is this stuff? Oh, that's perfect. (*He pulls out a portable phone and dials.*) Mona? Mona, it's Roy. What's with the voice, Mona? You're not cryin' again, are you? Well, you better not because I'm sick of it, woman, that's why. Listen, Mona, go to the closet...you got any mascara on your hands? Well, you wash them off, go to the closet, get my gray silk summer suit...gray suit...stop cryin', Mona...run that gray suit up to the July 4th reviewing stand...because I got nasty stuff on the Abe Lincoln suit...Mona, I can't give the Gettysburg Address covered in dog shit. Now give that gray suit to Luellen...my assistant Luellen...I am not sleepin' with Luellen, Mona...she is one year out of high school...what the hell are you cryin' about, I put your Prozac right where you could see it. Now I need that suit, woman; you do what I tell you. (*He cuts her off the phone.*) I can't stand that damn cryin'. (*He dials again.*) Luellen, sweetmeat, it's Long Dong Silver. You got any word where those fireworks are? Well, those damn Chinese don't know what U.P.S. means. Well, we'll shoot what we got. Listen, I'll be there...40, 45 minutes, max. (*Feels beard.*) Yeah, I got it on. This stick-on stuff stings like hell. Look, tell Carl keep the high school band a couple extra numbers 'cause we're missin' those Chinese fireworks. Well, you tell him to do it. I'm the damned mayor!

(*Puts phone back in pocket. A man appears above. It is Roy's younger brother Clem. He wears overalls and a work shirt, and carries an umbrella.*)

CLEM: That you, Roy?

(*Roy startles.*)

ROY: Damn, Clem.

CLEM: I tried not to scare you.

ROY: (*Scraping at his pants.*) Look at this? What are we doin' in the dump, Clem? What the hell are we doin' here?

CLEM: We promised her, Roy. It's a sacred trust.

ROY: (*Still looking at his clothes.*) A sacred trust.

CLEM: I get it. You're dressed up as a Smith Brothers cough drop.

ROY: This is Abe Lincoln, Clem.

CLEM: Oh, I see.

ROY: Seventy-five dollar rental, and I fell down the hill.

CLEM: Abe Lincoln, sure. We promised R.V. we'd come down here every 10 years.

ROY: I know that, Clem.

CLEM: Twenty years ago today. You want some Cheezits?

ROY: (*Another matter.*) Clem, I got to talk to you.

CLEM: It's Mama's birthday, too.

ROY: What?

CLEM: I know, you never like to think of her dead.

ROY: Our beautiful Mama.

CLEM: 'Member how she always called you "Tiny"?

ROY: Mama's birthday! Why did she leave us, Clem?

CLEM: She died, Roy.

ROY: I know she died, goddamnit.

CLEM: Our two beautiful ladies in the heavenly choir.

ROY: I miss you, Mama!

CLEM: Mama and R.V. Makes this a sacred trust.

ROY: All right, Clem. You hear anything from Moon?

CLEM: Can't make it. Wired R.V. a dozen white roses, just like when we did this in '84.

ROY: Well, I knew little brother wouldn't show. Where was the roses wired at?

CLEM: Liberia.

ROY: Well, brother Moon, he's seen the world. Hasn't *built* a damn thing. Hasn't *been* a damn thing. White roses every 10 years. I'm surprised he had the money.

CLEM: R.V. loved him.

ROY: She loved me.

CLEM: Well, Roy, I'd have to say...

ROY: I don't want to hear it! Three brothers, Clem, but everybody thought he was pure gold, didn't they?

CLEM: Oh, they did.

ROY: Well, I'm the gold and you're the gold, an' he's down in Liberia washing out his clothes in a stream full of fecal matter.

CLEM: I miss old Moon. He sure does love to kill people.

ROY: He always killed things. Back in elementary, he'd kill bugs, birds, squirrels, wild dogs...he just grew up, that's all. Clem, I got a time problem...

CLEM: Well, we'll do the toast.

ROY: There's somethin' else, Clem.

CLEM: What, Roy?

ROY: A real bad sign.

CLEM: Bad signs, that's right. You know that palomino horse old Gifford keeps out at four corners? Drivin' over here, seen that horse run mad, goes straight into the barbed wire, tangles himself up, goes to screamin', blood gettin' throwed up into the air, most horrible thing I ever saw, plus everybody's gettin' boils, the creek's turned red, and there's piles a dead frogs right downtown...

ROY: (*Hands him a letter.*) I'm not talkin' about that kind of sign, Clem.

CLEM: There's been three cases of rabid bats...

ROY: Just read the letter, Clem.
    (*Clem opens it.*)

ROY: I'm not worryin' about dead frogs or rabid bats; I'm worryin' about re-election, Clem.

CLEM: (*Referring to the letter.*) So the newspaper guy knows about the chemicals? (*So what?*)

ROY: What chemicals?

CLEM: (*Indicating the barrels stage right.*) Well...these ones.

ROY: They are food additives, Clem, not chemicals.

CLEM: Food additives.

ROY: I got the letter, I went over to the newspaper. Now that pissant editor has a load receipt from Long Island Petrochemical tells him how many barrels of this, how many barrels of that they sent down here.

CLEM: Food additives.

ROY: Food additives, that's right. I explained we have no barrel leakage or ground water problem on the site. I explained the value of the contract to the city; Hell, it's 37% of the municipal income, you'd think a damn moron could understand the economics, but he reads me a state statute says four of these additives—chloroethylene, hexochlorobenzine, polychlorinated biphenyls and...somethin' else—are prohibited from interstate transport. Too much damn government, Clem, that's what that is. Now where do you think he got that load receipt?

CLEM: Well...

ROY: You gave it to him.

CLEM: Well, he goes to our church, Roy.

ROY: You gave it to him.

CLEM: Well, he said, since it got the town so much money, just how many barrels was it? So I gave him the load receipts, and he was real impressed.

ROY: Now we got to go get it back.

CLEM: Why, Roy?

ROY: So he can't put it in the paper.

CLEM: It's just food additives, Roy.

ROY: Uh-huh, that's one thing, plus you and me set up the haulage company. You ever hear of nepotism?

CLEM: That's a positive word around here.

ROY: Never mind, Clem. Luckily you rent him the building he's in, so you got a key.

CLEM: Sure, but...

ROY: I'll go get the fireworks started. I got to be there 'cause the new poll says it's a real tight race. You go pick up your key...later on, we go on down to the newspaper, get that load receipt.

CLEM: Walk right in?

ROY: Uh-huh.

CLEM: That's not burglary?

ROY: It's fixin' the problem.

CLEM: I see.

ROY: Clem, there is America and there is not-America. America is the light. Not-America is the darkness. America isn't a place, Clem, it's an idea. Right now Clem, America isn't America, Japan is America. The problem is to get America back *in* America. Now, Clem, this is the idea that *is* America: see the problem, fix the problem, that makes a new problem, fix that problem. Whoever does that the best *is* America, and right now it's *not* America. Not-America, which right now *is* America, has two damn characteristics. Number one: fools. Fools, Clem, cannot see the problem and cannot fix the problem. These people are Democrats. Number two: idealists. These are fools who fix the wrong problem and tell the people who are fixing the right problem that they are short-sighted. For instance, Clem, let us posit this: the world's greatest bomb defuser is defusing a hydrogen bomb planted by Arabs under the Speaker's platform in the U.S. Senate. This is the only man who can defuse this bomb. He has defused bombs like this for years. Because fixing this problem is stressful, he is a chain smoker. Not-America number two, the goddamn idealists, Clem, pulls that expert defuser off the job because of the danger to United States senators of secondary smoke, and Washington, DC blows up! We are America, Clem—you, me, we fix the problem—but the forces of darkness, the non-America number one and the not-America number two is now America, and these not-Americans are saying the *real* Americans *are* the problem, which of course *is* the problem we, as real Americans, have to fix!

CLEM: We're the real Americans, right?

ROY: That's right.

CLEM: The good ones?

ROY: That's right.

(*Clem's face crumples. He pulls out a flask.*)

ROY: Don't you dare cry, Clem. You're a big businessman.

CLEM: Then how come Evelyn left me?

ROY: Because you drank her right out of the house.

CLEM: (*Taking a hit.*) I'm a bad person.

ROY: You got a haulin' business, you're into real estate. You run Gunworld, Clem, the biggest handgun retail outfit in a three-state area. You're a big success and you drive a damn Miata, how can you be a bad person?

CLEM: Evelyn still hasn't called, you know. She didn't call you, did she? How the hell am I going to raise those boys? They miss their mama. What kind of woman would run off like that and not even leave a note for those boys? How could she do that?

ROY: (*Handing him his handkerchief.*) She did it because women are a sorry damn lot, Clem. They are neurologically disadvantaged with the objectivity of a collie dog. They hate all systems, all logic, all authority, and any damn evidence runs contrary to their damn feelings. You take out the sex drive, there isn't one man in a million would stay in a house with 'em for 48 hours.

(*Clem weeps.*)

ROY: Stop cryin', goddamnit.

CLEM: Jimmy Peaslee...

ROY: What?

CLEM: His mama is the daughter of that woman used to run the Cherokee Diner.

ROY: I got the Gettysburg Address in 20 minutes. I got some colored lawyer dead even in the polls...

CLEM: Jimmy Peaslee took a gun to school, tried to shoot his second grade teacher.

ROY: When?

CLEM: Yesterday. An AK-47. He fired off a burst, but it went wild...

ROY: Down at Lincoln Elementary?

CLEM: Said his teacher was a damn lesbian.

ROY: Was she?

CLEM: I think she just wore a pantsuit.

ROY: We wouldn't have this kind of problem if we had prayer in the schools, Clem. Now let's do the damn toast.

CLEM: (*Heedless.*) That weapon come from Gunworld. It was mine, Roy.

ROY: You sold it to the boy?

CLEM: To the daddy.

ROY: So?

CLEM: I feel real guilty, Roy. (*He weeps.*)

ROY: Clem, I got 1,500, maybe 2,000 people showin' up for my fireworks show, and due to the Chinese I got five, six minutes of fireworks, tops. My wife's on a cryin' jag, I got a little girl on the side is gettin' real pushy, I got to break into the newspaper, I'm runnin' against a damn minority, and my Lincoln suit is covered with dog shit. *You* don't have a problem, Clem. You sold a legal weapon to a legal daddy, and if he is so damn dumb he leaves it where Junior can get it, it sure as hell is not your fault. Democracy honors the individual, Clem, at the cost of givin' him personal responsibility, and if he can't handle the responsibility, the state ought to castrate him so he can't mess up his kid! Plus you don't even know she *wasn't* a lesbian.

CLEM: You explained that real fine, Roy.

ROY: That's right. Now, I got to go to the fireworks. You meet me right after behind the Dairy Freeze. Bring the keys and a ski mask. (*He starts out of the dump.*)

CLEM: What about the sacred trust?

ROY: I don't have time for the sacred trust. (*Starts out.*)

CLEM: She was your wife, Roy.

ROY: That was 20 damn years ago!

CLEM: My wife left me, Roy. (*Weeping.*) My Evelyn left me!
    (*Roy stops.*)

ROY: Goddamnit Clem, you're gettin' me homocidal. (*Clem weeps.*) If I do the toast, will you stop cryin'?!

CLEM: You'll keep the sacred trust?

ROY: I will keep the goddamn, sonofabitchin' sacred trust. I'm givin' this five minutes, you understand me?

CLEM: You're a prince, Roy. You want some Cheezits?

ROY: Do it! (*He comes back down.*)

CLEM: (*Looking up.*) R.V.? It's me, Clem. I'm here with Roy, in the dump. It's about 8:30. Sky's a real funny color.

ROY: You gonna' do a weather report, Clem?

CLEM: Right, right.

ROY: Four minutes.

CLEM: So, R.V., it's Clem. I'm here with Roy in the dump.

ROY: You're drivin' me apeshit.

CLEM: R.V., we're here like we promised. Roy, me…well, Moon, he's tied up with fecal matter. Boy, I miss your shinin' face. You never loved me. Wasn't your fault. I know you loved Moon. I believe you loved Roy here…mainly. I don't know why you killed yourself, but that was just the worst thing ever happened to me. I still wake up cryin'. You asked in that death note would we hoist a beer every ten years on the pitcher's mount where we almost got to be state champs an' you sang the National Anthem. See, they sold the field for a dump site when they combined the high school over to Mayberry.

ROY: One minute.

CLEM: (*Quickly.*) I can still hear your beautiful voice. So clear and high. Sounded like Snow White or Cinderella singin' to the mice. Boy, I miss you, R.V.….it's just a dump now, but it's a world of memories to me. (*He weeps.*)

ROY: Goddamn it, Clem.

(*Clem stops.*)

ROY: R.V.? You were a damn fine woman with beautiful breasts and a good sense of humor. We shouldn't have got married with you still stuck on Moon, but that's 20-20 hindsight. You knew what a man is, but you didn't throw it in his face. You were mentally unbalanced, but you never let it show up in bed. That's a good woman in my book.

(*A middle-aged woman, Roy's wife Mona, wearing only a slip, high heels and a strand of pearls around her neck, appears on the ridge behind them. She carries a pistol.*)

ROY: You are my damn baby, R.V. honey, and any woman since you've gone is just passin' the time.

(*At this moment, Mona on the ridge raises the pistol and fires down on Roy. He and Clem scramble.*)

ROY: Hold it.

CLEM: (*Simultaneously.*) Don't shoot.

MONA: (*Holding Roy's gray suit on a hanger in her other hand.*) You are my nightmare, Roy Mannering! (*She fires again.*) You are a maggot b-b-born in the dung, b-burrowed down in my flesh eating me alive! I hitchhiked out here, so here's your g-g-gray suit! (*She flings it down into the dump.*)

ROY: You hitchhiked in your underwear?

(*She fires again.*)

ROY: Mona, that's enough now.

CLEM: Jeeminy.

MONA: I c-curse you, Roy. I c-call demons from their d-dank c-caves and crevices the c-creatures of the night to g-give you prostate cancer and Lou G-Gehrig's disease, and make you impotent that one t-time every c-couple of months you can still get it up.

ROY: You've got to relax if you want to stop stuttering, Mona.

(*She fires again.*)

MONA: Your teenage whore assistant called me up to say you were t-taking her to the Mayor's c-c-c-c-c-conference next week. She said you b-bought her a sapphire and d-d-diamond ring. Said you were divorcing me and m-m-m-m-marrying her. She said you called me a c-c-corpse with jewelry, Roy. Well, I am. I am eaten up with l-l-loathing for m-myself, and you taught m-me that with your fiendish c-c-c-criticism and little jokes and p-patronizing ways. I looked in the mirror t-t-tonight and I saw my b-bleached b-brain an' my d-dead eyes an' I said Mona, what b-became of you? Where are you, Mona?

(*The door of the junked car in the lot opens quietly, and Moon, dressed in jeans and a skull t-shirt with an army field jacket over it, boots and an old kerchief around his head, steps out. He is bearded and in every way piratical.*)

MONA: I curse your sons and your sons' sons that they should be b-born without testicles, blind as newts, and they should disinter your corpse and rifle through your pockets for spare change. Now I'm going to shoot your p-puffy head off, and that will make me feel considerably better. (*She raises the gun again.*)

MOON: (*In his left hand, he carries a stubby full automatic as if it were an extension of his arm. As she raises the gun, he speaks consolingly.*) Good evening, ma'am.

(*She turns, pointing the gun at him.*)

I had a friend used to stutter until his confidence caught up with his heart.

CLEM: Moon.

MOON: How you doin'? Well ma'am, I'd have to agree with you about Roy, untutored as he is, he probably thinks you're a household appliance. He just don't know what a woman is, ma'am, and he's just unteachable as a rooster.

ROY: What the hell, Moon?

MOON: Shut up, Roy. Now ma'am, I'm a brute killer for pay, and they tell me I'm one of the dozen best shots in the world, left-handed or right. May I call you Mona? Mona, what you're holdin' there is a Rossi 518 Tiger Cat Special, accurate up to about 40 feet and, combined with your understandable emotion and inexperience, you most likely won't hit me, whereas, my first couple of rounds will tear off your wrist, leavin' you with one hand for the rest of your life. They tell me the pain's unendurable unless we cauterized it with fire, and by the time we got some kindlin', you'd likely bleed to death. It's strange when you can see right inside your own body like you can when an extremity's gone. We never know what we are because we're covered with skin. Once you find out, you realize we're just walkin' meat. Now I'd feel more comfortable if you'd point that thing at Roy, if you don't mind.

(*She does.*)

ROY: Damn, Moon.

MOON: Well I feel a whole lot better. Much obliged. Now what can we do for you, ma'am?

MONA: K-K-K-Kill him.

ROY: Moon?

MOON: (*To Roy.*) There's no punishment in death, ma'am. It's over in the blink of an eye. The thing I like least about killin' people is how easy they get off. Hell, he stole your life from you. Wouldn't you say that's the situation?

MONA: I was...I was...I had dreams.

MOON: Sure, I know. You got some place you could go?

MONA: Clem's wife, Evelyn, she called from Arizona.

CLEM: Arizona?

MONA: She says it's n-nice. She l-lives with the Navajos.

CLEM: My Evelyn?

MONA: She said I could c-c-come out there.

MOON: You know what you get out there, ma'am? You get yourself a shadow, so you don't get lonely.

MONA: But I don't have the money. He didn't let me work.

MOON: Well see, he is so small. He is such a small person he could only enlarge himself at your expense.

ROY: Now that's just damned well enough.

MOON: She's going to kill you, Roy, we're lookin' for alternatives.

ROY: She can't hit the side of a barn.

MOON: She isn't stuttering, Roy. Her hand's steady. You ought to hold that with two hands, ma'am. Sort of like this.

(*He demonstrates. She changes her grip.*)

ROY: Dammit!

MOON: She might get lucky, put one right up your nose.

ROY: I don't know you.

MOON: Ma'am, I believe I'm goin' to take up a collection, how about that? Gimme' your wallets, boys.

(*They don't respond.*)

MOON: I said gimme' your goddamn wallets!

(*They throw them on the ground.*)

MOON: I get real pissed off at myself, the course I've taken. I should have got into robbery, it's just so damn easy. (*Picks them up. He looks.*) You don't mind if your pretty wife goes on a little shoppin' spree, will you, Roy?

(*Roy glowers.*)

MOON: So now I'm comin' up there, ma'am. Roy, throw me over your car keys, will you?

ROY: I am not givin' you my car keys.

MOON: What are you drivin' these days?

ROY: No way. No damn way.

MOON: Go ahead, ma'am, shoot him.

(*She fires. Roy hits the ground. She misses.*)

ROY: Goddammit to hell. Son of a bitch.

MOON: That was about a foot left, ma'am. And if you wouldn't mind a little advice, I wouldn't go for the head, I'd go for the gut.

ROY: All right. All right. I'm gettin' the keys.

MOON: How are you doin', Clem?

CLEM: Well, Evelyn run off.

MOON: Sorry to hear that. You better have a drink.

CLEM: (*Pulling out the flask.*) Okay, Moon.

MOON: There's a case to be made for finishin' the century blind drunk.

CLEM: Care for a dollop?

(*Clem, having taken a hit, passes the flask to Moon.*)

MOON: Well, I don't mind. (*Drinks.*) How about you, Mona?

MONA: (*A roar.*) I hate men!

MOON: Me too, ma'am. (*Drinks.*)

ROY: There. (*Tosses the keys.*) This is egregious damn car theft.

MOON: Tell him "shut up," ma'am.

MONA: Shut up!

MOON: Here I come now. (*Starts up toward Mona.*) Just bringin' the wallets and the car keys. Get you started, you know, before the divorce.

MONA: I was g-good at math.

MOON: Yes ma'am.

MONA: I was better than the boys.

(*He nods.*)

MOON: Yes ma'am.

MONA: I could have done r-research on the universe.

MOON: Well, you're still young, ma'am.

MONA: No, I'm not. I'm dried out.

MOON: (*Puts the wallets down near her.*) Well, you look a little chilly. You might like to put this around your shoulders. (*He puts his field jacket down on the ground. He looks off.*) Clem, are you drivin' that Mazda Miata or the Chrysler?

CLEM: I'm the Mazda, Moon.

MOON: Good for you, Roy, you bought American made. Hey, Clem, would she still take 79 South and then 64 West? It's been a long time.

CLEM: 64 to 44, then take Interstate 40 west all the way.

MOON: Down to Arizona?

CLEM: Yes sir, headin' west.

MOON: Nice two-day drive.

MONA: I'm too old, Moon.

MOON: Ma'am, Buddha said a good fire can only be made from seasoned wood. The point isn't to end the journey, the point is to make the journey.

MONA: I made the journey with you, Roy. I thought I would rest easy and you would care for me. I knew I wasn't a beautiful, wild creature like that R.V., but I thought we could make a quiet life, Roy. That's a horse laugh. A woman's just disposable goods to you. I gave myself over an' forgot who I was, but those days are over and gone, Roy. I'm makin' my own movie now, and you're just something in the rearview mirror to me. I let your tropical fish go free in the creek; I burned your Louis L'Amour first editions, and I pushed your satellite dish off the roof. I'm an outlaw now, Roy, no one will ever treat me that way again.

MOON: Louis L'Amour would despise you, Roy. (*To Roy and Clem.*) Take off those belts! Do it!

CLEM: I don't have a belt, Moon.

MOON: Lie down on your stomachs. (*Takes off his own belt and, with Roy's, expertly belts the two brothers' hands behind them.*) It took me four planes, an oxcart, and I forded a river on a man's back to get here, boys. Had to sell the gold teeth I'd been collectin' to get it done. See, I wanted to be here for R.V., do a little business, see my big brothers and take a little vacation from gettin' people down on the ground and tyin' them up with their belts. I guess it just shows you're a prisoner of your talents. That isn't too tight, is it?

CLEM: It feels real nice, Moon.

MOON: (*Looking over his handiwork.*) Well, okay... (*Up to Mona.*) You might want to get started, ma'am.

MONA: Are you the worst?

MOON: Beg pardon?

MONA: You have raped and pillaged and slaughtered?

MOON: More or less.

MONA: Are you the worst of men? I need a b-benchmark.

MOON: Well I don't know, ma'am. I guess I'm close enough to be competitive.

MONA: Then I'll k-keep the pistol.

MOON: Good idea. Say, you know what they do all over the world?

MONA: Who?

MOON: Those who have prevailed. Those who have brought their enemies to their knees and made them eat the dust of the road. It doesn't matter if it's Medellin or Kumasi or Kuala Lumpor, they fire their weapons in the air. They empty themselves into the universe in celebration. (*He hands her his automatic weapon.*)

ROY: My God, are you deranged?!

MOON: Go ahead, ma'am.

(*Mona looks at him and then fires a long burst in the air.*)

MOON: Feels good, huh?

MONA: It feels g-g-g-glorious! (*She hands back the automatic, keeping the pistol.*)

MOON: (*She smiles for the first time.*) Well, you might want to get goin', ma'am. Keep your mind real empty and close to hand, that'll let it heal up. You might want to put on some clothes, but everybody's got their own way.

MONA: Good-bye, Moon.

MOON: Adios, babe.

MONA: (*She turns to Roy and Clem.*) Good-bye, Clem. Good-bye, Roy. I'm sorry I was such a bad shot. I'm free now. When I'm out in Arizona, I'm going to take this money and raise b-bees. Millions of b-bees. Then with the aphrodisiac of my freedom, I will lure men to hotel rooms. I will tie them to the b-bed with silk scarves for a g-good time. Then I will place the queen b-bee on their penis and when they are completely covered with the swarm, I will leave them there to figure it out. (*She exits.*)

MOON: Nice night, beautiful stars, minimum of snipers. That's what I call perfect conditions.

ROY: Untie me, you bastard.

MOON: How come you're dressed up like an Amish farmer, Roy?

ROY: Do you know what a divorce is goin' to cost me?

MOON: That's just overhead, Roy, it was comin' on anyway, you just have to amortize it.

CLEM: There's ants in my shirt, Moon.

MOON: I'm goin' to smoke me a Cuban cigar, Clem. They roll these babies on the inside of a beautiful woman's thigh. One of the few luxuries left.

CLEM: My wife left me too.

MOON: Everybody's wife leaves, Clem, it's a shit job.

CLEM: How am I goin' to raise my boys?

MOON: Just tell 'em to do the opposite.

CLEM: The opposite?

MOON: I wouldn't worry about it, Clem. (*Moon lights up.*)

ROY: My own brother robbed me.

MOON: You can get on the phone and cancel the cards, they got all-night service.

ROY: I'm talkin' about my car! You stole my car.

MOON: A Chrysler ain't a car, Roy, it's just upholstery on wheels. (*Suddenly the dump is alive with movement. Small black shapes scurry everywhere.*)

ROY: My God, what's that?

MOON: Looks like the rats are leavin' the dump, Roy.

ROY: Untie me, goddamnit.

MOON: I once saw rats eat a man alive. They ate him in circles like a corn dog.

CLEM: I'm scared of rats, Moon.

MOON: (*Looks up at the stars.*) You both owe me money. (*Silence falls.*)

ROY: Now Moon, this isn't the time to talk about that. This is a time for three brothers, lost to each other by geography, to take hands, kneel down…

MOON: You owe me for the fishing cabin Pop left me that you sold for me in '86.

ROY: Moon, that cabin was in bad shape.

MOON: How much did you get for it?

ROY: …water damaged, rotted out.

MOON: How much, Roy?

ROY: Maybe $1,300, well, no, a little bit less.

MOON: You sold 1.3 acres down on the river for $1,300?

ROY: Hey little brother, this was eight years ago.

MOON: It was appraised 20 years ago at $7,500.

ROY: Are you accusing me of cheatin' my own damn family?

MOON: Yes.

ROY: There is no bond like blood, Moon, and there is nothing so despicable as to doubt it.

CLEM: Mighta been $5,000, Moon.

MOON: That's good, Clem, and when you started your pawnshop I fronted you $5,000, which was ten percent of the capital.

CLEM: Would you care for some Cheezits, Moon?

MOON: You sure that pawnshop didn't grow into your gun store? Because you would owe me ten cents on every dollar of profit.

CLEM: No. No, the pawnshop and the gun shop, that was two completely different enterprises.

MOON: I see. You still located down on the strip across from the Pentacostal Tabernacle of Simple Faith?

CLEM: Well, no, we kind of shifted over toward the water, when I changed over to family security.

MOON: Uh-huh.

CLEM: Riverfront development, you know.

MOON: It wouldn't be located on 1.3 acres of riverfront property, now would it? (*Pause.*) Would it, Clem?

CLEM: (*Pause.*) Come to think of it, Moon, Roy and me might owe you a small sum, and we'd sure like to settle up. Don't you think so, Roy?

ROY: Well, now that we think of it.

MOON: Sounds good to me, boys, because I'm thinkin' of openin' up a chain of coin laundries over in Albania.

CLEM: Albania.

MOON: Clem, those people really need their clothes done.

CLEM: Sounds like a real opportunity.

MOON: *(Rises.)* Well, boys, I look forward to settlin' up.

ROY: There's nothin' that people of good will can't work out.

MOON: There better not be. *(Moves to untie them.)* Say, Roy, there's some barrels in the dump labeled Phinoethylbarmetholine. Don't they use that stuff in nerve gas?

ROY: *(A beat.)* No, actually it's used in barbecue sauce, stuff like that.

MOON: Sure, that must be where I remembered it from.

ROY: We can work the money out, Moon.

MOON: Okay.

ROY: Well, I got a Fourth of July speech to give.

MOON: So.

ROY: I got to go *now*. Gimme your keys, Clem.

CLEM: We got to finish the sacred trust, Roy.

ROY: Goddammit.

MOON: We got to finish the sacred trust, Roy.

ROY: You can't have your community festivities until the mayor speaks to nail down the significance. That is *democracy* which you two wouldn't know a damn thing about.

MOON: Democracy, sure. Hey, I'm out there killin' people for the free enterprise system.

ROY: You're just out there killin' people.

MOON: When you start a democracy you have to kill a few people, if you know your history.

ROY: You don't know squat about history, Moon.

MOON: I was in Nam, man, I *am* history.

ROY: You're history all right, it was the first damn war we ever lost.

CLEM: Now hold on, Roy.

MOON: Are you mockin' my dead buddies?

CLEM: Now hold on, Moon.

ROY: I been workin' 20 years to fix what you and your buddies screwed up!

MOON: *(Starting for him.)* I'm gonna' rip your head off.

CLEM: *(Out of desperation.)* Mama's dead.
    (Moon stops in mid-charge.)

MOON: What's that?

CLEM: I didn't know if you knew Mama's dead?

MOON: When?

CLEM: July of '91. We didn't know where you were, Moon. We tried Soldier of Fortune magazine.

MOON: How'd Mama go?

CLEM: It was cancer, Moon, it wasn't too bad, she went pretty easy.

MOON: Goddamnit to hell! Was it the cigarettes?

CLEM: I don't know, Moon.

MOON: I told you to get her on to the low tar. I told you to take those Camel cigarettes away from her.

CLEM: I tried, Moon, but...

MOON: Damn! Buried or cremated?

CLEM: Moon, I just don't think...

MOON: Which was it?

CLEM: Cremated.

MOON: Aarrrgh! (*Moon, in a rage, slings trash across the dump.*) A man don't want his mother cremated! You understand that?

ROY: Well, she left instructions.

MOON: Instructions? Piss on the instructions! I want my Mama's grave! Where is she, goddamnit?

CLEM: Scattered.

MOON: (*Sitting down.*) You made bonemeal outta' my Mama.

CLEM: Well Moon, she didn't want to be a bother, see. She didn't want us worried about the upkeep. She just wanted to disperse.

MOON: You two morons went and dispersed her?

ROY: Well, we...

MOON: Dispersed her *where*, damnit?

CLEM: Wendy's.

MOON: Wendy's Fast Food?

CLEM: Well, she stopped cookin' with everybody gone and she liked to go down to the Wendy's.

MOON: You spread our Mama out at a fast food restaurant?

ROY: In the daylily garden.

MOON: I can't kneel down at a fast food restaurant and ask my Mama what to do.

CLEM: Well you could, Moon.

MOON: Never mind!

CLEM: It's a real busy corner though.

MOON: I don't want to talk about it. (*Throws his head back.*) R.V.!? The world's goin' to hell, R.V. Mama's dispersed. You're dead. Roy and Clem cheated on me. Communism wimped out. My trigger hand shakes. Where the hell are we? What the hell's goin' on?!!

CLEM: I'll get the beer.

MOON: (*A moment. He calms.*) I still remember your smell, R.V., the curve of your thigh. I don't know why you killed yourself, but you're sure as hell well out of it. You could gentle me down, I remember that. We never got to say good-bye, so I'm here to do it. Hell, I'm only 20 years late, that's not too bad. You asked for it, an' I'm doin' it, but I tell you what, R.V., I'm tired of dead people. They're piled up, one on top of the other, everywhere you go on this planet. Damn, I'm tired of *that* smell. You an' me were two crazy sons-of-bitches, and that always gave me some comfort. I tell you one thing, R.V., I hope wherever you are you still got that red dress and that snake tattoo.

(*R.V. appears again on the car behind them.*)

Heaven for climate, hell for company. Let's chug these beers.

(*They do. R.V. speaks from behind them.*)

R.V.: Did you love me, Moon?

(*The men turn, startled.*)

R.V.: Holy shit, you got old!

(*Clem slumps to the ground in a faint.*)

MOON: Is that you, R.V.?

R.V.: It's me, Moon.

ROY: (*To Moon.*) You see her, right?

MOON: I see her.

R.V.: I forgot you would get old.

ROY: Go on now, whatever you are. Go on, shoo! Shoo!

R.V.: Hello, Roy.

ROY: Looks just like the day she died.

MOON: What is it you want, R.V.?

R.V.: I bring the messenger to...say, is Clem all right?

ROY: Damn, but she looks real to the touch.

R.V.: Real to the touch?

(*She walks directly to Moon and involves him in a long kiss. Roy talks through it. Clem moans.*)

ROY: Shut up, Clem. Is she real, Moon? What's she feel like, Moon? I wouldn't do that, Moon. Hell, she could be a vampire.

(*She steps back from him. Their eyes are locked.*)

MOON: Your lips are cold.

R.V.: I wrote you 1,200 letters in Nam. I got two postcards.

MOON: It was a bad time.

R.V.: How's the Buddha, Moon?

MOON: I lost track.

R.V.: Where'd you go when you left Nam?

MOON: Angola for awhile, Rhodesia, Ghana, Yemen, Burundi, Salvador, Somalia, a little while in the Seychelles, Afghanistan, Azerbaijan, shacked up for a time in Albania, 26 days in Cambodia, two years near Zagreb, and I was down around Liberia when this came up.

R.V.: You know I married Roy.

MOON: Damn R.V., what'd you do that for?

R.V.: I was having nightmares.

MOON: Were you drunk?

R.V.: Some of the time. Shoot, Moon, back then he was the next best thing.

ROY: Thanks a helluva damn lot.

R.V.: Beggin' your pardon, Roy.

CLEM: (*Reviving.*) Roy! Roy!

ROY: (*Annoyed.*) What is it, Clem?

CLEM: (*Not seeing R.V.*) She was *here,* Roy.

ROY: Clem, damn it…

CLEM: No, no, I saw her. I saw R.V. So help me, no kiddin'. Wearin' the red dress just like the last night. I'm not foolin, Roy.
(*Roy points. Clem looks.*)

CLEM: Oh, my God, the graves are opening. It's the last judgment, Roy, it's on us. My God, humble yourself.

ROY: Will you be quiet, Clem?

CLEM: (*Drinks from his flask, sings.*) "Swing lo', sweet char-i-ot, comin' for to carry me home…"

MOON: Clem, knock that off!

R.V.: What's shakin', Clem?

CLEM: Oh my God, oh my God, oh my God, oh my God.

R.V.: (*R.V.: touches him on the cheek. He quiets.*) I had Clem one time, too. I had Clem and Roy 'cause you never answered my letters.

MOON: Come on, R.V.!

ROY: Clem!?

CLEM: Oh my God, oh my God.

ROY: You didn't have Clem? Not while we were married, was it?

R.V.: It was just one time, Roy.

ROY: While we were married?

CLEM: It was just one time, Roy.

ROY: (*To Clem.*) You're my own damn blood and you screwed my wife?!

MOON: That's pretty low, R.V.

ROY: It wasn't in my house, was it?

MOON: You said you were waitin' for me.

ROY: You better answer me, Clem!

CLEM: It was in the garden.

ROY: In the garden? It wasn't near Mama's daylilies, was it?

CLEM: Heck no, Roy, it was over in the phlox. You were sleepin'; it didn't mean to happen.

ROY: I just can't believe this!

R.V.: Roy, you and I were hardly makin' love at all.

ROY: Worst case, we always did it once a week.

R.V.: Yeah, Tuesdays.

ROY: It wasn't only on Tuesdays.

CLEM: We didn't do it on a Tuesday, Roy.

ROY: Shut up. Godawful, R.V., ol' Clem puffin' away in the missionary position.

R.V.: Not quite, Roy.

ROY: What do you mean, *not quite?*

CLEM: Well, I'm double-jointed, Roy.

ROY: Goddamnit!

R.V.: He was the only one of you boys ever loved me. Why the hell are you gettin' riled up? I'm dead, for one thing. He'd bring me coffee, get me car parts, roll my joints, remember my damn birthday, and come down every night to hear me sing at the Holiday Inn. He loved me like a dog; why shouldn't he get laid one time?

MOON: Because it's Clem, damn it!

R.V.: Roy was passed out. I couldn't sleep. The moon was real orange over the hills, so I walked out into the garden and there was Clem sittin' on the bench.

ROY: You didn't go out there naked, did you?

R.V.: I went out there naked all the time. It was 3:00 AM, who cared?

CLEM: I was just out walkin', Roy. I just sat down there for a minute.

ROY: You are a snake in the woodpile.

R.V.: We just sat there on the bench. He told me I looked like a statue in the moonlight. He said he come there some nights when we were asleep, he'd sit there and hope me and him were breathing in and out at the same time. We just sat there, whispering, with our shoulders touching, and after awhile we lay down in the phlox. You did real good, Clem.

CLEM: Thank you, R.V. You want some Cheezits?

R.V.: Sure.

ROY: Why the hell didn't you love me, R.V.? Goddamnit, I'm lovable. I'm a hard worker, ambitious, patriotic; I'm a damn fine provider, like to dance, I got a serious side. Why the hell didn't you love me?

R.V.: You're just too much man, Roy.

ROY: Well, I can't shrivel myself up to win a woman's love. I can't downsize what I am, R.V., I got to let it roll! It's like this country is what it's like. Those pissant third worlds can't stand the sheer magnificent expanse of us. They can't take their eyes off us, but they want to cut us down to size. It's tragic grandeur, that's what I got! Goddamnit, woman, you should have *loved* me!!

R.V.: It's not a function of the will, Roy.

(*A moment.*)

MOON: You're sure you're dead, R.V.?

R.V.: Deader than hell.

CLEM: There was omens, Roy, the Gifford horse, the frogs, the way the sky was. I must have seen 15 possum in a bunch headin' south on the highway, and a possum he travels alone.

R.V.: How about a beer, boys? A cold one for the road.

ROY: You want a beer?

R.V.: You get pretty dry when you're dead, Roy.

MOON: Get the lady a beer, will you?

ROY: I have got to get over to the...

R.V.: You can't go, Roy, you've been chosen.

ROY: What do you mean, chosen?

R.V.: Chosen, Roy.

(*Clem hands out the beer.*)

R.V.: How come you were sleeping in the dump, Moon?

MOON: I got in late last night. I can't sleep indoors, it makes me dream.

R.V.: Dream what?

MOON: Things I've done.

ROY: What do you mean chosen?

MOON: Outdoors, I've been dreaming about you.

R.V.: I know. (*She pops the beer and proposes a toast.*) To the white man, God help him.

(*Clem, Moon and R.V. drink.*)

ROY: What kind of toast is that?

MOON: Where are you, R.V.?

R.V.: Say what?

MOON: When you're not here?

R.V.: Heaven.

CLEM: Oh my Lord, there is life after death?

R.V.: Well, I'm drinkin' my beer, Clem.

CLEM: Moon, Roy, can you believe this. We're sittin' in the dump, and it's been revealed!

MOON: Take it easy, Clem.

CLEM: What do you do there? What's it like, R.V.?

R.V.: It's pure unadulterated longing. It's like you lost a leg but there's still feeling where the leg used to be. The feeling is for the life you didn't live, and you pass the time until you find some way to make yourself whole.

CLEM: Sure, but what's it like?

R.V.: The one you guys have is a celestial theme park with a thousand T.V. channels, continual sex and a 5,000 hole golf course.

ROY: Jee-sus!

R.V.: I go over sometimes for the salad bar.

MOON: Are you kiddin', R.V.?

R.V.: Could be.

ROY: I said chosen for what, damnit?

MOON: How you like it up there?

R.V.: Too damn serene.

MOON: Yeah?

R.V.: I tried to kill myself up there, too. Hell, you know, just for variety. Hurled myself down the cloud canyons. Forget it. Once you're immortal, you're immortal.

MOON: Sounds like a tough gig.

R.V.: It's a perception thing, Moon. See, I only got the perception I took up there, and that just doesn't cut it, you know. I took the messenger gig because I figured you could help me out. I'm locked inside 25 years, Moon. I only get the heaven 25 years can understand. Hell, you must be close to 50. Tell me what you know.

MOON: Shoot low and shoot first.

R.V.: Goddamnit Moon, I'm not jokin'.

MOON: Who said I was jokin', R.V.?

R.V.: Move me on, Moon, don't leave me where I am.

MOON: Got me a limited perspective.

R.V.: You lived all those years and only got smaller?

MOON: I yam what I yam, babe.

R.V.: Well, damn! (*She kicks something across the dump.*) How come this dump's sittin' on the ball field?

ROY: The dump's the whole point, R.V.

R.V.: What point?

ROY: The point. Town was fallin' apart, R.V. The town, the job pool, the tax base.

CLEM: Dollar movie closed down.

ROY: I said to myself, Roy, what is this country based on? And by God it came to me, it's based on garbage. There is nobody in the world has the garbage we do! (*He pulls stuff out of the dump.*) Blenders, TV's, Lazyboys, syringes! We did a little study showed that within one truck day of this town, two billion tons of garbage produced weekly. Bingo! You know where people want to put their garbage? Somewhere else, that's where. And there is no damn town in this country that is more somewhere else than we are. And I sold that idea, by God, and it saved the town. We got the dump here plus nine other locations. I'm not sayin' I can walk on water, but I'll tell you this here is a damn miracle.

R.V.: So the ball field's down there?

CLEM: Down there somewhere. (*Finishes the flask, throws it away.*)

R.V.: How come you started throwin' those change ups, Moon?

MOON: How come you drove off the bridge?

R.V.: You ever been airborne in a Corvette Stingray on a cool night at 145 miles an hour?

MOON: No ma'am.

R.V.: Hang time, it's a real rush. Damn, I love speed. What was I supposed to do, Moon? Stick around, do hair stylin' at Babettes, work part-time at the Seashell Gift Shop, make chocolate chip cookies down at Suzi's Love Oven?! Blow that crap out your ear, man.

CLEM: You could sing, R.V.

R.V.: Good enough for the Holiday Inn Lounge, huh, Clem?

CLEM: I came every night.

R.V.: Bunch of drunks in bad ties, yellin' out "Moon River." Yeah, I could sing that good.

CLEM: You was pearls before swine.

R.V.: Thanks, baby. Ol' Jimmy Dean an' me, we weren't countin' on tomorrow, see? You think I'm gonna drag a broke life behind me down Main Street, like some old rusty tailpipe kickin' up sparks? Hell with that, man! That night I flew the Corvette, I put on my red dress an' I looked fine! I was wearin' the hell out of that thing, you dig? Figured it was time to go out large, so I just slipped my good lookin' legs into some red rhinestone heels and put the pedal to the metal!

CLEM: We could see you go off the bridge from down at Bob's Big Boy parkin' lot. Slow motion right across the moon.

R.V.: Sure, I could see you boys standin' still lookin' up. Hell, 20 years later you're still there. You look sad, Moon. Is it me or the bridge?

MOON: What bridge?

R.V.: Your bridge.

MOON: What the hell are you talking about?

R.V.: The bridge in Liberia. (*A beat.*)

MOON: How do you know that, R.V.?

R.V.: I keep track, Moon.

MOON: Then why ask me?

R.V.: To see if you have the balls to tell me.

MOON: Just a bridge we held.

R.V.: Yeah?

MOON: Yeah.

R.V.: Just a bridge, huh?

MOON: Only way you could still get over into Sierra Leone. We didn't blow it 'cause we had to run transport through there once the town fell.

R.V.: Go on, Moon.

R.V. AND MOON: (*He is unaware that she speaks with him.*) The bridge stretched out like an old rusty skeleton between two hills…

R.V.: Tell it, Moon.

MOON: Those people...

R.V.: Those people...

MOON: Kept tryin' to come across it.

R.V.: That's right.

MOON: Everybody's snipers up in the hills.

R.V.: (*In sync, she sees it too.*) Man in a big brown coat...

MOON: Midday, somebody tried to run it.

R.V.: Uh-huh.

MOON: Looked like a man in a big coat. I was in the hills...

R.V.: Uh-huh.

MOON: I fired a rifle grenade into the coat...

R.V.: It didn't explode...

MOON: Didn't explode, but the coat opened up and it was a woman...

R.V. AND MOON: ...carrying a young child.

MOON: (*Hypnotized now by memory's image.*) That rifle grenade nailed the child to the mother's chest...

R.V.: Down there on the bridge...

MOON AND R.V.: ...and they lay, mother and child, nailed together on the bridge for two days...

MOON: See, nobody dared try to go out there and get 'em.

MOON AND R.V.: Lay there screaming...

R.V.: On the bridge...

MOON AND R.V.: Screaming.

MOON: Finally I took a rifle, blew up that grenade on the second shot.

R.V.: Then what, Moon?

MOON: I stayed there another day. Then I walked out, following the river. Took me three weeks.

R.V.: How come?

MOON: I figured I'd try something else.

R.V.: Like my bridge?

MOON: Your bridge?

R.V.: Right across the sky.

MOON: No thanks, R.V.

R.V..: What is it you know, Moon?

MOON: A piece of shit doesn't throw a perfect game.

ROY: You threw the damn game on purpose?

MOON: Shut up, Roy.

R.V.: It's getting late, Moon.

MOON: Could be.

R.V.: You don't have somethin' for me?

MOON: Not a damn thing.

R.V.: Well, it's time to get started, boys. (*She raises her arm, one finger pointing up, and there is a shattering crash of thunder. She raises her other arm.*) Spirits of wind, water, earth and fire, enwrap me here! (*Thunder, lightning.*) I am appeared before you, sent by the lord of hosts. She who is both the tumult and the eye of the hurricane. She who throweth up continents and maketh men from the fish of the sea. Hear me. Hear me!
(*The rain pours down on everyone except R.V. Clem raises his small umbrella. Roy and Moon are drenched.*)

R.V.: I come at her behest to be the harbinger of her great messenger. Through him will the blind see, the broken mend and the heart be made whole. (*A powerful beam of light pours down on her.*) Great spirit, King, right hand of the all-powerful, we welcome thee! Hold onto your seats, boys, he is upon us now!
(*A tremendous explosion, as if the stage had been struck in two by a lightning bolt. The rain stops. Smoke, debris and then sudden silence. Elvis appears. He is dressed in his "suit of lights," the famous white sequined performance suit. A driving guitar riff and final chord surround his entrance. He is the same age as at his death.*)

CLEM: My God, who are you?

ELVIS: I'm the King of the White Man, asshole, who are you?

CLEM: Elvis?

ELVIS: The Velvet Rocker, buddy, the Hillbilly Cat, the King of Western Bop.

CLEM: You thinned down, King.

ELVIS: I been dinin' on cumulus Nimbus.

ROY: Kinda' lost your magnitude.

ELVIS: Well, I'm not dressed up as a Smith Brothers cough drop. I'll tell y'all one thing, boys, there wasn't nobody, nowhere, no time, no way, ever seen a white boy move like me. They couldn't shake it where I shook it or take it where I took it. I was born with a guitar in one hand and the ruination of western civilization in the other. Y'all look a little tight there, boys, so the King's gotta' get you ready to party! Heck, have some Dexedrine... (*He scatters hundreds of pills in a multi-colored spray from his pockets as if they were coins for the multitudes.*) Have some Tuinal, Dilaudid, Quaaludes and Demerol! Get up, or get down, get wherever you need to be to hear the *word!* (*Lightning crackles, framing his figure in its flash.*)

CLEM: (*Picking some up.*) Thanks, King.

ELVIS: Uh-huh! Hit it! (*Another crash and sizzle of lightning.*) The Lord, she stood on the rim of the universe, and she did regard the earth, baby. And wherever her gaze did fall there was real bad doody goin' down. There was a sickly caste, a dread pigmentless, soulless, milky pale fungi suckin' the sustenance right out of the world, man, leavin' things undone, done badly, overlooked, overgrazed, snafued and skimmin' the cream right off the top. And who the hell was in the driver's seat takin' care of business? Buddy, it was a bunch of fat old white men, that's who it was! Greedy ol' farts livin' off the fat of the land while the land fell apart in their hands. They weren't gettin' it there, dudes! You can't rhumba in a sports car, baby. You can't do no Australian crawl in a shot glass. We had it, man, and we pissed it away! Regard me, brethren. I was the most beautiful cat ever rolled into Memphis in a '39 Plymouth. I could sing black boogie and the Mississippi Delta blues. I could shuck and jive like a funky angel. I was the white man triumphant, baby. If I wanted it *now,* I got it *now.* I was the boss, the king, El Presidente Grande, and I ended up fat as a grain-fed hog, down on my knees on the bathroom floor with my head floatin' in a toilet bowl. Hell, you're down in the bowl with me, boys. Y'all had played errorless, no-hit ball goin' into the eighth inning, and you took it from there to the dung heap, poisoned in spirit and your women flee you into the night with whatever they can carry.

CLEM: (*Delighted.*) He's talkin' about us, boys!

ELVIS: She-it, compadres! The last time the Lord saw somethin' like this, she had the game rained out, man but the Lord wouldn't even trust you cats to build an ark! Huh-uh! She was set to hurl the white man into the eternal dark and see what somebody else could do with it. My people were goin' down, baby, the bell was tollin' the midnight hour, cats, so I had the cherubim and seraphim deliver me to the Lord's right hand an' I whipped out my guitar and shucked out a tune, boys.

CLEM: We love you, Elvis!

ELVIS: (*He throws out his hand and an unseen band crashes into a rock and roll riff. Elvis' voice is now amplified.*) I rocked it, baby, laid down a hot lick, turned it every way but loose, like you know I can, and there amongst the beatific host, the Lord, she got down, she got tight, she got right with my music, and she boogied through the day, and a night, and a day and when I sent that last reverb down through the chambers of her immortal heart, she said, "Elvis, I thought I'd seen it all when I saw Lucifer, but the way you're rockin' tonight, I'm gonna give the white man one *(Chord.)* more *(Chord.)* chance." *(Chord. The music ends.)* And I said, "Lord, I'm hip and I'm on it, what's the deal?" And she laid her cool hand on my cheek and asked did I remember what my precious mama said to me when I done wrong and lied about it. And I said, "Yes Lord, I do." She said, "Sonny boy, there ain't nothin' done in this old world so debauched and brought low that you can't get right with your God and your mama with just two little words... *(The big finish.)* and listen here now, those two words, those two paradisiacal confections, sweet as plums or summer cherries, those two words are...I'm sorry!" *(A pause. Distant thunder rolls. The words "I'm Sorry" echo through the heavens.)*

MOON: Hey Elvis?

ELVIS: Yeah?

MOON: The Lord God wants us to say we're sorry?

ELVIS: Uh-huh.

MOON: Just "I'm sorry?"

ELVIS: Well, it's kind of a cosmic thing, man. But you got it, yeah. Otherwise she's gonna' send down the white flu, let it blanket the earth, uh-huh, all you white guys sneeze yourself right into eternity inside of two weeks.

CLEM: The white flu!?

ROY: What the hell are we s'posed to have done?

ELVIS: (*His arms wide.*) This.

ROY: Hey, everybody throws things away, okay?

ELVIS: But who was runnin' the store, buddy?

ROY: Well, it wasn't me, big guy.

ELVIS: Well, who the hell was it?

ROY: Hell, you got your media, your cartels, your multi-nationals, your big government.

ELVIS: And who was runnin' them?

ROY: How the hell am I supposed to know?

ELVIS: Well, let's just say they weren't purple, how about that?

ROY: I'm damn tired of everybody talkin' trash on the white man. Hell, we thought up about 90% of civilization. It was 12 of our own kind sat with Christ at his table. If these goddamn minorities shoulda' led us somewhere, why didn't they step up to the plate! (*He sneezes explosively.*)

ELVIS: Sounds like you're comin' down with somethin'. Say, R.V., how about some seraphim send us down a milkshake, maybe put an egg in it?

(*R.V. snaps her fingers.*)

CLEM: Say, King...

ELVIS: Uh-huh?

CLEM: You kinda lost me on the curve, King.

(*The milkshake descends from the flies.*)

ELVIS: Hell, y'all explain it, R.V., I'm gonna take a load off. (*Takes the milkshake and makes himself comfortable.*)

R.V.: Hear me, fishermen. (*Lightning.*) You, before me, of all those assembled, are the chosen. The bellwethers, the forerunners, you hold redemption in the palm of your hand!

ELVIS: She ain't kiddin'.

R.V.: See Clem, the Lord, she asked me did I know any white guys, and I said sure.

CLEM: How come she asked you, R.V.?

R.V.: I was just standin' there. She touched my snake tattoo, filling me with light, saying I should pave the way and we should proclaim the news.

ELVIS: (*Drinking his milkshake.*) Do it, iridescent one.

R.V.: Attend me, white ones! (*Sizzling lightning crash.*) The Lord God, the First Cause, the Celestial She, the Big Femina, instructs you here to prepare your hearts and set out on foot from this place to great Washington Monument in the city yclept "D.C." and to carry on that journey of the spirit a sign of apology.

CLEM: Gollee Roy, we could do that!

R.V.: Your garments shall you here divest, and your journey shall be unclothed. (*A pause.*)

MOON: Say what?

ELVIS: You got to do it butt-naked, buddy.

ROY: Now just hold on here.

ELVIS: (*Holding out the milkshake.*) You ever try one with an egg in it?

ROY: You want us to strip down and walk 600 miles from here to D.C. with a sign says "I'm sorry?"

ELVIS: Gonna' get a hell of a suntan.

ROY: When hell freezes over, boy! I'm the best damn thing genetics ever come up with, an' that's the American white man, runnin' the most powerful damn nation this world's ever seen, an' we don't strip down for some damn hallucination! (*He sneezes.*)

ELVIS: Have a Kleenex, Roy.

R.V.: Oh man, repent all and regard thee here thy immortal soul.

ROY: Damnit, Moon, listen to this.

MOON: I'm listenin'.

ROY: Clem?

CLEM: Well…

ROY: Stand up for your own blood, goddamnit!

CLEM: I guess God's my own blood, Roy.

R.V.: Lo, the plague will descend, your bodies be consumed and your heart sundered.

MOON: I don't have a heart, R.V.

R.V.: You just never turned it on, Moon.

ROY: R.V.?

R.V.: Sinner, save your kind and rejoice, lest you and all your tribe shall perish from the earth.

MOON: You comin', Elvis?

ELVIS: I'll be just above your head, man.

MOON: You sorry?

ELVIS: I failed my precious mama. I can't sleep the eternal sleep when I done like that.

ROY: The white man shouldn't have to take the rap for this!

ELVIS: Tough nuggies, Roy.

ROY: Who the hell has the moral authority to stand here in this dump and tell me I got to take off my underpants?!

ELVIS: I was you, I'd ask your precious mama.

ROY: How the hell am I gonna' ask my mama.

MOON: You can't ask her, you damn moron, you dispersed her!

(*A heavenly chord; a puff of smoke. Their mother appears on the ridge. She is in her early 70s, wearing a housedress. She has a halo.*)

CLEM: Holy smoke!

MRS. MANNERING: Hello, son.

ROY AND MOON: Mama!

MRS. MANNERING: Now you do what Elvis says, Roy. I only hope to goodness you took a shower.

CLEM: It's you, Mama.

MRS. MANNERING: Hello Bootsie. I just cannot believe you let an eight-year-old child get hold of an AK-47.

CLEM: I know, Mama.

MRS. MANNERING: I believe you've been imbibing hard liquor.

CLEM: It's only 80 proof, Mama.

MRS. MANNERING: Well, you had better pull up your bootstraps. Moon Mannering, what is that on your face?

MOON: Facial hair, Mama.

MRS. MANNERING: You got something to be ashamed of hid behind that mess?

MOON: Well, Mama...

MRS. MANNERING: You better not let your father catch you like that. Do you have blood on your hands, son?

MOON: I do, Mama.

MRS. MANNERING: I ought to whip your butt off. Thou shalt not kill, do you hear me? Tiny, what in heaven's name are you got up as?

ROY: Abraham Lincoln, Mama.

MRS. MANNERING: Remember the sin of pride, Tiny. Pride goeth before a fall. Look up sinner.

(*Roy does.*)

CLEM: Gollee Moses.

ROY: Oh, my God, Mama.

(*Clem lets out a long whistle.*)

ROY: It's the load receipt printed in fire on the sky.

CLEM: Those letters must be a mile high.

ROY: See what you did, Clem?

CLEM: It's real readable.

ROY: Shut up.

CLEM: (*Trying to make up.*) You want some Cheezits?

ROY: (*Ripping them from his hand. Stomps them.*) Arrrrrgh!

CLEM: You broke my Cheezits. Those were all the Cheezits I had.

ROY: Shut up!

CLEM: (*Suddenly twisted with rage; the straw that broke the camel's back.*) Don't...you...tell me...to...shut up!! You have... humiliated me...for 40 years. (*He reaches down and picks up an iron bar out of the dump.*) If you ever...ever speak to me in that tone of voice...Roy...I will mash you like a potato, tear out your liver and heart and devour them, whole.

MRS. MANNERING: (*Clapping her hands as you do with children.*) Now that is enough, now. You may not eat your brother. That is out of the question.

CLEM: (*Returning to himself.*) Golly, Mama...I didn't mean that.

MRS. MANNERING: Of course you didn't.

MOON: (*Looking at the sky.*) Well, they know what you got in your dump all over North America now, Roy.

MRS. MANNERING: (*With finality.*) People do not eat their own. (*She points up.*) Think of your mama seein' your dirty laundry bein' washed right across the night sky, Roy. You better get right with the deity. (*Roy hangs his head.*) Now have you boys been brushing your teeth?

THE BOYS: Yes Mama.

MRS. MANNERING: Then get undressed.

ROY: I don't want to, Mama.

MRS. MANNERING: It is very, very late.

ROY: I...just can't...Mama.

MRS. MANNERING: Why not, Roy?

ROY: I'm ashamed of the size of my sexual member.

MRS. MANNERING: God gave you that body, there is no reason to be ashamed of it. You think I haven't seen your thing before?

ROY: Yes Mama.

MRS. MANNERING: You have a responsibility to your fellow creatures, Roy Mannering, now I don't want to hear anymore about it. Your sweet Grandpa Abbey, 100 years old, your kind Uncle William always sent five dollars on your birthday, you want them to die of this flu?

THE BOYS: No Mama.

MRS. MANNERING: Well, I would think not. I carried you inside me, boys, and you were, every one of you, breech births. I have cradled your tiny fevered bodies in my arms and sang to you from the opera Aida by the immortal Verdi. I watched you grow from beautiful, tiny, tow-headed perfections into big, splotchy, gangly things who masturbated. I paid your car insurance long after it should have been your responsibility. Yes, Jesus, I have suffered! You could see me draining out into you like a bottle emptying. There wasn't a drop, not a scintilla, left for my thoughts or feelings or dreams. I could have been a supply-side economist or the President of the United States. After you were born, your father was afraid to have marital relations with me because you boys never learned to knock. I dreamed of Mr. Presley drenching my body with scented oils and creamy peanut butter and taking his will with me, but none of you would ever drive me to Memphis! I died as I had lived, a housewife, a mother, a cleaning lady and, when that time came, when I did die, when I was no longer your lifelong wet nurse, you irresponsible sons-of-bitches dispersed me to the wrong place!

ROY: Mama!

MRS. MANNERING: I said Hardee's, goddamnit, not Wendy's! Wendy's Big Bacon Classic is pigeon piss compared to Hardee's Frisco-burger! I wanted to be at Hardee's in amongst the begonias, across from the drive-thru!

CLEM: It wasn't Wendy's?

MRS. MANNERING: Never mind! That was then, this is now. You can make it up to me *here, after death*. You can give me what I never had, my dreams, my glory, my raison d'être. You three, my spawn, have been chosen by the apogee, the highest of the high, to save the white man! All is forgiven; seize the day, do it for your mama!!

(*They stand astounded.*)

MRS. MANNERING: Go on, I'm waiting.

(*Clem unbuttons his work shirt. Roy and Moon are still. Clem takes off the shirt.*)

MRS. MANNERING: Don't make me get the strap, Roy.

(*A beat, and then Roy sits and starts taking off his shoes. Moon stands dead still, arms at his side.*)

R.V.: Did you ever love me, Moon?

MOON: I did.

R.V.: Then why the hell didn't you write?

MOON: I was ashamed.

R.V.: You damn fool, Moon. Look what became of us.

(*He stands for another moment and then starts unbuckling his belt.*)

R.V.: Cool.

(*She takes a step back.*)

MRS. MANNERING: Good night, R.V.

R.V.: Good night, Chlotilda.

MRS. MANNERING: I've still got ironing to do. Good night, Clem.

CLEM: Good night, Mommy.

MRS. MANNERING: Good night, Tiny.

(*Roy's hands move instinctively in front of his genitals.*)

MRS. MANNERING: Good night, Moon.

(*He lifts a hand in farewell. She starts to exit.*)

MRS. MANNERING: Everybody sleep tight now.

(*Humming a hymn, she disappears. A harmonica, somewhere in the universe, picks up the hymn. R.V. raises one hand and speaks.*)

R.V.: And lo, grace descended…

ELVIS: …and they divested themselves, and the harbinger said to them…

R.V.: As you journey, oh chosen ones, men where they stand in the fields will lay down the tools of the harvest and join with you…

ELVIS: Yeah, baby…

R.V.: From far off will men hear your righteous tread and stream weeping from the corporate headquarters…

ELVIS: From the condominiums and nouvelle restaurants…

R.V.: From the universities and the oak-paneled boardrooms…

ELVIS: Outta Wall Street and the Silicone Valley.

R.V. AND ELVIS: See them, this multitude of white guys of a certain age…

ELVIS: CEO's, estate lawyers, congressmen…

R.V.: Pediatric allergists, downsizers, aldermen…

ELVIS: Gettin' on their Harleys and their Swiss Alpine snowmobiles, their longin' palpable…

R.V.: Their eyes regretful, their hands joined.

ELVIS: They are comin', baby!

R.V.: The Catholics, the Jews, the Episcopalians…

ELVIS: The down and dirty Baptists…

R.V. AND ELVIS: And all the lesser faiths!

ELVIS: And Roy, my man, you're in the front, dude.

R.V.: You too, Moon…

ELVIS: And Clem, you swingin' dick, you're drivin' the vanguard forward…

R.V.: Until at last these pale multitudes envelope the Washington Monument, as the muscles surround the heart, and from their throats will spring one single cry…

ELVIS: The cry of sins committed…

R.V.: The cry of sins repented…

ELVIS: The cry of old white guys everywhere…

R.V. AND ELVIS: "I…am…sorry!"

(*The word "sorry" echoes through the heavens. Roy's fireworks begin overhead. Three rockets in various colors illuminate those below.*)

ROY: Luellen started the show.

(*More fireworks.*)

R.V.: Oh, boys, you were beautiful that day; your crisp, cream, pin-striped uniforms against that emerald green infield.

(*Rocket overhead. The brothers remove their last items of clothing.*)

R.V.: You boys, like music box figures, spinnin' and divin'. The endless arching beauty of that final mile-high pop-up.

(*Another rocket.*)

R.V.: You were gods, boys…

ELVIS: Gods of summer.

R.V.: Think what you might have done?!

(*A tattoo of explosions and bursts of color. The brothers are finally naked. They look up at the display. R.V. scribbles on the back of an old "For Rent" sign with her lipstick.*)

CLEM: (*A particularly glorious rocket.*) Ooooooo, look at that one!

(*A golden light plays down the sequined rope by Elvis. He puts one foot in a loop at the bottom and takes hold of the rope with one hand.*)

ELVIS: We've got to get on that resurrection express, boys. (*Making his exit.*) Hail and farewell, buddies. Y'all bring it on home.

(*He is gone. A series of sharp explosions. R.V. moves down and hands the sign to Moon.*)

R.V.: Let's go, boys. I'd go south on Rural 501 and then east down the turnpike. They'll be comin' that way. Hold it up, Moon. Hold it high, my darlin'!

(*He does. It says, "I'm sorry." In the distance the Mayberry High School band strikes up a traditional march, the fireworks redouble. It is the finale of Roy's display. The brothers stare out at us; Moon*) *holds up the sign. R.V.:, in her red dress, stands on the remains of the car behind them.*)

R.V.: Fishers of men! The night is fallen, but the lark yet sings. Oh, you Euro-centric Anglo Saxons, (*They turn front.*) there is still one inning left to play!

(*There is a final tattoo of airborne explosions and a dying scutter of fireworks. The Mayberry High School band plays bravely on. The lights fade.*)

END OF PLAY

Pomp and Circumstance

THE CAST
  King
  Composer

TIME
  18th Century, perhaps

PLACE
  A throne room

POMP AND
CIRCUMSTANCE

A king. He waits. He does accounts. A musician enters. He kneels. The king looks up.

KING: Ah. Didn't see you come in. You're a…

COMPOSER: Bachweist, your Majesty.

KING: Ah. You wouldn't know anything about ships' keels, would you?

COMPOSER: Keels, your Majesty?

KING: Keels. What it costs to build one, more specifically?

COMPOSER: I know nothing of keels, your majesty.

KING: Nor do I. Nor does any generalist. Do you know what a millwright does or how many a country ought to have?

COMPOSER: It is beyond me, your Majesty.

KING: Of course it is, and you are doubtless an intelligent man. *(A pause.)* You are an intelligent man?

COMPOSER: Of a sort, your Majesty.

KING: Exactly. Of a sort. As am I. My intelligence has to do with power, and yours has to do with…?

COMPOSER: Harmonics, your Majesty.

KING: Really? Oh, yes, you're Bachweist. Well, Bachweist, power in the end has to do with the treasury. I'm the King, you see, I dispense. And if I'm cagey about it, the key people stay indebted, and the monarchy thrives. Dispensing, however, isn't easy because it's all value judgments. Millwrights, Bachweist, who are they and what should I put down for them? I could find out, of course, I have advisors, but advisors, Bachweist, have agendas... agendas. There is no such thing, Bachweist, as objective advice, and there is never enough money...I'm sure you understand?

COMPOSER: Yes, your Majesty.

KING: I see I've left you groveling. Please rise if you'd be more comfortable.

COMPOSER: If you don't mind.

KING: They say you're a genius, Bachweist. Are you?

COMPOSER: Yes, your Majesty.

KING: Ah. What is that?

COMPOSER: A genius?

KING: How does one know? That you are, I mean?

COMPOSER: One's work surpasses all expectations. It is nonpareil. Logic cannot explain it. It is beyond definition.

KING: Like a millwright. I'm quite hostile toward anything I can't define, Bachweist. It's one of the problems I've always had with music. Plus, it never fits in with my mood, whereas everything else, certainly every*one* else, does if he/she has any sense. Anything that doesn't accommodate me, opposes me. You catch my drift? Well, this is all bullshit isn't it, Bachweist? The point is I need a court composer. Austria has one. Lichtenstein has one. Budapest has one. I mustn't be caught short. People feel more comfortable with power if it has taste. You're available, I take it?

COMPOSER: I would be...honored.

KING: Of course you would. Go ahead, sell yourself.

COMPOSER: Your Majesty?

KING: Sell yourself. Sell yourself, man. We've only got ten minutes here before the millwrights.

COMPOSER: (*A set piece.*) At two, my father put down his French horn and I, picking it up, played by ear the exercises he had struggled with by the fire. At four, I composed my "30 Etudes for Piano and Violin." At five, my first symphony. At seven, I was presented on violin with the Imperial orchestra. At nine, I toured Europe giving concerts of my own work before nine heads of state, three kings, two queens, and a parliamentary democracy. At fourteen, I completed an opera that brought a convention of musicologists screaming to their feet and, in my maturity, am a recognized master of sixteen instruments, have thirty-one published symphonies, have performed in twenty-three nations, and have been offered astonishing fees at stud. To put it briefly.

KING: (*Applauding lightly.*) Well done, Bachweist. And what can you do for me?

COMPOSER: I can make you immortal.

KING: Already been taken care of.

COMPOSER: I can delight you.

KING: Kings don't delight, Bachweist, children delight.

COMPOSER: I can carry you away on gossamer wings of melody.

KING: Bachweist, you better kneel down again. *(He does.)* I'm not interested in your talent, man, it's peripheral to the real business of governing, or even living for that matter. Oh, it's useful with women, but my position is a stronger aphrodisiac than that. Only other musicians could possibly be interested in music in any meaningful way. And critics, of course, as a way of making a reputation. No, Bachweist, what I want from you is the following: a few ceremonial pieces on demand, hummable, naturally. A printable paragraph on my respect for and understanding of art. Some good groveling to make clear my position, and a resolute and articulated belief that you haven't been censored in anyway. Satire might sometime be a problem, Bachweist, but that's beyond the province of serious music, in any case. But this is trifling. You're eccentric, I hope? I hear you're eccentric?

COMPOSER: I have been so described, your Majesty.

KING: Really kinky?

COMPOSER: Pit bulls, your Majesty.

KING: *(Impressed.)* First rate, by God! You're well dressed, Bachweist, that's a drawback.

COMPOSER: I compose wearing only a codpiece made from the hearts of salamanders.

KING: Now, we're getting somewhere. Food?

COMPOSER: The skin of cucumbers.

KING: Sleep?

COMPOSER: Never, your Majesty.

KING: Living arrangement?

COMPOSER: I prefer to pass the evening inside a freshly killed horse.

KING: Are these inclinations, Bachweist?

COMPOSER: They are necessary to a career in the arts.

KING: Quite so. A nation needs distraction, Bachweist. If the populace seriously thought about the situation we find ourselves in they would go mad. This is the role of the artist. A bourgeois artist would be as useless as the ox coccyges. You don't mind dying young?

COMPOSER: It's expected.

KING: The suicide of a great artist is the creme de la creme of distraction. How would you do it?

COMPOSER: I would publicly eat, over the period of one month, a large civic statue of no distinction.

KING: Very distracting.

COMPOSER: I hope so, your Majesty.

KING: Compensation?

COMPOSER: Beyond my wildest dreams.

KING: That won't be much. You won't be wanting me to appreciate you, will you?

COMPOSER: I do without.

KING: *(Holding out his hand.)* Good choice. *(Bachweist takes it.)* We'll have a proclamation out presently.

COMPOSER: Do you find power satisfactory, your Majesty?

KING: Only when I consider the alternatives. And art?

COMPOSER: It's a fraud, Majesty, but someone has to do it.

KING: I know exactly what you mean. Well, time for the wheelwrights. I suppose for form's sake I ought to hear you play something. Something short.

COMPOSER: I would be honored.

KING: Of course you would. You won't mind if I work?

COMPOSER: Pay no attention.

KING: You're a useful luxury, Bachweist. Play away.

(Bachweist raises his violin and begins to play superbly. The king eyes him icily.)

KING: Thrilling.

(Bachweist plays on dramatically. The king opens his account book and works. A moment. Light s out.)

END OF PLAY